JOB PAY FOR JOB WORTH

Designing, Managing, and Involving Employees in an Equitable Job Classification System

Second Edition

Richard I. Henderson
Professor Emeritus
Department of Management
Georgia State University

Kitty Williams Clarke
Management Consultant

Georgia State University Business Press
Atlanta, Georgia

NEW ENGLAND INSTITUTE OF TECHNOLOGY
LEARNING RESOURCES CENTER

4/96

#30474920

The Library of Congress Cataloging-in-Publication Data

Henderson, Richard I., 1926-
    Job pay for job worth: designing, managing, and involving employees in an
equitable job classification system / Richard I. Henderson, Kitty Williams Clarke.—
2nd ed.
        p.   cm.
    Includes bibliographical references and index.
    ISBN 0-88406-246-5
        1. Job evaluation. 2. Job analysis 3. Wages. 4. Equal pay for equal work
    I. Clarke, Kitty Williams. II. Title.
HF5549.5.J62H37 1994   94-12464
658.3'06—dc20   CIP

Georgia State University Business Press
University Plaza
Atlanta, Georgia 30303-3093

© 1981, 1994 by Georgia State University
Published 1981. Second edition 1994.

98 97 96 95 94   5 4 3 2 1

Georgia State University, a unit of the University System of Georgia, is an equal
educational opportunity institution and an equal opportunity/affirmative action
employer.

Printed in the United States of America.

Cover design by Richard Shannon and Jim Kerr
Typography by Jim Kerr

Contents

Part III: Solving Human Problems   **187**

Appendix

Index   **311**

Preface

The process of translating theory into action is a dynamic one, especially when money is involved. Employee compensation must keep pace with a changing work environment. It is becoming increasingly important for organizations to spend their personnel dollars wisely. At the same time, however, employee perceptions of the value of goals and products provided by the employer dollar are changing. The need for employer-employee cooperation to provide each customer with quality goods and services becomes increasingly more important.

The authors feel that the Factor Evaluation System (FES) can be used effectively to develop an equitable pay system for an organization. They also believe that it lends itself better to employee involvement than does any currently practiced method of job evaluation. As an additional bonus, an organization can, if it wishes, implement and maintain the system with a minimal amount of training and without the expense of outside consultants.

The authors' confidence in the ability of FES to meet the compensation needs of many types of organizations resulted in this book. Dr. Richard I. Henderson, then a professor of management at Georgia State University, and Kitty Williams Clarke, former director of personnel for the city of East Point, Georgia, and currently a human resources consultant, worked together to design and implement a metropolitan area pay survey. This survey provided pay comparability information for both public and private sector organizations. At the conclusion of this project, four survey participants used the federal government's then newly developed Factor Evaluation System (FES) to evaluate six benchmark jobs for which they had provided pay information. From this evaluation, it became apparent that the jobs selected from the four involved organizations for matching with the six benchmark jobs were not comparable. This, in turn, placed a cloud on the entire survey.

Shortly after completing this pay survey, Clarke, Henderson, and a team consisting of human resources professionals and two graduate students from Georgia State University joined forces to perform a classification and pay study for a city in the metropolitan Atlanta area. This book is a direct result and product of that effort. Today, many of the same issues that faced the classification and pay consulting team continue to arise.

The design of this book first presents the major areas of concern that must be addressed when performing a classification and pay study. The second part focuses on the activities and results achieved by the study team. There are additions to this part that are products of further classification and pay efforts by the authors. The final part of the book centers on the human aspects of any classification and pay study and what was done in particular in this study to gain employee acceptance and cooperation.

The additional and new how-to information include (1) techniques that facilitate the collection of valid and useful job content information; (2) recommendations for writing task statement, how to convert task statements into responsibility and duty statements, and then how to group responsibility and duty statements into responsibility modules that describe positions or jobs completely and accurately; (3) procedures for translating job content information into FES points; and—possibly most useful— (4) how to design a pay structure that will either replicate market conditions or support the compensation policy of the organization. The step-by-step process described herein can be used by any organization to develop a pay system.

The authors wish to thank the staff of Georgia State University Business Press, and in particular R. Cary Bynum, director, and Margaret F. Stanley, managing editor, for their suggestions and guidance in developing this second edition.

PART I

THE CLASSIFICATION PROCESS

Installing and maintaining a rational, logical, orderly, and workable pay system is a primary concern to anyone responsible for managing a productive and profitable organization. A major reason people work is to acquire the resources necessary to purchase the goods and services that not only make survival possible but also ensure an acceptable lifestyle. The major work-related reward offered by practically all organizations to their members is money. The actual amount of money earned by any one employee depends on a wide variety of factors. The identification and ordering of the pay factors related to the scope and complexity of the job and the making of pay decisions relative to these factors are performed in the classification process. Chapters 1 through 4 describe recognized and accepted methods and procedures used by many different kinds of organizations to make job-related pay decisions.

Chapter 1

DETERMINING JOB WORTH

Once a person accepts a job and the various rewards offered in exchange for his or her availability, capabilities, and performance, the question of internal equity arises. If the only issues involved in developing and designing reward packages were the absolute amounts of the rewards, the problems facing personnel or compensation staffs would be much less complex. Related issues arise as employees compare the kind and amount of their rewards with the rewards others receive.

The comparison and perception process determines to a very large degree the amount of satisfaction an employee has and maintains from rewards received. This satisfaction with rewards, in turn, has a significant impact on the quality and quantity of efforts made by employees to help an organization achieve desired end results.

Exhibit 1-1 shows the employer-employee exchange process. The observable, identifiable, and measurable components of this model are integrated within the brain of each employee. It is there that individual perceptions and comparisons influence employee decisions concerning the quantity and quality of effort to be expended for the benefit of the organization. Exhibit 1-2 is a simple representation of the process leading to establishment of a workplace environment that either stimulates employee effort in a way that benefits the organization and all of its members or fails in this mission. When perception and comparison lead

3

to the feeling that employer-provided rewards are insufficient, employee efforts are far from optimal. When employees refrain from putting forth their best efforts or misdirect their efforts through such actions as tardiness, absenteeism, poor utilization of material and equipment, or even sabotage or malicious damage of employer resources, the organization is the loser and, in reality, so are the employees.

This book identifies the tools, processes, and procedures that enable organizations to (1) design and manage efficient and effective pay components of a compensation system, and (2) take positive steps toward communicating the what, why, when, where, and how of these tools, processes, and procedures, so that employees understand and accept the pay system as fair return for effort expended. Exhibit 1-3 identi-

Exhibit 1-1: Rewards-Behavior Interface

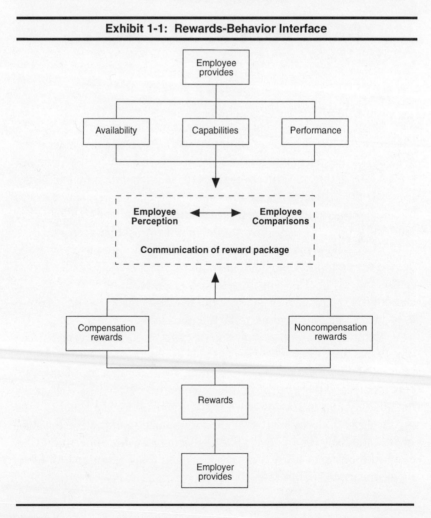

fies some of the principal forces that influence employee perception and comparison processes.

Even in a model as simple as this, the complexity of the perception and comparison processes becomes readily apparent. Organizations frequently have minimal opportunities to influence the internal forces that have an impact on employee decisions. Even forces external to the employee provide organizations with limited opportunities for influence. Recognizing these limitations emphasizes how critical

Exhibit 1-2: Establishing a Motivated Workplace Environment (Directing Employee Behavior)

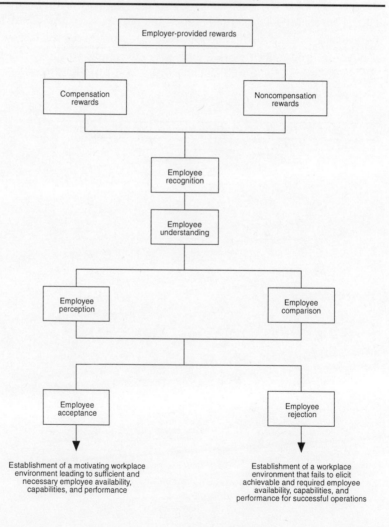

it is for organizations to seize and make good use of the opportunities they do have. There is possibly no single area where organizations have a greater chance to influence workplace behavior than through the pay they provide for employee skills and effort.

Four major components of any well-designed pay system are (1) the amount of pay established for jobs requiring different kinds and amounts of knowledge, skills, and responsibilities; (2) recognition, through variations in pay, of adverse physical and emotional conditions that affect the jobholder; (3) recognition, through seniority pay, of loyalty to the organization; and (4) pay that recognizes the quality and quantity of actual performance provided by the jobholder (incumbent). Establishing an internally equitable pay relationship among jobs requires the development of an idealized structure of the relative worth of different jobs. From work started a century ago, various processes and procedures have combined to evolve a discipline known as job evaluation.

Exhibit 1-3: Forces Influencing Employee Perceptions and Comparisons

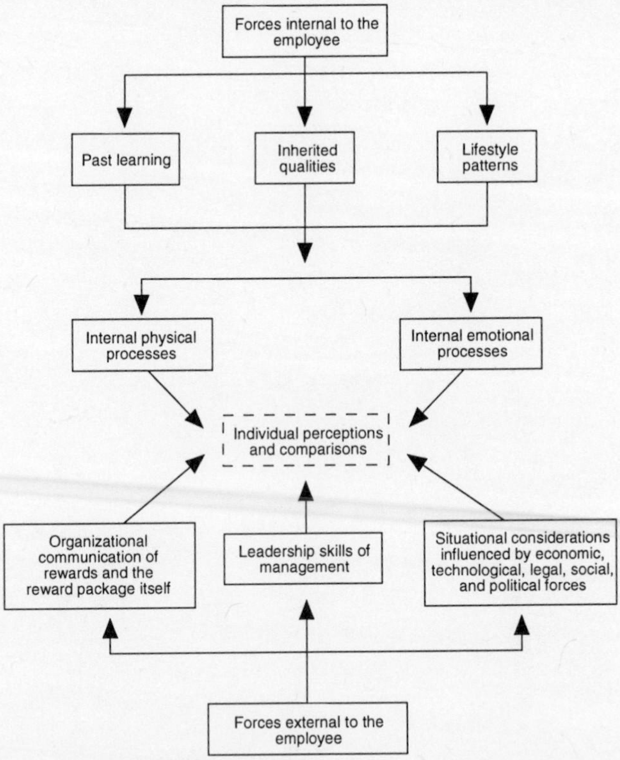

Introduction to Job Evaluation

The goal of job evaluation is to establish an objective ordering of jobs relative to their worth to the organization. The key words are *objective, ordering,* and *worth.* These key words, in themselves, establish areas of conflict. An objective ordering and an ordering by worth focus on the conflicting topics of subjectivity and objectivity. Relative worth of jobs requires individual judgments. The broad spectrum of forces that have an impact on individual decisions strongly influences judgment. These forces, in turn, influence perceptions, and perceptions will vary when worth is being determined. Worth is the value of something measured by its qualities or by the esteem in which it is held. When esteem is part of the measurement criteria, the influence of subjective considerations becomes a primary issue. This is especially true when the worth of a job is being evaluated.

Job evaluation is a major input in establishing rates of pay. The rate paid to a job incumbent is, in most cases, the major determinant of the lifestyle of that individual and his or her dependents. Lifestyle security (for most people) depends on job earnings. Threatening this security in any way will usually vary employees' perceptions of the worth of the jobs they occupy and the quality of their performance. The issue then becomes the difference between reality and perception. This touches a major building block of the process developed in this book. What a person perceives is reality. If employers wish to develop a closer relationship between their employees' perceptions of reality and the organization's view of reality, every effort possible must be made to communicate and develop understanding and acceptance of methods and procedures that relate compensation rewards to individual knowledge, skills, efforts, and accepted responsibilities. In a nutshell, this is the purpose of a formal (organizationally instituted) job evaluation. A review and analysis of job evaluation methods will assist in identifying the ones that may be most useful to compensation professionals.

Over the past one-hundred years, at least three major methods of job evaluation have been developed. These three methods are (1) those that focus on the whole job, including plans that in some manner compare jobs and job rates of pay within an identified labor market—market pricing; (2) those that use compensable factors; and (3) those that use a statistical procedure—regression analysis, which, in reality, is a mathematical algorithm using compensable factors.

Whole-job Ranking Method of Job Evaluation

The *whole-job ranking* method of job evaluation is undoubtedly the oldest and by far the simplest method of determining job worth. It is commonly known as job ranking. In this method, those involved in the evaluation process compare each job with all other jobs and establish a ranking or job hierarchy, from most valuable or important to least valuable or important (or vice versa). When the evaluator is intimately familiar with all jobs to be ranked, this can be a very effective and low-cost process. The method may use the opinion of only one evaluator—perhaps the top manager or owner of the business. This individual reviews the jobs of the organization and simply states that job A is worth more to the organization than job B, and so on, moving through this process until a hierarchy of jobs (ranked by pay) has been established. Or, the ranking process may include the opinions of a group of individuals who collectively are intimately familiar with all jobs being evaluated.

When whole-job ranking is done in its purest form, it only determines which job is ranked first, which is second, third, and so on, down to the lowest-ranked job. Since pay determination is an essential part of the equitable pay-setting process, ranking of the jobs in itself is not sufficient. Pay is both an absolute amount and a rate (rate of pay) and, as such, both a ranking as well as a relative relationship must be developed.

The establishment of a rate of pay may come about when the person responsible for setting the pay rate says "this" is the amount the organization will pay for "this" job. Even when this decision is made in a very unilateral manner, the variables affecting the decision usually follow a very logical, rational process. The major variables, in most cases, are (1) What do I have to pay? (2) What can I afford? and (3) What am I paying other job incumbents?

Another job evaluation method that is closely related to whole-job ranking is commonly known as *market pricing*. This procedure requires a description of the jobs under review. Using this description, a survey is made of relevant labor markets, and the jobs under review are matched with jobs in other organizations. Pay data gathered from other organizations are analyzed, and statistics are developed to identify the market or "going" rate for the jobs. When an organization uses a pure market-pricing method, it, in essence, allows the market to determine the relative worth of its jobs.

A job evaluation method that combines whole-job ranking and market pricing is the *Market Pricing Guide Line Method*. This method first requires the establishment of a guideline (a diagonal line). On this line, points are located certain distances apart (one major method has points 5 percent apart, another one has points 6 percent apart). Jobs are then described and a market survey is conducted. From the pay data generated by the survey, each job is placed on the point of the guideline that most closely approximates the average or median of the pay survey data. If those responsible for the final design of the pay plan do not agree with the placement and determine that the rank of the job is higher or lower relative to other jobs, they have the right to move the job up or down one point on the guideline.

The ranking method establishes an ordinal scale (first, second, and so forth), while job worth requires the determination of relative values. After one job is ranked as being worth more than another, the issue of "how much more" must still be answered.

When undertaking market pricing (which may be preceded by a ranking of jobs), organizations competing in the same labor market are requested to supply pay information on comparable jobs. Controversial questions regarding the establishment of job worth based on market pricing include:

1. Are the same or comparable jobs being matched? Are the responsibilities and duties of the two jobs similar or identical? (Even when jobs in two different organizations have similar if not identical responsibilities and duties, a difference in emphasis on certain responsibilities and duties within each organization could vary the worth or value of the job and the pay of the jobholder. This kind of difference is seldom, if ever, recognized in job matching for the completion of a pay survey.)

2. Is the survey respondent providing useful pay information—actual incumbent rates of pay versus minimum and maximum rates of pay for the job or average rate of pay for those performing the job?

3. What influence does job tenure or incumbent performance have on job rates of pay?

4. What influence does the design of the total compensation package have on the amount of pay provided to jobholders?

5. What influences do noncompensation rewards have on the design of the pay package and the total compensation package?

6. Does the market relate to past discriminatory practices on hiring and thus perpetuate pay practices that have an adverse impact on women and minorities?

When analyzing the value or usefulness of market pricing, the problem of word usage or definition again comes to the forefront. The underlying purpose or use of job evaluation is to establish an internally *equitable* ordering of jobs. Market surveys provide information on the competitive rates of pay for similar jobs. Surveys do *not* provide external or *market-equity* information. There is no such thing as equity in the marketplace. Many writers discuss internal and external equity relationships and relate market rates of pay to external equity. This kind of thinking and writing colors or places into jeopardy any evaluation method used for determining equitable relationships. Equity with regard to the employer-employee exchange process is simply the right to certain rewards based on job requirements and the contributions of the jobholder.

Compensable-factor Methods of Job Evaluation

By the latter part of the nineteenth century, industrial engineers responsible for improving the productivity of organizations began performing very detailed analyses of jobs. Using their analytic skills, they studied human efforts and identified and described improved ways of doing various kinds of work. Following this path of work-motion and work-method study, others working in the area of job evaluation focused their attention on what an employee does in performing job assignments and the desired and actual results obtained from these efforts.

In attempting to develop procedures and methods for evaluating the worth of jobs, these investigators recognized the weakness of whole-job evaluation and ranking. It is all too easy to miss or underestimate some of the decisive and critical requirements when looking at a job in its entirety. Recognition of this weakness opened the door to the identification, development, and use of compensable factors. A compensable factor is a paid for, measurable quality or feature that is common to many different kinds of jobs. Through a detailed analysis, synthetic qualities (features) that are common to these various jobs are defined. This is where a compensable-factor job evaluation plan differs significantly from any evaluation plan using the whole job. The whole job is real. It is directly observable. A compensable factor, however, is a synthetic variable. It describes certain features or qualities of a job. The factor is not directly observable, but the interaction of its features produces observable results that are measurable. The easier it is for those involved in job-related efforts to recognize the relationship between the compensable factor and the job being evaluated, the more useful and valuable the factor.

To be useful, a compensable factor must be common to a wide variety of jobs. This characteristic, in turn, requires that the compensable factor be abstract. The broader the job universe covered by a compensable factor, the more abstract it must be. The more abstract the factor, the more difficult to describe it with words and terms that have meaning to those having a vested interest in job evaluation.

Because most compensable-factor job evaluation plans are designed to cover many different kinds and levels of jobs, the factor-classification scheme normally consists of two or more redefinitions of the primary compensable factor. A typical compensable-factor job evaluation plan includes universal factors, subfactors, and degrees. Universal factors are the general, relatively abstract and complex qualities that relate to all kinds of jobs. The subfactors further describe the universal factors, making them more understandable and useful in relating to a specific job. Degrees (or levels) provide a yardstick or measurement scale that assists in identifying a specific amount or level of the factor in the evaluation of a job.

To facilitate the assignment of worth to a job, compensable factors are frequently weighted, and the degrees are given specific point scores. When using more than one compensable factor in a job evaluation method, weighting of each factor is critical if the factors are of varying importance. (It is very unlikely that all factors in a compensable-factor job evaluation plan are of identical worth.) The weighting of factors and the assignment of a particular value to each degree becomes critical in designing a point-factor job evaluation plan.

Some compensable-factor job evaluation plans narratively describe universal factors and levels of factors in an ordinal manner. It is still possible to sum the ordinal rankings received from a job evaluation and arrive at a specific quantitative value of worth for the job.

When using more than one compensable factor, the set of factors should theoretically cover all features of a job. Factors should be mutually exclusive and possess an additive relationship. Each factor must describe a different quality of the job, and all qualities to be compensated must be identified. If this is not done, an important feature of the job may inadvertently be overweighted, another quality underweighted, while another quality may be totally unrecognized. Most compensable-factor job evaluation plans have more than one compensable factor because the analysis and synthesis process reveals that job payment relates to more than one synthetic quality. When using only one compensable factor, the same problem occurs that arises when performing whole-job ranking—difficulty in recognizing all compensable features of a job.

It must be recognized, however, that compensable factors do not cover 100 percent of the compensable features of a job. For example, working conditions is frequently included as a compensable factor in a compensable-factor job evaluation plan. This quality could just as easily be excluded. (Working conditions would still be a compensable feature but would be recognized outside of the job evaluation plan.)

One of the authors favors a separate payment for dangerous and distressing (D&D) conditions, the compensable element of working conditions. All workers involved in similar D&D conditions would receive identical D&D pay regardless of the worth of their jobs. This approach removes working conditions as a job evaluation compensable factor but includes it as a compensable component of the job. In essence, this is no different from separate premium and differential payments that recognize variations in hours worked (overtime premiums), second- and third-shift work, weekend and holiday work, and so forth. The compensable factors that compose a compensable-factor job evaluation plan must cover 100 percent of the features to be described in establishing an ordering of job worth. Total compensation received by a jobholder will normally include other compensable items that affect the pay of the jobholder but do not relate to the relative worth of the job.

Over the past seventy years, many different kinds of compensable-factor job evaluation methods have been developed. These may be classified under two general headings: methods that are qualitative in design and methods that are quantitative. *Qualitative methods* use narratives to describe factors and the differences between them. In *quantitative methods*, points are assigned to factors, indicating differences in worth. Relative magnitudes of differences in factors are further defined through the use of a point-scored measuring scale.

Position Classification Method

The qualitative compensable-factor job evaluation method that has been widely used by public-sector organizations is the *Position Classification Method*. Used by the federal government since 1920 for establishing the worth of General Schedule (GS) jobs, this method uses eight compensable factors developed in a narrative format. All eight factors are not used to describe and determine the worth of all jobs. The narrative format is not consistent, and the narratives frequently do not relate to changing job responsibilities and requirements. Overall, the system is cumbersome, difficult to understand, and leads to inconsistency in evaluation.

The most important document developed in a position classification plan is the classification standard. It describes knowledge requirements, major responsibilities and duties, and basic qualifications for a class of jobs. The narrative becomes long and complex because it must provide data in sufficient detail to differentiate the various jobs included within the particular class.

Other Qualitative Methods

Other compensable-factor methods that use a narrative format for describing compensable factors include Elliot Jaques' *Time Span of Discretion* (TSD) *Method*. Jaques contends that differences in the time span of discretion relate to differences in job worth.[1] T. T. Paterson and T. M. Husband developed the *Broadbanding Method.*[2] In this method, six levels or bands of decision make it possible to differentiate all jobs that are identified. Other organizations have developed variations of this method by expanding the broadbanding method to include a number of compensable factors (for example, knowledge, judgment, accountability, and level of content).

Jobs that supposedly defy precise description, such as managerial and professional jobs, may use such criteria as age of incumbent, years of experience in a specific occupation, and years since receipt of undergraduate or graduate degree. The use of these criteria is based on the hypothesis that there is a direct relationship between years of service, job knowledge, job level, and job performance. These broad classification methods include the Maturity Curve Method and the Frequency Distribution Method.

From their beginning over seventy years ago, various types of quantitative job evaluation methods have been designed to improve precision and orderliness and to minimize the subjectivity inherent in job evaluation.

Point Method

One of the first quantitative job evaluation methods using compensable factors was the *Point Method* developed by Merrill R. Lott in the mid-1920s. Lott recognized that in order to determine a quantitative value for each job, it would be necessary to identify and describe those factors that create pay differentials. Lott identified, described, and weighted fifteen factors. His method uses the following procedure:

1. Identify and define fifteen compensable factors useful in describing the fundamental elements or general nature of jobs to be studied.
2. Weight each of the fifteen factors so that the total weight of all factors equals one hundred. (Lott's fifteen factors were weighted from three to twenty-three).
3. Identify a sufficient number of key or benchmark jobs to cover the entire range of difficulty or importance of each factor. (In recent years the word *benchmark* has replaced the word *key*.)

The ordering of jobs relative to each factor provides a yardstick or scale of values for assigning a value to other jobs through the use of slotting or the paired-comparison technique.

4. Using each factor, assign a value from one to ten to each key job. The job demanding the greatest degree of a factor receives a ten, and the job demanding the least amount of a factor receives a one. Values between one and ten are assigned to other jobs by comparing them with the key jobs.

5. Multiply weighted factor value (Step 2) by the key job value (Step 4). This provides a point score for each job.

6. Add scores for all factors for each job.

7. Order jobs relative to total points earned.

In the seventy years following Lott's efforts, point-factor evaluation methods have witnessed many changes. These changes have made the point-factor approach to job evaluation more practical and useful for businesses with a wide variety of jobs.

Factor Comparison Method

Following in the footsteps of Lott, Eugene J. Benge and associates developed the *Factor Comparison Method* for the Philadelphia Rapid Transit Company in 1926 by reducing the number of Lott's factors from fifteen to five: (1) skill, (2) mental demands, (3) physical demands, (4) responsibilities, and (5) working conditions. Although the title and descriptions of the factors may vary, they are to this day an integral part of many point-factor methods.

Benge's factor comparison method was another step in the development of universal compensable factors. It also used key jobs to develop factor scales that adequately represented the level of requirements basic to each factor and allowed for a slotting procedure to determine the relative value and absolute worth of jobs.

Instead of using a point scale like Lott's, Benge developed a wage-rate scale for each factor. After assigning a wage rate to each key job and defining the universal compensable factors, a wage rate or monetary scale was developed for each factor. All other jobs in the business could then be evaluated. (This scaling method gave rise to the other name for this evaluation process—*weighted-in-money method*). Summing the monetary value of all factors for a particular job established its pay rate.

The weakness of Benge's method, as of Lott's, is in the establishment of a scale of values. In the factor comparison method, the evaluators must know the existing rate of pay for a benchmark job. However, the dynamic work environment that exerts so much influence on work content and job requirements reduces the stability of pay relationships among jobs. In addition, the pervasiveness of the marketplace and inflationary conditions result in market variations and constantly changing rates of pay. These two conditions in themselves are sufficient to limit the value of any plan that uses dollars and cents as the primary measuring scale for determining relative job worth. Using the factor-weighting process in the Benge method, it is extremely difficult to allocate a specific dollar and cents pay rate among five or more factors of a specific benchmark job. The determination of the weight of a factor and its scoring is the most crucial and difficult part in developing any numerically scored factor-evaluation method. The use of wage rates, as in the factor comparison method, does not make the development of a measuring scale any easier.

Point-factor Method

The application of a point-factor job evaluation plan within many business settings gave rise to a further modification of the factor methods of job evaluation. Various associations like the National Metal Trades Association (NMTA), the National Electrical Manufacturers Association (NEMA), and such large private employers as Western Electric developed point-factor methods that are still in use today.

A widely used spin-off of these plans is the job evaluation method currently presented by the American Association of Industrial Management (AAIM).[5] The AAIM Plan (or close facsimiles) is used by thousands of businesses. These plans more closely resemble Lott's point plan.

The NMTA, NEMA, and the AAIM plans have eleven factors; each factor is further divided into five degrees. Both the factors and their associated degrees are described in universal terms, making these methods useful for job evaluation purposes in a wide variety of settings. These methods establish weighting for each factor and each degree is assigned a specific number of points. This standard scale of values permits an understandable and precise approach for comparing and evaluating unlike jobs. By preassigning weights to factors and setting points for each degree, the *point-factor method* overcomes weaknesses in both the point method and the factor comparison methods.

The point-factor method eliminates the need to review key jobs and assign a value ranging from one to ten to describe the relative importance or value of a factor to the jobs in an organization (as required by the point method). The point-factor method also does not require the allocation of a certain amount of money to the various factors of the plan or the determination of how much of that share should be further allocated to a specific job relative to the importance or value of the factor in the design and operation of the job (as is necessary in the factor comparison method). Point-scored degrees describe the magnitude of differences or levels of difficulty existing within a compensable factor.

The Hay Plan

In the mid- to late 1940s, Edward N. Hay and Dale E. Purves modified the point-factor method by combining two or more universal factors on one guidechart. Their *Factor Guide Chart* or *Hay Plan* became one of the most widely used evaluation methods of the 1950s and is still very popular.[6] This method uses three universal factors for measurement purposes. These are know-how, problem solving, and accountability. (When necessary, a fourth guide chart profiling working conditions is available.) The three factors are further defined through the use of factor comparison guide charts. A guide chart is a two-dimensional matrix with one or more subfactors assigned to the *y*-axis or rows and one or more subfactors assigned to the *x*-axis or columns. A specific value or number of points is assigned to the intersection of each row and column. The various rows and columns then define the degrees or levels of the factor.

Factor-Ranking Benchmark Guidechart Method

In 1970, in response to a two-year Congressional study of job evaluation, competence, and capabilities of government workers, the U.S. Civil Service Commission (CSC), now known as the Office of Personnel Management (OPM), established a Job Evaluation and Pay Review Task Force—the Oliver Task Force. In 1972 this task force recommended a factor-ranking approach as a basis for job evaluation. At that time, the CSC established the Test and Implementation Group (TIG) to design, develop, test, evaluate, and revise, as necessary, a method to replace the existing job evaluation method.

The first output of the TIG was a job evaluation plan called the *Factor-Ranking Benchmark Guidechart Evaluation System*. This plan used eight factors: (1) knowledge required by the job, (2) responsibility, (3) difficulty of work, (4) personal relationships, (5) physical and environmental demands, (6) supervisory functions, (7) accountability, and (8) scope of work operations.

The factor-ranking benchmark guidechart method evaluated jobs in six different major occupational groups:

- Clerical Personnel, Office Machine Operators, and Technicians (COMOT)

- Professional, Administrative, and Technological occupations (PAT)
- Protective Occupations/Law Enforcement (POLE)
- Supervisory and Managerial (SAM)
- Executive, Scientific, and Medical (ESM)
- Trade and Craft (TAC)

This method did not use the same factors or combination of factors to evaluate the jobs in each of the six occupational groups. In addition, the same factor was weighted differently when used in evaluating jobs in the various occupational groups. The very design of a guidechart precluded easy identification of the weight of a specific factor because the points assigned in a guidechart represented the interrelationship between two or more factors.

The use of different sets of factors for evaluating jobs in different occupational groups may foster significant apprehension and could lead to misunderstanding. After reviewing the benchmark guidechart system, the OPM decided that the benefits of flexibility obtained through a plan that related to six major occupational groups would not be as great as the benefits derived through using one set of compensable factors for all kinds of jobs.

The Factor Evaluation System (FES)

Based on the philosophy that one set of compensable factors should be used for all jobs, the OPM then developed the *Factor Evaluation System of Position Classification* (FES). FES is a point-factor evaluation system that uses nine factors. In themselves, the nine factors defined in broad, general terminology provide no great innovation or advancement in the point-factor methods. These nine factors, defined in universal terms applicable to all General Schedule (GS) nonsupervisory jobs from Grades 1 to 15, form what the OPM calls *Primary Standards* or Standard-of-Standards. Defined and weighted factors within the Primary Standards relate to every GS position; consistent use of these factors assures grade alignment for positions within an occupation, between occupations, and across organizational lines.

After research, field testing, and the use of various statistical procedures, the factors were weighted and points were assigned to each. Because of the large number and variety of GS jobs to be evaluated and the broad range of pay ($11,015-$80,138), a total point score of 4,480 was assigned to the nine factors. Exhibit 1-4 identifies these nine factors.

Statements describing levels (degrees) within a factor facilitate comparison of the relative magnitude of a factor in one job with the same factor in another job. Although the number of levels developed for each factor differ significantly (for example, Knowledge has nine levels; Work Environment, three levels), each factor contains a sufficient number of levels to develop an observable scale of differences. The levels adequately define each factor in terms of increasing importance or increasing difficulty. Appendix A includes a complete description of the nine FES factors.

After establishing the Primary Standards, the next step in the FES is the development of what the OPM calls *Factor-Level Descriptions* for the Series (the application of the Primary Standards to a specific occupation or group of closely related occupations). By further defining the factors in terms of the work/job content performed by a specific occupation, the system is applicable to a wide variety of jobs and provides the system with a significant amount of flexibility. The development of Factor-Level Descriptions for the Series (occupational standards) is the major contribution of FES to the field of job evaluation. Appendix B includes an example of an occupational standard.

Each occupational standard (or factor-level description for the series) follows the exact format set by the Primary Standards. The occupational standard, however, describes the factors in words and terms that relate directly to the *work performed* by the positions within that occupation. The levels that describe magnitudes of differences of a factor are also described in words and terms that apply directly to the *type of work* performed within that occupation.

Exhibit 1-4: Factor Description Table

Factor	Points for Factor	Value Factor of Percentage of Total	Number of Levels	Points for Each Level
1. Knowledge Required by the Position	1850	41.3%	9	50, 200, 350, 550, 750 950, 1250, 1550, 1850
2. Supervisory Controls	650	14.5	5	25, 125, 275, 450, 650
3. Guidelines	650	14.5	5	25, 125, 275, 450, 650
4. Complexity	450	10.0	6	25, 75, 150, 225, 325, 450
5. Scope and Effect	450	10.0	6	25, 75, 150, 225, 325, 450
6. Personal Contacts	110	2.5	4	10, 25, 60, 110
7. Purpose of Contacts	220	4.9	4	20, 50, 120, 220
8. Physical Demands	50	1.1	3	5, 20, 50
9. Work Environment	50	1.1	3	5, 20, 50
Total	4480	99.9%		

The only design variation between the Primary Standards and an occupational standard is that the occupational standard may not have the complete range of levels that appears in the Primary Standards. This variation occurs because the jobs in the occupation may not cover the complete range of differences for a factor as described in the Primary Standards.

The second major contribution provided by FES is the development of *Patterns of Concepts*. The Patterns of Concepts describes the underlying concepts relative to each factor. (These underlying concepts should be considered the equivalent of subfactors when using a universal, subfactor, degree approach.) The Patterns of Concepts (1) provides an excellent outline for developing checkoff-type questions to be included in job analysis questionnaires (this reduces the amount of writing an employee must do to complete the questionnaire); (2) assists those writing a position, job, or class description to describe the essential or critical components of the job and maintain a high degree of uniformity of information presented in each description; and (3) improves the evaluation and the appeals process, since the information provided in the position or job description relates directly to the levels of the factors in FES. (Many point-factor methods use job descriptions that have a job specification section. The specification section normally provides substantiating data relating directly to the job evaluation factors that are equivalent to this part of FES.)

The contribution made by the Patterns of Concepts within FES is the degree of direction it provides to those responsible for analyzing jobs, writing job descriptions, and evaluating the worth of these jobs. It is unlikely that the same individuals are going to be involved in every phase of the evaluation process. Therefore, the Patterns of Concepts guidelines provide continuity of thought and improve acceptance and the potential for success. Exhibit 1-5 provides a summary of the Patterns of Concepts.

Criteria for the assignment of factor levels to a job being evaluated also provide for greater uniformity in the evaluation process. Although the approach used by FES is not new, its clarity and preciseness of instruction minimize misunderstanding and evaluation differences.

The following six criteria must be observed when evaluating jobs using FES:

1. Only the specific point values indicated in FES standards may be used. *Intermediate point values may not be used.*
2. For a position factor to warrant a given point value, it must be fully equivalent to the overall intent of the selected factor level description.

3. Point values assigned to the factors in a position description must relate only to one set of responsibilities and duties. Usually, these duties take a majority of the employee's time and have obvious weight and influence for point-rating purposes. If a particular set of responsibilities and duties is performed for less than the majority of time, it may be considered as a basis for point rating only under the following conditions:

   • Such responsibilities and duties are paramount in influence and weight, occupy a substantial portion of the employee's time, are regularly assigned on a reasonably frequent basis, and are not of an emergency, incidental, or temporary nature.

   • They are so different from other responsibilities and duties in the position that they require a materially higher level of qualifications, which are used as a basis for staffing the position.

4. Because all factors of a position description must reflect a relationship to the same set of responsibilities and duties, Factor 2, Supervisory Controls, and all other factors, are assigned point values relating to the responsibilities and duties that served as a basis for point rating Factor 1, Knowledge Required by the Position.

Exhibit 1-5: Summary of the Patterns of Concepts

Factor 1, Knowledge Required by the Position
Kind or nature of knowledges and skills needed; and
How these knowledges and skills are used in doing the work.

Factor 2, Supervisory Controls
How the work is assigned,
The employee's responsibility for carrying out the work, and
Judgment needed to apply the guidelines or develop new guides.

Factor 4, Complexity
Nature of the assignment,
Difficulty in identifying what needs to be done, and
Difficulty and originality involved in performing the work.

Factor 5, Scope and Effect
Purpose of the work, and
Impact of the work product or service.

Factor 6, Personal Contacts
People and conditions under which contacts are made (except supervisor).

Factor 7, Purpose of Contacts
Reasons for contacts in Factor 6; skill needed to accomplish work through person-to-person activities.

Factor 8, Physical Demands
The nature, frequency, and intensity of physical activity.

Factor 9, Work Environment
The risks and discomforts imposed by physical surroundings and the safety precautions necessary to avoid accidents or discomfort.

---

5. Because the factors are weighted differently, it is not possible to balance a high rating for one factor with a low rating for another. *Each factor must be rated independently.*
6. Some combinations of factor levels are highly improbable. For example, it is unlikely that a position requiring skill and a wide range of professional knowledge (Level 1-7 of Knowledge Required by the Position) would have very close supervision (Level 2-1 of Supervisory Controls) or specific guidelines (Level 3-1 of Guidelines).

The third step in FES is the development of *benchmarks*. Benchmarks describe a typical job situation that represents a significant number of jobs in an occupation. Thus, FES provides three sets of standards for evaluating the worth of jobs ranging from the broad, universal definition in the Primary Standards to the more specific definition in the Series Standard to the very precise definition in the Benchmarks. These provide job evaluators with a wide range of job-standard information to facilitate quick and accurate evaluation of a job and allow a wide degree of flexibility in matching a job under study with an appropriate standard.

Through its design, the FES provides sufficient structure to facilitate its application with maximum consistency in a wide variety of situations and organizations. These design features also provide maximum flexibility, since the nine factors can be redefined in terms applicable to almost any job or occupation without changing the meaning as defined in the Primary Standards.

Regression Analysis

Over the past four decades, mathematical models have been developed to evaluate the worth of jobs. The mathematical procedure that has gained the greatest recognition uses a linear multiple regression technique. Linear multiple regression has been used to accurately predict rates of pay. A regression model has a dependent variable and one (simple regression) or more (multiple regression) independent variables. The value of the independent variables and their interrelationships predict the value of the dependent variable. The quality of the regression model relates directly to its predictive ability.

In using regression models to predict the rates of pay, evaluators must first make certain basic assumptions about the important factors that operate in the real world. The independent variables used in the regression model are comparable to the compensable factors used in the more traditional approaches to job evaluation. The major difference, however, is that the regression model variables are more objective and less abstract than the traditional compensable factors. Regression models may use such objective variables as years since last degree, age of incumbent, annual dollar sales of business, number of subordinates directly supervised, and number of levels from chief executive officer.

Another job evaluation method that captures pay policy uses regression analysis with a structured and weighted task list of jobs. The development of structured and weighted task lists starts with the detailed analysis of a wide variety of jobs that results in a lengthy list of job tasks. Experts review this list and develop more concise and manageable task lists. Individual jobholders then identify which tasks are or are not part of their jobs. They also identify, through various scaling procedures, the relative difficulty, complexity, importance, or frequency of occurrence of these tasks. They may also be asked to describe the kind and amount of education and skill required to perform the task when first entering the job or when the job is performed in a completely proficient manner. The best known example of a structured and weighted task list is the Position Analysis Questionnaire (PAQ) developed at Purdue University.

From their initial analysis of approximately 171 jobs—later expanded to over 3,000—behavioral scientists at Purdue identified 189 elements that they claim will cover all jobs. Through factor analysis, these elements were further grouped into thirty-two dimensions. Then, through the use of a stepwise regression-analysis procedure, it was found that nine dimensions could predict the pay of jobs. The nine dimensions, which are composites for a number of job elements, act as compensable factors.

The development of structured and weighted task lists becomes enmeshed in many of the same issues that relate to compensable factors. A list of job task statements of manageable size and adequately covering differing levels and kinds of jobs requires that the task statements be general and, to some degree, abstract. Since abstraction involves varying differences in recognition, understanding, and perception, these differences ultimately result in conflict over which tasks relate to which job. The problem of semantics thus becomes an issue in developing task lists.

A major characteristic of a structured task list is the listing and description of task statements that are recognized and understood by incumbents completing a task list questionnaire. Task lists now in use require incumbents to identify those tasks they perform while doing their work assignments. Incumbents frequently encounter difficulty in recognizing and comprehending the tasks in the inventory and in relating them to the work they do. A structured task list provides very general task statements to describe the specific task of a job; therefore care must be taken to ensure that the inventory of task statements relates in a useful and meaningful way to the real experiences of the person on the job.

In addition to the development of recognizable task statements, scales are developed to permit the weighting of each task. Some of the scales commonly used to measure task worth or value are task part of the job, relative difficulty, relative importance, relative complexity, relative amount of time spent on the task, and frequency of occurrence. To answer these questions concerning tasks, a respondent must use very personal and extremely subjective values, and the results of the specific answers may be questioned.

The structured and weighted task lists provide both indicators (task statements) and indications (specific weighted values of the tasks). It is critical that the indicator and indication relate in some manner to a perceived value held by incumbents. The inventory of task statements must be logically sound and have a genuine real-world relationship to the job it describes.

At least one potential area of difference exists between the more traditional compensable-factor job evaluation plans and the regression-analysis-based plans: regression-analysis-based plans are designed to capture company pay actions, while the compensable-factor job evaluation plans may or may not be designed to capture pay policies.

As mentioned earlier in this chapter, the rewards provided by employers in exchange for employee services are far broader and more complex than base pay. Pay is only one component, albeit an important one, of the compensation system, and compensation is but one major component of the reward system. Each organization has its own unique mixture of reward components, and that mix uses not only different compensation components by kind but also by degree. When using job evaluation to establish an equitable ordering of jobs, organizations may not, and most likely, do not, follow this listing without changes.

Equitable Job Ordering and Differences in Pay

There are at least six major forces that influence pay decisions and may result in pay relationships that are different from the ordering of jobs as established through job evaluation. These forces include (1) differences in the reward and compensation package, (2) traditional considerations, (3) political considerations, (4) demonstrated employee behavior, (5) ability to pay, and (6) market demands.

Differences in the Reward and Compensation Package. The opportunity to earn different reward and compensation components and the differences in the size of these payments may drastically alter the compensation package. An example of this may be where one group of jobs has more job security. Incumbents in this group have never been laid off, and they know that as long as they behave in an acceptable manner they will have a job. Another group of jobs may receive higher pay but be evaluated lower than the high security jobs because the jobholders must endure frequent but temporary layoffs. Another example is where compensable features of a job, (for example, overtime, premiums, shift differentials, and weekend premiums) are not covered by the job evaluation plan but still have a significant influence on the actual size of the paycheck.

Traditional Considerations. From the early days in the development of the organization, certain pay relationships have existed in organizations and these relationships continue to exist although the results of job evaluations do not support them.

Political Considerations. For whatever the political reason (the incumbent is the owner's son-in-law, or the boss's companion, or close friend, for instance), rates of pay are adjusted because of subjective personal reasons. Again, job evaluation does not justify these pay relationships.

Demonstrated Employee Behavior. Job evaluation places a worth on a job independent of the jobholder. Pay rates, however, are significantly influenced by employee job-related and organizationally related behavior, such as tenure on the job or with the organization and the quality and quantity of work performance.

Ability to Pay. Another reason for job rates of pay that differ from an established ordering of jobs according to worth is that many organizations have a limited amount of money available for employee compensation. To make more effective use of the available funds, they are allocated in a manner peculiar to the organization; thus pay reflects neither market relationships nor internal worth considerations.

Market Demands. Other than internal relationships, possibly the most important influence on rates of pay is the market. Many individuals who question the ability of job evaluation to establish an internally equitable ordering of jobs say job evaluation is a waste of time because the market still establishes the rate of pay. In a macro sense, this may be true, but it is absolutely false in a micro or organizational sense. All one has to do is look at the wide ranges of pay identified for comparable jobs by highly respected surveying organizations. One may say that the data collected was faulty (poor job matching), but there is always the possibility that job matching was accurate and that factors other than job comparability significantly influenced pay-rate decisions.

Examples of Job Evaluation Practices Currently in Use

Over the past twenty years, the American Compensation Association (ACA) of Scottsdale, Arizona has conducted surveys to determine (1) what kinds of job evaluation methods (plans) are being used, (2) groups of employees covered by these plans, and (3) overall satisfaction with these plans. Exhibit 1-6 provides a summary of ACA's 1989 Survey of Job Evaluation Practices of 1,845 organizations. Highlights of this survey include the following:

Frequency of Job Evaluation

- The majority of organizations (more than 50 percent) evaluate job content on an as-needed basis.
- The majority of companies also evaluate job content when requested to do so or when the job has obviously changed.
- Less than one-fourth of companies evaluate jobs on a fixed schedule such as annually or every two years.
- Union positions are the least likely to be evaluated regardless of the stimulus for evaluation.
- Nonprofit/government/educational institutions are more likely to evaluate jobs when requested to do so and less likely to evaluate jobs on a fixed schedule.
- Companies with fewer than 500 employees are more likely to evaluate jobs on a fixed schedule than are larger companies.

Satisfaction with the Job Evaluation Plan

- The vast majority of organizations feel their job evaluation plans meet their needs or are excellent.
- About one-third of organizations describe their job evaluation plan as more than meeting their needs.
- Job evaluation plan satisfaction is weakest when job evaluation is applied to union positions.
- Large organizations are more likely to rate their job evaluation plan as more than satisfactory.
- Nonprofit/government/educational institutions are less satisfied with their job evaluation plans.

Exhibit 1-6: Summary of Survey Results

Types of Jobs
(Expressed as a percent* of respondents)

QUESTIONS	Executive	Middle Management	Engineering & Scientific	Administrative	Sales	Technical	Clerical/Office	Service	Production & Maintenance	Union Salaried	Union Hourly
1. Type of Plan											
Nonquantitative	8%	6%	6%	6%	5%	7%	8%	8%	8%	9%	16%
Quantitative	32	43	40	44	34	42	43	39	39	11	20
Point Factor	27	37	34	38	29	37	38	34	34	9	16
Market Pricing	24	14	15	14	18	14	14	14	15	10	15
2. Evaluated by											
Analyst	29	41	42	42	36	44	44	43	41	22	22
Committee	27	34	28	31	28	29	29	25	26	11	13
Personnel Manager	20	21	19	20	20	20	21	18	19	11	16
Automated	2	3	2	2	2	2	2	2	2	1	1
Consultant	11	2	1	1	2	1	2	1	1	1	1

3. Frequency of Review										
As Needed	55	61	58	60	56	60	59	56	55	27	33
Request	40	49	46	50	43	48	48	46	44	22	24
Job Change	40	47	43	47	42	45	47	44	42	23	25
Fixed Schedule	23	23	16	18	16	17	19	16	17	6	8
4. Satisfaction										
More than Satisfactory	28	37	34	33	31	34	34	32	32	17	20
OK	43	42	39	40	39	40	40	40	41	24	36
Less than Satisfactory	13	17	16	18	18	19	21	17	16	11	12
5. Considering Change?										
No	80	75	74	75	76	74	74	76	75	82	82
Yes	20	25	26	25	24	26	26	24	25	18	18
If Yes,										
Quantitative	29	38	37	38	31	38	37	37	33	12	14
Point Factor	22	29	28	30	25	32	30	28	26	10	13
Market Pricing	8	5	6	5	6	5	6	5	5	2	1
Custom Design	10	10	9	10	10	11	10	9	8	2	4
6. Types of Surveys Used										
National	17	18	18	13	15	8	5	6	4	6	3
Industry	13	17	17	14	16	14	9	10	8	8	9
Regional	9	15	15	14	12	14	10	9	7	7	6
Local	12	12	15	10	20	24	20	21	13	14	14
Own	4	5	5	5	3	7	7	6	6	5	5

*Totals may not equal 100% where no answer was given.

Source: Survey of Job Evaluation Practices, August 1989, American Compensation Association, Scottsdale AZ 85260-3601.

Analyzing Survey Data

An issue to be faced when using data developed by ACA, or any organization that collects data on job evaluation practices, concerns the accuracy of the data. This concern is not with falsification of data, but rather with the ability of respondents to match correctly the job evaluation methods they use with terms such as point factor, point system, factor comparison, job classification, job component, and Hay Associates plan, all of which are used in some surveys. There is significant lack of agreement or common understanding among compensation practitioners as to what is meant by a point system, a factor comparison, or a job classification method of job evaluation. This issue of definition is not only a problem in the area of job evaluation, but occurs in many different compensation-related areas. One word having different meanings and different words having the same meaning form barriers to communication between these specialists and other managers as well as the work force as a whole. Any investigation into this area must ensure complete and common understanding relative to words and terms used to describe concepts, methods, procedures, and so forth.

In summary, over the years the major classification scheme used to group job evaluation methods has been to separate them into quantitative methods and nonquantitative methods. Nonquantitative methods normally include the ranking method, slotting method, and the job-classification method. Quantitative methods include the factor comparison method and the point method. According to the particular compensation specialist doing the writing, many other job evaluation methods are included within these two general classes.

ENDNOTES

1. Elliot Jaques, *Time-span Handbook* (London: Heinemann Educational Books, 1964).
2. T. T. Paterson and T. M. Husband, "Decision-Making Responsibility: Yardstick for Job Evaluation," *Compensation Review,* Second Quarter 1970, 21-31.
3. Merrill R. Lott, *Wage Scales and Job Evaluation: Scientific Determination of Wages and Rates on the Basis of Services Rendered* (New York: Ronald Press, 1926), 46-59.
4. Eugene J. Benge, *Job Evaluation and Merit Rating* (New York: National Foremen's Institute, 1946).
5. American Association of Industrial Management, *Job Rating Manual (Shop)* (1969 Edition) (Melrose Park: Pennsylvania, AAIM, 1969).
6. Edward N. Hay and Dale Purves, "The Profile Method of High-Level Job Evaluation," *Personnel,* September 1951, 162-170; and "A New Method of Job Evaluation: The Guide Chart-Profile Method," *Personnel,* July 1954, 72-80.

Chapter 2

COLLECTING JOB CONTENT INFORMATION

It is difficult to find a human resource function that does not have a significant relationship to the content of the job. In some cases, the input-output relationship between the human resource function and job content may be indirect, while in other cases it is quite direct. The kinds and degrees of job content information vary according to the use of the information within a particular human resource function. Since the primary purpose of this book is to identify a means for establishing a base pay for incumbents performing a wide variety of assignments, particular attention and interest focus on the relationship between job content information and differences in rates of pay. A procedure used for collecting job content information is job analysis.

Job analysis is a systematic process of collecting, recording, and effectively describing information that facilitates an accurate identification of responsibilities, duties, and qualification requirements of a jobholder. Trained individuals using one or more of a number of job analysis procedures collect job content information. With this information, it is possible to describe the job in a manner that enables (1) employees performing jobs to recognize and accept written models that accurately reflect what they do, (2) supervisors to approve of written models that accurately identify what incumbents should be doing, and (3) individuals who may not personally be familiar with the job to recognize the contributions of the job toward the overall success of the organization in accomplishing its objectives.

Although the mission of job analysis is very straightforward, the actual implementation of a successful job analysis program is difficult and costly. Job analysis programs frequently consume large amounts of the work time of those who provide job information and those who record and translate it for specialized uses. What at first glance appears to be a simple assignment quickly becomes complex and laborious. Such areas as differences in perception, lack of common understanding or misunderstanding, special interests or self-interests, and inability to communicate become significant barriers to successful job analysis.

One opportunity to improve both the efficiency and effectiveness of job analysis is through employee participation. In fact, employee participation in the entire job analysis process is crucial to the success of any program of this type in the modern organization. But participation, in itself, is a time consuming, costly process. Throughout this book, a major area of focus will be the identification and description of employee participation opportunities.

One approach to understanding the participation issue is to answer this question: Why do individuals agree to provide availability, capability, and performance for an employer? One answer must be, "For rewards." The rewards an employer can offer are almost limitless, but each reward varies in importance from one individual to another, depending on unique individual demands and specific situational requirements. A reward that in some way influences the behavior of each individual is the monetary payment provided by the employer in return for employee efforts. If job pay is to relate to work content, then an early and extremely important opportunity for employee participation opens when the organization permits, requests, even requires all employees to describe what they do, so that valid and complete descriptions of their jobs can be developed.

The costs related to job analysis efforts have led some experts in the personnel field to conclude that job analysis is a waste of time, especially job analysis as it relates to the setting of pay rates. Before investigating the worthiness of these kinds of statements, it may be useful to identify specifically some of the more important personnel-related uses of job analysis and methods used for collecting job content information.

Basic Uses of Job Analysis Outputs

There are at least four extremely important uses of job content information. One use involves all aspects of staffing; a second relates to the pay assigned a particular job; the third focuses on the appraisal of incumbent performance; and the fourth, and possibly most important use, is to ensure compliance with various pieces of government legislation. If staffing, pay, and appraisal decisions are not firmly rooted in the content of the job, the likelihood of decisions based on highly subjective criteria becomes a distinct possibility.

Staffing begins with employment-related decisions. Testing and selecting candidates for job openings requires valid information about the knowledge and skills necessary for job entry, the responsibilities that must be accepted by an incumbent, and the environmental conditions existing at the workplace. After job entry, staffing involves training and development activities and employee movement from lateral transfer to promotion to even demotion or termination. Action related to these areas normally involves job content information.

Determining job worth and making decisions regarding the assignment of specific rates of pay to specific jobs also require job content information. The needs here differ somewhat from those required for hiring or selection decisions. At this stage, job content information must relate to the knowledge and skills needed by a fully proficient employee and the responsibilities that an employee of that caliber must be capable of performing.

Performance appraisal goes a step beyond traditional job definition by insuring that the dynamic nature of the job and the influences of the environment on successful job performance are fully recognized. The identification of desired results and the establishment of acceptable performance standards again relate to job content.

The major difference between evaluating job worth and appraising incumbent performance is that job worth determinations are made in a relatively static environment, while performance is real-time demonstrated job behavior. Both personnel functions, however, have an audit trail that originates with identified job content information.

Government legislation, including the Fair Labor Standards Act and its amendments and a number of Civil Rights Acts, including the Americans with Disabilities Act (ADA), have critical parts that relate to job content. The more accurate and complete the job content information, the better an organization can comply with these legislated mandates.

Job Content Collection Procedures

Although kind and degree of job content information may vary according to specific use, the procedures available for collecting it are very stable. The four basic job content information collection procedures are (1) questionnaire, (2) observation, (3) interview, and (4) diary/log. A wide variety of approaches are available for designing and using questionnaires and interviews; in addition, the four procedures can be used in any combination. Because of the barriers involved in collecting job information, it is often necessary to combine two or more collection procedures in order to obtain a sufficient quality and quantity of necessary information.

A brief discussion of each of the four basic information-gathering procedures provides some idea of the variety of available approaches.

Questionnaire

For the amount of information collected and the time required to collect it from many incumbents, the questionnaire may be the most useful approach. When using a questionnaire, it is critical that it (1) be designed so that it is easily understood by all who must complete it, (2) collect information on all aspects of the job, and (3) be properly completed.

Questionnaire design varies significantly from the use of a few open-ended questions to a large number of checklist statements. Both of these procedures solicit job content information from respondees. Unlike observation and interview techniques, there is the risk that the respondee will not complete the questionnaire or will complete it inaccurately or take an excessively long time to return it.

Observation

When using this procedure, the analyst observes and records what the incumbent is doing. An analyst must be able to observe the entire work cycle or all activities that a worker must perform. In the service world, where the majority of jobs exist, many assignments must be performed on an irregular basis. The work routine of many workers does not have a linear relationship. Many activities must be performed because of situational requirements that occur in a nonroutine manner. Other activities occur at definite periods of time or on conclusion of a specific set of activities. These activities may be performed once a week, once a month, or only once a year. When using the observation method for identifying work activities, the likelihood of missing nonlinear activities or those that occur infrequently is a distinct possibility. The result is a less than complete picture of the job content.

Another issue faced by any observer who is not intimately familiar with the job under review relates to the often-discussed issue of perception. Is what the observer sees and records actually what is happening? An observer's interpretation and description of what is visualized may not, in reality, validly describe what actually occurs. It is for these reasons that observations normally are linked with the interview procedure. By combining observations with the interview, the analyst (observer) can

- clarify aspects of the job that were not completely understood.
- inquire about activities performed by the worker that were not detected by the observer or were not performed while the observer was on the scene.
- include comments or feelings of the worker as to which aspects of the job should be emphasized and which should be deemphasized.

Interview

The interview is a face-to-face situation in which the job analyst attempts to gather job content information by discussion with one or more individuals who have knowledge of the job. A title frequently given to these individuals is *Subject Matter Experts* or SMEs. The interview may be conducted with an incumbent; with groups of employees performing jobs that are similar, closely related, or interacting; with supervisors of jobs under study; or with individuals who do not perform the job but who are intimately familiar with the job activities, the behaviors demonstrated by proficient workers, and the results expected when the job is performed in a satisfactory manner.

When conducting a group interview that includes job incumbents and higher levels of management (possibly the immediate supervisor), care must be taken to ensure that the presence of these higher levels of management does not inhibit the incumbent from discussing the job content. In many cases, when an employee perceives the presence of a supervisor (immediate or otherwise) as threatening or coercive, valid and useful information will not be forthcoming.

Many of the same design issues that affect the value and usefulness of a questionnaire also affect the design of an interview. Kinds of questions and their sequence have a direct influence on the quality of information collected in an interview. In addition, when interviewing groups, the analyst must exhibit extreme care in determining who will and who will not interviewed.

Diary/Log

The least used of the four job content information collection procedures is the diary/log. In this approach, the analyst asks job incumbents to keep daily logs of work activities. When an incumbent changes from one activity to another, a description of the new activity is recorded along with the time of occurrence. As with the observation, it is critical that the incumbent record all significant work activities, including those that occur infrequently or at irregular intervals. The primary advantage of using this procedure is its comprehensiveness. However, the diary/log requires much effort and diligence on the part of the incumbent. In addition, many people do not like to write or to spend time writing, and this blocks success with this procedure. One alternative to writing in a diary is to provide a handy tape recorder that allows the incumbent to record his or her work activities as they occur. Administrative or staff personnel can then transcribe from the tape to a written document.

Combination or Multiple Approach

Because of the usefulness and importance to both employer and employee, job content information of sufficient quantity and quality may require the use of two or more of these information collection procedures. A multiple approach provides these benefits.

Questionnaires can provide the largest amount of information for an extended number of jobs in the shortest amount of time and are probably the least costly approach. Observation gives the analyst a deeper understanding and appreciation of what the job is all about. Interviewing may develop specific kinds of information not readily obtainable through either the questionnaire or observation and permit a validation of information and the interpretation of the information gathered through other procedures. Diary/logs can provide specific and more detailed information than that obtained through any other collection approach. Because a quality job analysis program must identify and describe the activities an incumbent performs and the knowledge and skills required in the satisfactory performance of these activities, multiple job information collection techniques that involve more than one jobholder are frequently used.

Job Analysis Criticisms

One of America's most successful football coaches, Vince Lombardi, stated many times that what separates champion football teams from others is skill in blocking and tackling. To acquire these two fundamental skills, patience, perseverance, diligence, and hard work are necessary. Developing a group that blocks and tackles as a coordinated team is extremely costly in terms of time and effort.

The blocking and tackling concept also applies to the personnel function, as managers work toward the development of first-class workers who perform their activities in a first-class work environment. Nowhere is the requirement for "doing your homework" or "learning the fundamentals" more applicable than in the many personnel-related functions directly associated with the identification and description of job content. The time-consuming fundamentals discussed in collecting, analyzing, and summarizing job information have a direct impact on decisions that critically influence employee job behavior and organizational success.

Over the years, however, criticisms by professionals in the human resources field have been leveled at job analysis procedures. Here are some of the more common criticisms:

1. Completion of a job analysis questionnaire requires an excessive amount of the incumbent's time or that of a supervisor who may be required to complete it.
2. Adequate and acceptable review by supervisors consumes an inordinate amount of their time.
3. Analysis, validation, additions, and deletions by the analyst are very costly.
4. Analysts are unable to separate fact from fiction; incumbents can easily inflate or deflate their jobs.
5. Questionnaire completion requires too much writing.
6. Information provided by questionnaires is inconsistent and varies significantly from one jobholder to another.
7. In many jobs, activities are frequently added and deleted, and it is almost impossible to keep any description current.

Reviewing and Analyzing Critical Comments

A major criticism of job analysis is that it consumes an excessive amount of time. In the short-term perspective, a job analysis that requires incumbent, supervisor, and analyst to review current work-content of jobs can consume as much as three to five hours. Multiply that by the compensation received by each employee and the number of incumbents to be interviewed, and the cost can be substantial.

The first rebuttal is that if the analysis is done properly the first time, and if the job content information is complete and correct, updating requires a minimal amount of time.

If money is not spent on an effective job analysis program, the scenario may look like this:

1. Employee does not understand what he or she is supposed to be doing on the job.
2. Results expected by the organization fail to materialize.

3. Supervisor and employee fail to agree on the quality of demonstrated job behavior.
4. Organization does not generate revenues to maintain work force or provide rewards employees expect.
5. Employees do not receive rewards expected, and they reduce their outputs in relation to rewards received and those they expect to receive.

While it is possible to measure the effectiveness of our human resource management through the use of turnover rates, grievance frequency, and employee morale questionnaires, these measures can only scratch the surface. In manufacturing environments, industrial engineers concentrate primarily on efficiency in the use of available human resources. But this does not ensure that these resources are being utilized effectively. In addition, the efforts of the industrial engineer often conflict with those attempting to reduce turnover rates and improve overall worker performance.

An intensive job content analysis can be viewed as a foundation on which to build an efficient and effective human resource system. While accountants would revolt at the idea, a complete job analysis project can be viewed as a capital outlay, the benefits of which the organization will realize over an extended period of time. In any case, the cost of job analysis in the long term is not expensive and does not present an extreme burden on organizational revenues.

Any response to job analysis criticisms must also take into consideration available alternatives.

Alternative 1. Ask employees what they do, and in ten minutes or less they can orally describe their jobs.

The response to Alternative 1 is poppycock! This approach is not worth the paper it is written on. Sooner or later, someone, somehow must describe in writing what the incumbent does in performing the job. The description must include all significant work activities, must be in a uniform format, must be useful for various purposes to a number of people who may not be personally familiar with the job, and must adequately describe the complexity, scope, and purpose of the job.

Alternative 2. Use a canned approach. A number of structured task-analysis checklists are available. Job incumbents merely review the list, checking those items that most closely describe the work they do.

The response to Alternative 2 is that no checklist has yet been developed that (1) identifies the activities included within all jobs of an organization and (2) provides an accurate estimate of the criticality, complexity, importance, or intensity of the activity as performed in a specific job for a specific organization. Structured task lists provide cookbook approaches or bird's-eye views that describe how a job should be performed, not how it is being performed.

Within the next decade, however, the use of computer-generated, occupation-based task inventories will significantly change the entire job- analysis process. Task inventories consisting of from 200 to 500 statements for most occupations will be available on disks. Employees will be able to sit in front of a terminal and select those statements that define their jobs. They will also be given instructions on how to modify an occupation generic task statement to provide a unique description of their own work activities.

Alternative 3. Eliminate the questionnaire and use either an observation by the analyst or a review by the supervisor to provide job information.

The response to Alternative 3 is that although it may significantly reduce the amount of time consumed in collecting job content information, the problem of completeness remains an unresolved issue, and it does not promote incumbent participation.

Designing a Job Analysis Questionnaire

Because job analysis questionnaires are the most commonly used procedures for collecting job content information to be used for the writing of job descriptions and the eventual evaluation of a job, the alternatives for designing a questionnaire should be reviewed.

When the eventual output of job analysis is the determination of a rate of pay for jobs based on their worth, the selection of the job evaluation method assumes immediate importance. This selection must precede the design of the questionnaire. Kinds of questions and the particular design of information-capturing devices must relate directly to the job- evaluation method. Different job evaluation methods require different kinds and degrees of job content information.

Format Considerations

The format of the questionnaire should facilitate accurate completion by the respondee. The kinds of questions and their flow should direct the respondee's attention to job activities in a manner that simulates what actually occurs when performing job assignments. It should assist in identifying both the obscure and the obvious work activities.

A questionnaire normally has four distinct sections. The first section is an identification section that requires the respondee to identify him or herself, to state his or her current job title, and to provide other individual and organizational information. The second section requests job activity information. The third section focuses specifically on compensable factor information that identifies significant features or qualities of the job.

The fourth is the review section. Here, the immediate supervisor or manager having the closest working relationship with the incumbent reviews the information provided by the respondee for completeness and accuracy. (In *no* case, however, does a reviewer ever delete or modify what the respondee reports. In such cases the reviewer will complete a separate section describing inaccuracies or providing additional information.)

As is readily apparent, the second and third sections are the heart of the questionnaire, and it is here that questionnaires may have significantly different design characteristics. An initial issue facing the questionnaire designer relates to the use of open-ended questions or checklist statements.

Open-ended Questions. The open-ended, verbalized narrative certainly grants respondees a "day in court." If the quest is to find out what is happening now at the work site, the open-ended narrative excels. In responding to this kind of question, incumbents can describe all their activities, including those that supervisors or the personnel department may not know about; those activities they feel they should be doing as part of their jobs, but are not; and those they are not doing, but should be doing.

Open-ended questions allow incumbents to use their own terminology in answering the questions. This kind of question is useful when considerable variation in responses can be expected. The primary disadvantage of open-ended questions is that they are often answered too sketchily (sometimes not at all), or they are answered too verbosely. This may leave the job analyst with the task of having to return to the incumbent or other sources to obtain the information originally required or sifting through superfluous information to identify that which is necessary.

Checklist Statements. A checklist allows the respondee to make a choice among a number of potential or alternative responses rather than having to write detailed answers to open-ended questions. A properly designed set of checklist statements provides a broad spectrum of possible responses, which enhances the probability that the respondee will find the right description of his or her job with respect to the job content feature under study.

There are also disadvantages in using checklist questions. Employees are unlikely to formulate responses that do not appear as alternative responses for a specific job feature. What may be more harmful is that employees may interpret the alternative responses in a context other than that intended. And, of course, there are employees who will select responses that they feel will place their jobs in the most favorable light, not necessarily the ones that most closely relate to their particular jobs.

The two basic kinds of job information obtained through the use of checklist statements are task or job activity information and features or qualities of the job that include environmental conditions influencing employee performance.

Task or Activity Checklist Statements must be extensive if they are to cover all the essential tasks/activities performed by an incumbent. When designing a questionnaire that contains the basic tasks/activities of various kinds of jobs, it is necessary to develop a different set of checklist statements for each occupational group. This means that there would be a different questionnaire for each job family or occupation. The actual development of a set of checklist statements initially requires some kind of open-ended questionnaire or interview session in which people very familiar with a specific kind of work identify the tasks/activities performed in the job under review. After considerable amounts of analysis and review, a set of checklist statements is developed. The preliminary work required to design sets of checklist task/activity statements is, in itself, time-consuming and costly. Following identification of job tasks or activities, the principal knowledge and skills required to perform each task/activity must also be identified in a satisfactory manner.

Once developed, the checklist statements must then be placed on a scale. The scales assist the analyst to identify not only the tasks/activities that are part of a particular job but also the level or degree of the task/activity.

Scales relate to dimensions of the task as it relates to the job. Such scale dimensions are (1) criticality, (2) complexity, (3) importance, (4) frequency of occurrence, and (5) difficulty. One very simple scale requests the respondee to identify whether or not the task is part of the job. Those involved in designing structured task lists frequently add another dimension to their investigation by weighting each task statement. Responses to the previously identified scales assist in developing weights for each task/activity.

Job Feature or Quality Checklists normally relate to the specific compensable factors used in the job evaluation method. The purpose of developing job-feature checklists is to focus the respondee's attention on the specific kinds and degrees of information needed for job evaluation purposes. By using checklist statements, alternative responses can be couched in terminology that closely relates to the description of the various degrees/levels of the compensable factors used in the job evaluation method.

Most questionnaires using checklist statements (for job tasks/activities or job qualities/features) will also request respondees to provide alternative responses when the list of statements does not, from the respondee's point of view, provide an adequate response. The use of the open-ended opportunity with the structured checklist once again underscores the need for a mixed approach for gathering job-related information. The complexity of jobs, variations in individual interpretations, and differences in skill among analysts require the use of all the techniques available for collecting job information.

Jobs in a Team-based Organization Environment

A new problem facing many organizations is the definition of a job in a team-based organization environment. The grouping of employees into teams and the delegation of authority to teams that once was the sole prerogative of management has clouded the area of job-based responsibilities and duties.

Instead of making job analysis less critical, the movement toward team-based management makes job analysis more critical. Team members frequently have responsibilities that once were assigned to managers, such as (1) assignment of team members to certain duties and the flexibility to change duty assignments; (2) selection of personnel for team membership; (3) rating of team-member knowledge and skills for assignment of rates of pay; (4) requesting training and development opportunities for team members; and (5) training team members for team-performed assignments.

The definition of jobs in a team-based environment is *not* significantly different than the definition of jobs in a knowledge-based operation. Job assignments change frequently; some assignments are performed at infrequent intervals; and assignments are extremely situational-based. Assignment of additional duties that must be accepted and performed by team members when certain conditions occur is quite likely.

The dynamics related to change in working assignments makes many believe it is now more difficult if not almost impossible to define jobs, especially team-member jobs. No doubt from an administrative and record-keeping process the defining of a team-member job is far more complex than that of defining the job of a factory worker in a typical manufacturing environment. However, with the great advances in computer-based technology that can maintain inventories to identify every task performed within a work unit or an occupation or by an employee, as well as the word processing capabilities to transfer this information to job descriptions, it is now possible to identify precisely, accurately, and completely what a specific employee is doing at any point in time—in other words, to identify the *job* of any employee.

Job definitions in a team-based environment start with a definition of all tasks or responsibilities and duties performed by the team members. Specific team-member responsibilities and duties may be related to a work station. A work station is a physical location where the assigned individual must perform certain tasks or respond to specific well-identified inputs. The job of a team member would include all assignments made to a specific individual, recognizing that individual's level of knowledge, skills, and physical capabilities.

Because team-based environments may require employees to perform wider and more extensive sets of responsibilities and duties, it is critical that a list of responsibilities and duties be established for each team member and that the member be qualified to perform them. By prioritizing these sets of responsibilities and duties, it is also possible to recognize their importance or their frequency of occurrence, just as would be done with the responsibilities and duties of an employee in a typical job setting. The major difference in a team-based environment is that the list of responsibilities and duties may be more extensive and, for certain team members, may include every assignment completed by the team.

Chapter 3

WRITING THE JOB DESCRIPTION

After incumbents have provided job content information and the supervisors have reviewed it for accuracy and completeness, the questionnaires are given to job analysts for further checking, reviewing, and clarification. As important as the collection of job information may be, it is an exercise in futility if the information is not processed, summarized, and made valuable for other uses. The transition stage from the job analysis to further use of the information for a variety of human resource functions is the writing of the job description.

Once again, the appearance of simplicity and ease is misleading and may be a trap for those who fail to recognize the difficulties and costs involved in writing a job description. On the other hand, the importance of a job description cannot be overstated. It may be the most important document linking employer obligations to employee responsibilities. The job description has a number of the major components of an employer-employee quasi-contract. It does not detail what rewards the employer offers for employee availability, capability, and performance. It also does not detail specific results expected of the employee. But, it does outline job requirements and the typical activities expected of a jobholder in performing job assignments. In addition, the job description may contain sections that identify job specifications and a general list of desired end results.

Definitions of Critical Words and Terms

In most cases, each job, like the jobholder, is unique, and the requirements and content of each unique job must be documented accurately and precisely. An existing barrier to the writing of valid and useful job descriptions and, for that matter, the implementation and completion of a successful classification and pay project is that many of the words and terms common to the field of human resources management and, in particular, to job analysis are often used interchangeably and inconsistently and are poorly defined. This situation has led to considerable misunderstanding, which is a problem not only for the newcomer trying to develop skills in this area but also for experienced practitioners, consultants, and researchers. To establish a sound basis for understanding the processes and methods developed throughout this book, the following commonly used words and terms are defined.

Position: Work consisting of responsibilities and duties assignable to one employee (there are as many positions as there are employees; in fact, there can be more positions than employees when there are unfilled positions). Example: Mary Jones, Secretary, Purchasing Department.

Job: Work consisting of responsibilities and duties that are sufficiently alike to justify being covered by a single job analysis/job description. A job may be assignable to one or more employees. Example: Secretary, Purchasing Department.

Class: A group of jobs sufficiently similar as to kinds of subject matter; education and experience requirements; levels of difficulty, complexity, and responsibility; and qualification requirements of the work. (It is possible to have a single-job class.) Example: Secretary II.

Class-series: A grouping of job classes having similar job content but differing in degree of difficulty, complexity, and responsibility; level of skill; knowledge; and qualification requirements. The jobs within a class can form a career ladder. Example: Secretarial Series (I to IV).

Family: Two or more class-series within an organization that have related or common work content. Example: Administrative Support Occupation (Secretarial-Clerical).

Occupation: A grouping of jobs or job classes within a number of different organizations that have similar skill, effort, and responsibility requirements. Example: Administrative Support Occupation (Secretarial-Clerical).

Activity: A word with broad general meaning that includes any kind of action or movement required of a jobholder in performing job assignments. The word *activity* is often used as a generic in lieu of the following words: *function, element, task, duty,* and *responsibility.*

Major Activity or Responsibility: A term that relates to an important or critical area of the job. Major activity statements are statements that, taken together, describe the general nature of the job. They organize the job into distinct categories. They provide the top of a funnel classification scheme that moves from major activities to tasks to procedures. (The word *responsibility* is used in lieu of major activity when identifying the "major activities" in a job description.)

Function: The natural or proper actions an individual, work unit, or mechanism performs. The activities required in the performance of a job; could be synonymous with a major activity or responsibility.

Element: The smallest step into which it is practical to subdivide any work activity without analyzing separate motions and mental processes. Elements are the individual activity units of identifiable and definable physical and intellectual work that produces an output.

Task: A coordinated series of work activity elements used to produce an identifiable and definable output that can be independently consumed or used.

Duty: One or more tasks performed in carrying out a job responsibility. (The words *responsibility* and *duty* are used to identify the activities in a job description.)

Behavior: The actions an individual takes under certain circumstances. Behavior may be used as a generic term to describe a set of interacting activities.

Essential Job Function: An Americans with Disabilities Act (ADA)-related term that is equivalent to an activity as previously defined, or possibly equivalent to a responsibility or a duty. It is an activity that the individual who holds the position must be able to perform unaided or with the assistance of a reasonable accommodation.

There are definitional problems related not only to these words, but to practically every word used in defining what a person does. The same word has different meanings to people in different situations. Conversely, different words have common meanings to individuals in different situations. For example, Eskimos have over fifty words to describe snow.

To ensure common understanding of the words and terms used in describing a job, the job analysis process should follow accepted rules in sentence or phrase structure and in defining words and terms.

Design of a Typical Job Description

Job descriptions may take almost limitless forms, but many will include five basic sections: (1) identification, (2) summary, (3) responsibility and duty statements (job definition), (4) minimum qualifications or specifications, and (5) accountabilities.

The job identification section may consist only of a job title, or it may include a dozen or so items such as job title, department, name of supervisor, date written, and so forth. The two most important identification items are (1) job title and (2) date written. The date the job description was written should absolutely appear somewhere on the job description. This date is critical for review and update purposes.

The job summary section will normally consist of from two to five sentences that provide a capstone or thumbnail description of the essential parts of the job.

The responsibility and duty section is the heart of the job description. Responsibilities identify the primary reasons for the existence of the job or its major activities. Duties further describe the responsibilities and could also be called subresponsibilities. The sets of responsibilities and duties define the job.

Practically all jobs can be completely described by anywhere from three to seven responsibility statements. Some jobs, however, may have only one responsibility. The major functional areas in which the jobholder has work assignments identify the responsibilities. Analyzing these responsibilities, in turn, identifies the major knowledge and skills required of the jobholder. These activities may relate to such general areas as (1) operational (things the employee does); (2) technical (formal kinds and levels of knowledge and skills required of the employee); (3) financial; and (4) interpersonal.

Responsibilities and duties establish not only the what and how of the job, but also why the job exists. The important point to remember in defining them is that the key issue is why the work is being performed, although these statements also normally provide what and how information.

The minimum qualifications section identifies the knowledge and skills a candidate should have prior to being selected for the job. This section may also include a listing of any certificates, registrations, and licenses required of an incumbent before that person can legally perform job assignments.

A specification section normally is included when the organization uses a compensable-factor job evaluation method. The specification section provides substantiating data for the compensable factors as they relate to the job. Examples of typical compensable qualities or features of a job that may be included within a specification section are:

1. Frequency and type of supervision received.
2. Frequency and type of supervision given.
3. Interaction or involvement in teaching, counseling, coaching, training, or development of others.
4. Ability and requirements for analyzing and evaluating action-oriented information.
5. Requirements for following instructions or orders.
6. Amount and quality of direction, instructions, and suggestions transmitted.
7. Degree of accountability for human and nonhuman resources in planning, operations, and control of the job.
8. Physical demands.
9. Emotional demands.
10. Special demands.

An accountability section identifies desired results in very general terms. Actual results required of a jobholder are influenced daily by all kinds and variations of situational and environmental demands. These demands may vary significantly, but the general results expected of the jobholder are rather static.

General Guidelines for Writing Job Descriptions

The first requirement for writing a useful job description is to have valid and sufficient job content information available for the writing exercise. The entire purpose of Chapter 2 was to describe procedures available for identifying and collecting job information. In addition to the procedures described in Chapter 2, additional job information may be obtained by reviewing existing job descriptions, organizational charts, and manuals that describe in detail the methods used in performing assignments. These manuals may describe material use, machine operation, and purpose of operation. The manual may also describe the "best way" to do the assignment, detailing the sequence of methods and procedures for accomplishing job requirements.

The most difficult part of writing a job description involves the identification and description of responsibilities and duties. Because of the confusion that results when asking a job incumbent to identify and describe responsibilities and duties, it is far better to ask incumbents to provide task/activity information. An individual trained and skilled in the writing of job descriptions then takes the task/activity information provided through questionnaires, observation, interviews, or diary/logs and develops responsibility and duty statements. Performing this assignment requires an appreciation of the work being performed and knowledge of the correct verbs to use in describing the specific activity.

A job responsibility, duty, or activity statement should describe the *what* requirements of the job. Sloppy thinking, poor writing skills, and excessive use of jargon can minimize success.

In writing the responsibility and duty statements, the first assignment is to review the task/activity statement provided through the job analysis. In most cases, employees will identify from fifteen to fifty activities that they perform. From these task/activity statements, the analyst selects one or more statements that identify a general characteristic or function of the job and its organizational relationship. These general characteristic statements then become the responsibility statements for the job. When identifying and describing a responsibility, it may be necessary at times to combine two or more activities into one responsibility.

After identifying the responsibilities, the analyst then reviews the task/activity list and places under a specific responsibility those tasks/activities that best describe or relate to it. Normally, three to seven activities or duties are sufficient to adequately describe major features of a responsibility.

After developing a first draft of the responsibilities, the analyst should review the information provided by the job incumbent for (1) order of importance, (2) time spent or frequency of occurrence, (3) difficulty, and (4) complexity. This review should provide the analyst with enough information to establish an ordering of responsibilities. The same procedure is then used to establish a ranking of duties for each responsibility.

When the final draft of responsibility and duty statements is written, the responsibilities should follow a natural order. The list of responsibilities (when more than one is identified) may be an ordering of the characteristics or functions by importance or a description of a sequential relationship to the overall work performed. The list of duties may also relate to the sequence of occurrence of the duty or the relative importance of the duty within the specific responsibility. This procedure allows for a needed uniformity among job responsibility and duty statements. Anyone reviewing such a list would know that the first responsibility listed is the most important or comes first in a sequence of occurrence, the second listed is the second most important or the second in sequence of occurrence, and so on. Likewise, the ordering of duties within a responsibility also would easily carry the same meaning to a reviewer.

In a compensable-factor job evaluation plan, the job description writers should include information that substantiates or identifies the specific level or degree of each compensable factor included within the job evaluation method. This is called the job specification section of the job description.

The job specification information should clearly describe different kinds or levels of work. Care should be taken in describing the precise nature of the compensable factor as it relates to the job. To ensure a proper description of the specification, the analyst must thoroughly understand the compensable factor and be able to recognize differences among the levels/degrees of the factor.

The writer of the job specification must thoroughly understand both the job and the compensable factors so that the parts of the job as they relate to the compensable factor of the job evaluation method can be precisely described.

Formatting is also extremely important when writing the job specification section. All compensable factors should appear in the same order in all job descriptions. The specification statements should provide level/degree distinguishing features. This can be accomplished by (1) underlining or otherwise highlighting those words, phrases, and sentences that distinguish the levels/degrees, and (2) distinguishing between major and minor aspects of the factor as it relates to the job.

The responsibilities and duties of the job should complement and support the job specification. Information provided within the responsibilities and duties could be repeated and expanded in the specification section.

Benefits and Costs

Under the general title of job description, an organization may have a position description (one relating specifically to the work of each employee); a job description (one describing work that is similarly if not identically performed by one or more incumbents); or a class description (one describing comparable work performed by one or more incumbents). The descriptions may be so general that they are of minimal value to anyone or so specific that they could be used as an industrial engineering workplace study. In addition to acceptable degrees of specificity, the other major issue involving job descriptions is the validity and up-to-date value of the job information provided.

No doubt many job descriptions in a large number of organizations are inadequate. They do not describe the job in terms that aid the varied human resource functions, and the descriptions are often obsolete. It is also true that, from a narrow frame of reference, the collection and analysis of job data and the writing and printing of job descriptions is a costly process.

A short review of validity, obsolescence, and costs may be helpful here. Job content changes. Sometimes there are dramatic changes caused by new technology or the addition or removal of major responsibilities and duties.

At other times, jobs change slowly, and over an extended period of time they evolve into something significantly different. Identification of job changes rests primarily with three groups: (1) the human resources (HR) department, (2) the immediate supervisor, and (3) the incumbent.

HR department members become involved in reclassification of jobs. Every time a reclassification arrives in the department, an immediate question that must be answered is: Are these additional assignments currently part of another job? If yes, then the other job must also be audited and reclassified. (It is important to recognize that requests for upward reclassification will occur readily, but requests for downward reclassification seldom occur spontaneously.) Auditing and reclassification often require intense investigation on the part of the HR department.

Immediate supervisors usually are the first to know of changing work activities. They should inform the HR department of these changes. However, as mentioned, there is a great likelihood of such communication when job responsibilities and duties increase, but nothing may occur when responsibilities and duties diminish.

The job incumbent is the key figure in keeping a job description current and valid. If incumbents initially have a vital role in the development of their descriptions and recognize the impact of the descriptions on the pay rates established for their jobs, relationship to performance appraisal, transfer, promotion, and other reward opportunities, the great majority of incumbents will make certain that their job descriptions are up-to-date and valid.

An accurate, well-written job description could cost an organization from $100 to $400. That appears to be a high price to pay for a sheet of paper that does nothing more than describe a job. In addition, other funds must be spent to ensure that all job descriptions are current.

A major concern to those involved in maintaining accurate job descriptions is the job that evolves slowly over a period of years. These slow changes are often imperceptible to the incumbent and the immediate supervisor. For this reason, a massive review of all descriptions should be done every three to five years. This review could add another $100 to $300 to the cost of maintaining a valid job description.

An organization that wants up-to-date, accurate job descriptions may have to invest as much as $300 to $500 per job over a period of five years. Thus, an organization with 2,500 employees who perform approximately one thousand different jobs may have to spend as much as $300,000 over a five-year period to maintain a worthwhile job description portfolio:

$200 (per updated job description) x 1,000 jobs = $200,000
Reviewing jobs that do not require the writing
    of job descriptions   <u>100,000</u>
                                           $300,000

Even at half the cost—$150,000—many managers would consider this too high a price to pay.

Looking at this cost from another perspective provides yet another insight to the value of this expenditure. Total compensation (monetary payments plus all in-kind benefit costs) now range from $30,000 to $40,000 per average employee. A minimum average employee compensation cost of $30,000 x 2,500 employees x 5 years equals $375 million dollars in labor costs over a five-year period; $300,000 ÷ $375 million equals less than one-tenth of 1 percent of total labor costs.

Is this too high a price to pay for the only document in the organization that explicitly describes the activities a jobholder should perform, the knowledge and skills required, and the scope and complexity of the job? The job description forms a major building block for many human resources-related functions that impact directly on employee quality of work life and performance.

Chapter 4

DESIGNING A PAY STRUCTURE

A pay structure that eventually sets limits on the base pay for a job is a blend of organizational policies and values, senior management philosophy, external influences, and technical considerations. Pay structure design is neither a complex nor a scientifically pure procedure. However, many issues require recognition and consideration if a pay structure is to achieve its primary purpose of attracting sufficient individuals who will stay with the organization and make the quality of contributions necessary for the organization to achieve its objectives and goals. Decisions affecting the design of the pay structure are frequently made in an arbitrary manner, while information that should be reviewed relative to specific design issues is often neglected.

Pay Structure Design Issues

The following considerations must be acknowledged in one manner or another when designing a pay structure. The more objective the review of these critical areas, the greater the likelihood that pay structure-related decisions will benefit both the employees and the employer:

1. What is the lowest rate of pay that can be offered for a job that will entice the quality of employees the organization desires to have as its members?
2. What is the rate of pay that must be offered to incumbents to ensure that they remain with the organization?

3. Does the organization desire to recognize seniority and meritorious performance through the base pay schedule?

4. Is it wise or necessary to offer more than one rate of pay to employees performing either identical or similar types of work?

5. What is considered a sufficient difference in base rates of pay among jobs requiring varying levels of knowledge and skills and responsibilities and duties of increasing complexity?

6. Does the organization wish to recognize dangerous and distressing working conditions within the base pay schedule?

7. Should there be a difference in changes in base pay progression opportunities among jobs of varying worth?

8. Do employees have a significant opportunity to progress to higher level jobs? If so, what should be the relationship between promotion to a higher job and changes in base pay?

9. Will policies and regulations permit incumbents to earn rates of pay higher than established maximums and lower than established minimums? What would be the reasons for allowing such deviations?

10. How will the pay structure accommodate across-the-board, cost-of-living, or other adjustments not related to employee tenure, performance, or responsibility and duty changes?

Pay Structure Design Features

An initial issue in designing a pay structure is the determination of the lowest and highest rates of pay. Between these minimum and maximum rates of pay there will be a slotting of job rates of pay that vary because of differences in job worth as determined by (1) variations in knowledge and skill requirements, (2) assigned responsibilities and duties, (3) dangerous and distressing conditions within which the job must be performed, (4) traditional pay practices of the organization, (5) political relationships that exist between individuals who can influence pay practices, and (6) the pressures exerted by relevant labor markets.

With the identification of lower and upper limits to the pay scale, it becomes possible to establish a pay line (also known as a trend line, regression line, or line of least squares). Following this step comes the determination of pay grades, the number of pay grades, structural considerations within and between grades, and, finally, pay structure changes that recognize wide-scale economic changes in the market place.

Establishing a Pay Line

In developing a pay line, the minimum pay may be influenced by a number of considerations. For many businesses, the most influential consideration is the legal issue. What minimum standards are prescribed by the federal government through regulations set under the Fair Labor Standards Act of 1938 (FLSA) and its many amendments? In some cases, the Davis-Bacon Act (1931) and the Walsh-Healey Public Contracts Act (1936) may also influence the lower end of the pay scale or set a floor for base pay.

Some states set even more rigorous minimum requirements than those set by the federal government, and when this is the case, state laws preempt federal regulations. Organizations that must collectively bargain will normally have their lowest rates of pay set through negotiations with their representative unions. Even when an organization is nonunion, collectively bargained wage rates have a significant influence on practices followed by nonunionized organizations. Another major consideration beyond union influence in the labor market is the general influence a particular labor market has on wage rates. Where employment is high and insufficient numbers of people are seeking entry-level jobs or specific kinds of jobs, minimum wage rates must be high enough to attract enough job seekers who are able and willing to adequately perform job assignments.

The upper limit or highest rate of pay is a more subjective consideration. In this case, senior policymakers determine an acceptable rate of pay for jobs they consider most valuable to the business. Some factors that normally influence policymakers when making these decisions include:

1. Traditional or past practices.
2. Ability of the organization to pay.
3. Pay provided by other organizations for comparable jobs.
4. Need to attract sufficient personnel or individuals with specific talents and skills.
5. Other compensation components provided to high-level personnel.
6. Political pressures exerted by certain groups external to the organization, such as unions or groups of employees within the organization, that have significant influence.

With the establishment of a lower and upper limit to rates of pay, it becomes possible to develop a *pay line* (Exhibit 4-1). The simplest approach would be to connect the lower- and upper-rates of pay.

Exhibit 4-1: Pay or Trend Line Development

*   Rates set by individual(s) with compensation decision authority.
**   Midpoint value obtainable through a survey of relevant labor markets. A competitive midpoint is the "going rate"
     or average or median rate of pay for a surveyed job

The line connecting the lowest-offered to highest-offered rates of pay could be the pay line for the organization, or it could be a first approximation of a pay line. Pay structure designers normally find that even for entry-level jobs, a higher rate of pay is provided once an employee demonstrates acceptable performance and remains on the job for some probationary period. For the highest rate of pay offered in the most highly paid job, the process works in an opposite manner. In this instance, the employee receives a rate of pay lower than the maximum rate and, through tenure and demonstrated performance, works to gain the maximum attainable pay. Another very simple procedure for establishing a pay line is to obtain the market-rate or going-rate of pay for the lowest-paid and highest-paid jobs. Connecting these two points provides a first approximation for a pay line.

The procedure most organizations normally follow in establishing a pay line is to identify the market rates for various benchmark jobs that cover the entire pay spectrum from lowest to highest rates of pay. (A benchmark job is commonly found in the marketplace and has responsibilities and duties so clearly identified that it permits other organizations to match it with their jobs for pay comparison purposes.) By plotting the pay-rate information obtained through surveys on a chart, a scatter diagram can be developed (Exhibit 4-2).

When placing a pay line through the use of a scatter diagram, the line can be established very simply by "eye-balling" the various points and drawing a line (either freehand or with a straight edge) that cuts through the middle of the points. A more scientific procedure would be to use the least-squares method for determining the direction of the line. Least-squares is a mathematical procedure that establishes a line that minimizes the squared differences between the points plotted on the graph and the line itself.

Pay Grade Determination

After establishing a pay line, the next step in the design of a pay structure relates to the pay grade. Here, such issues as these arise:

1. What is the relationship between job worth and pay grade assignments?
2. Should there be variations in the pay of incumbents performing jobs assigned to a specific pay grade?
3. How many grades should there be?
4. If there is a range or spread of pay within a pay grade, what factors influence the setting of lower and upper limits to a pay grade, and what should be the internal design characteristics of a pay grade?
5. What should be the relationship between adjacent pay grades?
6. How should seniority and performance be recognized through pay grade design?

In establishing job worth, especially when using some type of a point system, the relationship between the score received by the job and the pay provided for performing the job is an important consideration. The first point to remember is that internal equity is *not* the only criterion used for establishing job rates of pay. Other criteria include market, traditional, and political considerations, which have already been discussed. Second, even when using a point-factor, job evaluation method, the precision related to the score or evaluated worth that is finally derived should

---

Exhibit 4-2: Developing a Scatter Diagram

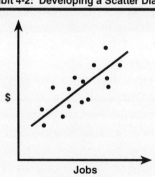

$

Jobs

not hide the fact that this value is not by any means a perfect indicator. Rather, it is a good indicator of worth. When a point-factor job evaluation method has been properly designed, the factors and their assigned weights have a high degree of validity and reliability.

In an organization with only a few types of jobs, it is certainly possible to assign a different rate of pay to each job and have the difference in rates of pay reflect evaluated differences in job worth. But once an organization requires a wide variety of jobs to accomplish its mission, individual pay rates for each job become administratively burdensome, if not impractical, and, above all, an area of contention. In addition, when pay relates directly to job worth, expectations may develop for adjustments in base pay whenever duty assignments change. This condition also would be a nightmare for supervisors and compensation administrators.

Single-rate pay grades are frequently found in organizations where employees are members of an industrial union. Union workers frequently perform jobs that require minimum levels of knowledge and skills, are easy to learn, and have similar work procedures that are constantly repeated. Craft jobs also have historical relationships to single rates of pay. The traditional apprentice, journeyman, master classifications require a rate of pay for each level, but workers performing different assignments that may require different skills do not receive different rates of pay. Jobs assigned to pay grades that have a range of pay are found in clerical, administrative, professional, and managerial areas of work. In these types of jobs, the individual has a greater opportunity to make the job more valuable. Movement through the pay grade recognizes changes in individual contributions.

Throughout this book we have emphasized the importance of individual perception and the influence of subjective considerations in compensation practices. One of the more interesting propositions supporting this philosophy was developed approximately sixty years ago by Edward N. Hay, who used the nineteenth century work of Ernst H. Weber to investigate the concept of observable differences. Weber's law states, "The increase of stimulus necessary to produce an increase of sensation is not an absolute quantity but depends on the proportion which the increase bears to the immediate preceding stimulus."[1] Or, more simply stated, the small perceptible difference in two objects is not absolutely the same, but remains relatively the same. That is, it remains the same fraction (percentage) of the preceding stimulus. For example, if we can distinguish between sixteen and seventeen ounces, we should be able to distinguish between thirty-two and thirty-four ounces, but possibly not between thirty-two and thirty-three ounces.

In the 1940s Hay conducted a series of studies based on Weber's *Law of Just Observable Differences* and noted that a 15 percent difference in the importance of one factor, as compared with the preceding factor, was discernible by trained raters at least 75 percent of the time.[2] This 15 percent difference provides compensation specialists with an extremely valuable criterion, index, or rule-of-thumb for a variety of uses. One use could be in relating jobs to pay grades.

Even with the best of systems or methods and under favorable working conditions, it is possible to have a 15 percent error in measurement. Also, taking Weber's law into consideration, individual perceptions will recognize that certain factors, issues, or values that differ by as much as 15 percent are, in fact, identical or similar. Herein lies the foundation for establishing pay grades. A pay grade permits the grouping of jobs or classes of jobs that—although different with respect to kind of subject matter, type of knowledge demands, or type of work— are sufficiently equivalent by level of difficulty and responsibility and by qualification requirements. When attempting to determine a more precise definition of "sufficiently equivalent," Weber's law may be most helpful. If, through some grouping of criteria, one job is no more than 15 percent different than another, most people will consider the two jobs equivalent and worthy of similar compensation.

The number of pay grades included within a pay structure varies with the circumstances—there is no right number. Therefore, compensation system designers and managers all face the same answer—it all depends. It all depends on demands of the organization: What is acceptable to top management? What do employees perceive as fair? What is administratively practical? What best recognizes differences in job worth, employee behavior, and the opportunity to maintain a logical and rational control over wage payments?

Some organizations use market surveys and guidecharts to establish job rates of pay that have seventy to eighty and possibly more pay grades. Alternatively, some behavioral scientists are promoting the use of as few as four to six pay grades.

The issues to consider and the results of using a large number of pay grades versus the use of a very small number of pay grades are as follows:

1. Is there to be only one pay structure that will include all jobs from the lowest entry-level job—requiring minimum education, experience, and skill—to that of the chief executive officer—

demanding a considerable knowledge and skill? If this is the case, it is likely that even a small organization with, say, five-hundred employees would require eighteen to thirty pay grades.

2. Is it desirable to have a small monetary variation between pay grades—somewhere between 4 and 6 percent? If this is the case, and the organization is using only one pay structure, then it would not be unusual to find fifty to seventy-five pay grades being used. By having a small variation in pay grades, a mistake made in assigning a job to a pay grade that is one or even two grades too high or too low relative to job worth would hardly be noted (remember Weber's law). More grades also allow for assignment of jobs with different evaluations to different pay grades. With a large number of pay grades, the overlap between pay grades will be large—in the vicinity of 70 to 85 percent.

3. A small number of pay grades will normally result in less overlap between them. It will also require the assignment of more jobs to the same pay grade. Having fewer pay grades permits a greater spread, allowing increased recognition of growth of job knowledge through seniority and merit in-grade pay increases. The larger the range in a pay grade, the greater the opportunity to pay employees differently while performing the same or equivalent types of work.

Pay Grade Design. A number of design features must be considered when designing the pay grades for the pay structure. The following are major considerations:

1. Range or height of the pay grade.
2. Width of the pay grade.
3. Relationship between midpoints of adjacent pay grades.
4. Overlap between pay grades.
5. Internal structuring of a pay grade.

Range. The range or spread of the range of a pay grade is the difference between the upper and lower limits of the pay grade. The range may be expressed in absolute dollar amounts or as a percentage. When expressed as a percentage, the range is the

$$\frac{maximum\ dollar\ limit - minimum\ dollar\ limit}{minimum\ dollar\ limit}.$$

In some pay structures, the range is identical for all pay grades. In other structures, the pay range will vary. A commonly used pay structure that has grades with variable ranges is the fan-type pay structure. Lower-level grades in a fan-type pay structure will have ranges of from

20 to 30 percent. Grades for jobs in the middle of the organization vary from 30 to 50 percent. Grades for jobs at the top of the organization have a range of from 50 to 100 percent (Exhibit 4-3).

The rationale for this type of a pay structure is that employees occupying jobs in lower pay grades are in a transition stage and will, in a fairly short period of time, either move to jobs in higher pay grades or leave the organization. However, as an employee progresses to higher-level jobs, the opportunity for promotion and promotion-related pay increases becomes less. Thus, in-grade pay increases become the best way of recognizing growth of job knowledge and experience and the contributions made through above-average performance. An additional reason for significant increases in the size of the range at the upper levels is that the individuals in these jobs have greater opportunity to influence the scope and effect of the jobs, and the larger ranges permit recognition of these valuable individual contributions.

Design of a pay structure follows the establishment of the pay or trend line. Market or going rates for jobs are normally located on the pay line and are usually found at the midpoint of the pay grade. Policymakers then provide direction or make determinations regarding what is an acceptable range of pay or just what the range should be for the pay grades.

Once the midpoint and the desired spread or range is known, it is a matter of simple mathematics to identify the upper and lower limits of the pay grade. If the midpoint is $30,000 and the spread to the maximum rate of the grade is 20 percent and the spread to the minimum rate is also

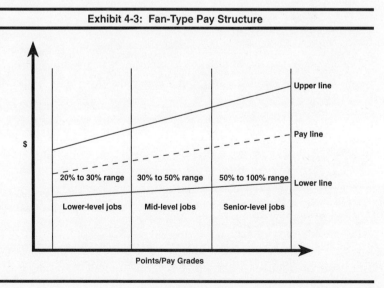

Exhibit 4-3: Fan-Type Pay Structure

20 percent, the maximum is equal to $30,000 multiplied by 1.0 plus 20 percent or 1.20, which is $18,000. The minimum is $15,000 multiplied by 1.0 minus 20 percent or 0.80, which is $12,000.

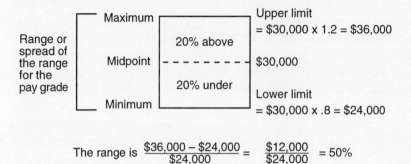

The range is $\dfrac{\$36,000 - \$24,000}{\$24,000} = \dfrac{\$12,000}{\$24,000} = 50\%$

When the midpoint and the range are known, a slightly different mathematical procedure can be used to obtain the maximum and minimum of the pay grade. The first step is to determine the minimum of the pay grade. The minimum is obtained by first adding half of the spread of the range to 1.0 and then dividing the midpoint by this amount. For example, the midpoint is $30,000 and the range is 50 percent. To obtain the minimum:

$$\frac{\$30,000}{(1.0 + 0.25)} = \frac{\$30,000}{1.25} = \$24,000$$

The maximum is then obtained by multiplying the minimum by 1 plus the spread of the range. Continuing with the above example with $24,000 being the minimum and the spread of the range being 50 percent:

$$\$24,000 \times (1.0 + 0.50) = \$24,000 \times 1.50 = \$36,000$$

The actual range of a pay grade is frequently an amount arbitrarily selected by an individual or individuals with compensation policy decision-making responsibilities. There are, however, some issues that could affect the final value selected. If the range is small and the minimum or lower limit relates closely to the market, the entry rate of pay is more attractive to those looking for employment. There is also an unsatisfactory side to this story. When entry and maximum limits are too close, long-term employees feel that the organization does not recognize their services and loyalty, and there is an unsatisfactory compression of pay rates within the pay grade.

Width. This feature of a pay grade design may be the most arbitrary of the five features. The width figure may represent nothing more than a pay grade number, e.g., 1, 2, 3, etc. or it may represent a specific number of points. Points are applicable when using a point-factor job evaluation plan. Each grade may have the same number of points, i.e., the difference between the maximum and minimum width limits is the same for all pay grades, or the pay plan architect may have an increasingly greater point-width spread with succeeding pay grades or group of pay grades. The actual number of points assigned to the width dimension will depend on (1) total points in the job evaluation plan, (2) number of pay grades in the pay plan, (3) some statistical or arbitrary value determined by the designer of the pay plan.

Midpoint-to-Midpoint Relationship. Midpoint to midpoint relationships determine the number of pay grades in a pay plan. Small midpoint to midpoint differences, i.e., 4 to 6 percent, permit the development of a large number of pay grades, while large midpoint to midpoint differences of 10 to 15 percent will result in a small number of pay grades.

Overlap. Following the identification of the midpoint, upper limit, and lower limit of the pay grade, the next step is to establish the relationship between adjacent pay grades. The pay structure may have no overlap between pay grades and look like this:

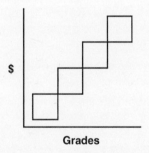

Grades

or the pay structure may have overlapping pay grades and look like this:

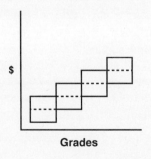

Grades

The overlaps between pay grades are those pay opportunities that are identical in adjacent pay grades:

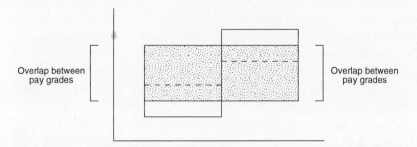

When a pay structure has a small difference between adjacent midpoints (4 to 6 percent), there will be a considerable overlap between pay grades (70 to 85 percent). A theory underlying overlap between pay grades is that the amount of overlap should equal the similarity of responsibilities, duties, knowledge, and skills that exist among jobs in the adjacent pay grades (i.e., 80 percent overlap equates to an 80 percent comparability in responsibilities and duties, knowledge, and skills in jobs assigned to these pay grades).

Another underlying reason for having overlapping pay grades is that a high-performing employee in a lower pay grade may make a greater contribution to the success of the organization than a new or less efficient employee in a higher-rated job, and these contributions should be recognized through the receipt of more pay.

A major problem with pay grades that have significant overlap is that an employee already in the upper end of a pay grade who receives a promotion to a job in the next pay grade—even one in two pay grades up the pay structure—may not receive much of a pay increase or an opportunity to increase the amount of pay earned in the future. Many compensation-policy decision makers feel that in order for a promotion to have a true incentive value, it should carry with it at least a 10 percent increase in pay. This is one of the major reasons for the warning that in a well-designed pay structure there should be no overlap between pay grades that are four grades apart.

When establishing differences between midpoints, it may again be valuable to consider Weber's law. Such values as 3, 5, 10, or 15 percent are divisible into fifteen; the impact of just perceptible differences may be an important consideration when it is desirable to demonstrate through pay policies that there is a significant difference in the worth of the various jobs in an organization.

Internal Pay Grade Design. After establishing the trend line and fitting the pay grades to the trend line, the final step in this process is to complete the internal design of the pay grade itself. A pay grade may include nothing more than the minimum, midpoint, and maximum rates of pay. It may, however, be structured with a number of well-identified steps.

A structure using only minimum, midpoint, and maximum values may identify the minimum as an entry-level rate; midpoint as the rate for demonstrated acceptable job performance; and maximum as the rate paid to highly proficient performers. Other structures may commonly have anywhere from five to ten steps. An incumbent may progress through all steps strictly on a seniority basis. For example, the movement from Step 1 to Step 2 may require one year of service and satisfactory performance; movement from Step 2 to Step 3 may require eighteen months of acceptable service, and so on.

When using step increases, the amount of difference between each step in a pay grade may relate to some specific arithmetical difference (absolute amount of difference is the same for each step); geometric difference (difference between steps is some given percentage); or random difference (the amount between steps varies by no regular amount or percentage).

Another way of using steps within a pay grade is to base movement through steps to midpoint on a seniority base (provided performance is satisfactory), while movement from midpoint to maximum is based strictly on merit. The issue then is how the organization defines and identifies meritorious performance. The decade of the 90s is witnessing a strong interest in pay for performance. This interest has placed a cloud on the basic concept of merit pay.

Over the past twenty years, many organizations have instituted a merit guidechart progression process through the pay grades. This process requires the establishment of no clearly defined steps in the pay grade. Instead, the 25th, 50th, and 75th percentiles are identified for each pay grade. Each employee then receives a regular, formal appraisal of performance. (Again, the performance appraisal and measurement issue arises.) The actual amount of increase received by an incumbent depends on (1) the location of that individual's pay in the pay grade (in the first quartile, up to the 25th percentile; in the second quartile, up to the midpoint or 50th percentile; in the third quartile, up to the 75th percentile; or in the fourth quartile, up to the maximum or 100th percentile); and (2) the appraised quality of the individual's performance. A simple merit guidechart could take the form of Exhibit 4-4.

Exhibit 4-4: A Simple Merit Guidechart

		Performance rating (percentage pay adjustments)			
	Location in pay grade	Superior	Good	Improvement desired	Unacceptable
Maximum— 100th Percentile					
	4th Quartile	5	2	0	0
75th Percentile					
	3rd Quartile	6	3	0	0
Midpoint— 50th Percentile					
	2nd Quartile	7	4	2	0
40th Percentile					
	1st Quartile	8	5	3	0
Minimum— 0 Percentile					

The rationale for paying different rates of pay to individuals receiving identical performance ratings is that those in the upper quartiles are already receiving more pay and this permits those in the lower levels of the pay range to improve their situations.

An additional element frequently inserted into this type of process is to vary the performance review dates relative to the location of the employee in the pay grade. Employees in the lower quartiles of the pay grade are reviewed more frequently and thus have the opportunity to receive more frequent pay increases. A schedule of performance review and subsequent pay adjustments may take this form:

Location in Grade	Minimum Period Until Next Review
Above maximum	By exception only
Fourth quartile	15 - 18 months
Third quartile	12 - 15 months
Second quartile	9 - 12 months
First quartile	6 months
Below minimum	6 months

Rates Above Maximum and Below Minimum

Some organizations permit no employees to receive rates of pay that fall either below or above the established limits of the pay grade. Other organizations have a number of well-defined exceptions that allow the payment of rates of pay above the maximum or below the minimum of the pay grade. Here are some examples and reasons for their occurrence:

Red Circle employees are those individuals receiving rates of pay higher than the established maximum for the job. Frequently, these employees receive no pay increases, even when there is a wage-structure adjustment or some other economic-related realignment of the entire pay structure, until such time as their pay rate is within the maximum limit of the pay grade. The most common reason for an employee being red-circled is that the job has been reevaluated and downgraded, but the employee's pay has been left unchanged. Another reason for a red circle rate is that an employee has been demoted but retains the pay received in the prior job.

Silver Circle employees are high seniority employees who have been given a special increase above established maximum in recognition of long-term employment.

Gold Circle employees are those in the upper limits of a pay grade who receive excellent performance ratings and are granted an increase that takes their rate of pay beyond the established maximum.

Many organizations limit silver and gold circle adjustments to pay rates of 10 to 15 percent above maximum.

Green Circle employees are those receiving rates of pay below established minimums. These employees may have jobs that have been reevaluated, but the new rate of pay requires an increase greater than that permitted by the compensation policy. In this case, the employee receives the maximum permissible increase and continues to receive such increases until reaching at least the minimum of the pay grade. A similar situation may occur when an employee receives a promotion to a job where the difference between current pay and the minimum pay in the new job exceeds the maximum amount granted at any one time. The employee will normally receive maximum allowable increases until reaching the minimum rate of the new job.

Organizations with policies limiting one-time pay increases frequently set the amount and time restrictions at no more than a 15 (in some cases, 25) percent increase in any six-month or twelve-month period.

Use of Multiple Pay Structures

The need for multiple pay structures occurs when an organization feels that employees performing different types of jobs require pay treatment that uses pay scales with different relationships. Groupings of jobs that typically receive different pay treatment are:

1. Assembly, maintenance, craft, and trade jobs
2. Clerical, secretarial, and other lower-level administrative-type jobs
3. Professional jobs

4. Managerial and higher-level administrative jobs
5. Senior management (executive and senior manager) jobs
6. Exempt vs. nonexempt jobs
7. Hourly vs. salary jobs

The principal design feature that differentiates one pay structure from another is the slope of the pay or trend line. In moving from structures for lower-level jobs to structures for higher-level jobs, the slope of the trend line will increase at a faster rate. (The slope of a line is its average rate of change between any two points or over the entire range of points.) See Exhibit 4-5.

The larger the value of the slope, the faster the rate of change. The impact of the slope on the pay structure is that the greater the slope of the pay line, the greater the difference in pay between jobs in adjacent pay grades. Some point-factor job evaluation methods result in employees in different types of jobs receiving the same or similar amounts of job evaluation points. Through the use of pay lines with different slopes, the same number of points (x-axis coordinate) results in a higher rate of pay (y-axis coordinate) for jobs assigned to the pay line having the larger slope.

Pay Structure Adjustments

Once the pay structure is designed and put into operation, the relative relationship it identifies and measures should be stable. The major

---

Exhibit 4-5: Determining the Slope of a Line

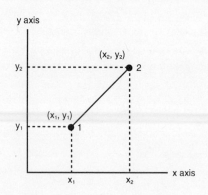

$$\text{Slope of line 1-2} = \frac{\Delta y}{\Delta x} = \frac{y_2 - y_1}{x_2 - x_1}$$

If $\begin{aligned} x_1 &= 2, x_2 = 7, \\ y_1 &= 3, y_2 = 6 \end{aligned}$ then $\dfrac{6 - 3}{7 - 2} = \dfrac{3}{5} = 0.6 = \text{Slope of the line}$

reason for changing job relationships, once jobs have been evaluated and assigned to a pay grade, would be changes in job responsibilities and duties. These could occur for many reasons (i.e., redesign of job, changes in technology, and so on). The concept of the range is to grant some flexibility to individual rates of pay in order to recognize seniority and performance criteria.

The major factors influencing pay structure changes are changes in economics that affect all of society or a specific labor market. For example, the major economic issue facing all employers and employees is inflation. To stay abreast of changes in cost-of-living caused by inflation, employees demand that their work-related income provide for a continuation of the standard-of-living to which they have become accustomed. Employers attempt to maintain the "real income" of their employees ("real income" means that the purchasing power of the income provides a consistent quantity and quality of goods and services) by adjusting the pay structure.

When pay-structure adjustments are made because of national economic conditions, the Consumer Price Index (CPI) of the Bureau of Labor Statistics of the U.S. Department of Labor provides the measuring device for adjustments. When adjustments relate to local or specific market conditions, surveys will normally be the most useful approach for identifying changes and amounts of adjustments.

A frequent method of adjusting the rates of pay is to provide a one-time or annual across-the-board pay raise. An across-the-board pay raise provides an identical raise to all employees in all jobs. When this occurs, and since the design of most pay structures uses relative relationships (percentage difference from minimum to maximum of a pay grade or percentage difference between midpoints), the entire structure becomes distorted and the relationships become invalid.

Part of the philosophy underlying across-the-board raises relates to the fact that the increase in the price of bread is the same for everyone. The problem here is that man does not live by bread alone, and most workers design their lifestyles around their job-related earnings. Lifestyle includes subsistence (food, clothing, shelter, and transportation), luxuries, and savings for the future. Considering all of these complex issues, the argument for across-the-board pay raises becomes much weaker.

The underlying philosophy of an across-the-board pay increase is that it treats every employee equally. This has a sweet ring to employees in the lower end of the pay scale, but what about the employees who perform jobs requiring more responsibility and greater levels of knowledge and skill? A basic feature of any well-designed compensation system is that it provides compensation on an equitable basis and offers rewards that relate to the contributions made or offered by the employee.

Cost-of-living adjustments need not mean an automatic increase in pay to all employees. If an organization increases its entire pay structure by 6 percent, it means that the minimums, midpoints, and maximums of all pay grades increase by 6 percent:

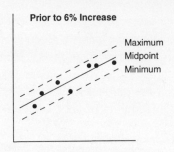
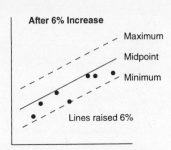

Actual rates of pay remain unchanged

This now provides an additional opportunity for the organization to increase pay relative to some type of merit or performance criteria. Organizations using the merit guidechart procedure for determining pay increases can include a factor in the guidechart that would add a pay-structure adjustment to the merit increase (Exhibit 4-6).

The x in the guidechart represents the percentage change in the pay structure. If, for example, the structure were increased by 6 percent, then each employee receiving an x increase would receive a 6 percent plus

Exhibit 4-6: Merit Guidechart Combining Performance Ratings and Pay Structure Adjustments

		Performance rating (percentage pay adjustments)			
	Location in pay grade	Superior	Good	Improvement desired	Unacceptable
Maximum— 100th Percentile					
	4th Quartile	5+x	2+x	0	0
75th Percentile					
	3rd Quartile	6+x	3+x	0	0
Midpoint— 50th Percentile					
	2nd Quartile	7+x	4+x	$2+{}^x/_2$	0
40th Percentile					
	1st Quartile	8+x	5+x	$3+{}^x/_4$	0
Minimum— 0 Percentile					

the performance rating increase. Those receiving no x increase would be receiving a relative pay cut and would regress within the pay grade. Those receiving a fraction of the x ($^x/_4$, $^x/_2$) would also not be receiving the full benefit of the pay structure change.

Another major reason for structural change occurs when workers with specific kinds of knowledge and skills come into short supply. This is possibly the most difficult problem that pay structure designers face. If the shortage is temporary, it may be possible to provide some type of a bonus to recruit employees with the required knowledge and skills, but this opens up the problem of what to do with employees currently performing these jobs. It may be possible to bring the new employees into a job at an advanced step or location in the pay grade, but this also causes conflict with employees currently on the job who are at lower levels of pay. This situation may be a sign of an improperly evaluated job, and it may be that a reevaluation would place the job in a higher pay grade. It may be possible to add some responsibilities and duties to the job, resulting in a higher evaluation and grade assignment.

The final solution may require the establishment of a separate pay structure for exotic or high-demand jobs. Possibly the only design structure that satisfies problems related to these types of jobs is the market-pricing approach to job evaluation and the assignment of pay. As discussed in Chapter 1, market pricing or its offshoot, the guideline method, surveys the market, identifies the pay that incumbents currently receive, and provides an amount that closely relates to what those who compete in the market are paying.

Pay Adjustments Made Outside the Pay Structure

It is possible to use the pay structure for recognizing differences in job worth, and any adjustment would relate only to time on the job. As previously discussed in this chapter, the job is assigned a pay grade. The grade may have one rate of pay or a range of rates. Where there is a range of rates, it may take, for example, three years to achieve the midpoint of the pay grade and seven years to reach the maximum. There are, however, options to using the grades for recognizing high-quality performance, tenure, and working conditions.

Performance. When not using the pay structure to recognize levels of performance, certain high-quality performance ratings could be the basis for a one-time bonus given annually or on demonstration of highly desirable behavior. These types of rewards would have to be re-earned through actual workplace behavior and would not be a once-earned/maintained-forever type of reward.

Tenure. Some organizations provide a seniority bonus to recognize service. Examples may be a 5 percent cash bonus at the end of the fifth year of employment, a 10 percent cash bonus at the end of the tenth year, and possibly fifteen, twenty, and twenty-five year bonuses.

Working Conditions. Where the job evaluation method does not include working conditions as a compensable factor, employees who perform work assignments under dangerous and distressing conditions, or who face emotional or physical fatigue significantly greater than the average employee, may receive a supplement. This supplement may be provided as a bonus to the paycheck when the employee performs under such conditions. The amount of the working-condition pay supplement would not vary because of kind or level of work, but would relate equally to all employees who must perform under these unacceptable conditions.

ENDNOTES

1. *Encyclopaedia Britannica,* 15th ed., *Micropedia,* vol X, 593.
2. Edward N. Hay, "The Application of Weber's Law to Job Evaluation Estimates," *Journal of Applied Psychology* 34 (1950), 102-104.

PART II

DEVELOPING A PAY SYSTEM FOR OLYMPIA

The chapters in Part II provide insights to the major processes included in a classification and pay study. The how-to information includes (1) techniques that facilitate the collection of valid and useful job content information; (2) recommendations for writing a task statement, including how to convert task statements into responsibility and duty statements, and then how to group responsibility and duty statements into responsibility modules that describe positions or jobs completely, accurately, and honestly; (3) procedures for translating job content information into FES points; and possibly most useful, (4) how to design a pay structure that will either replicate market conditions or support the compensation policy of the organization. The step-by-step process described herein can be used by any organization to develop a pay system.

Chapter 5

SELECTING THE FACTOR EVALUATION SYSTEM FOR OLYMPIA

The city of Olympia is located in the southeast section of Spartan County. The city has a council-manager form of government—an elected mayor, and eight city council members who serve four-year terms. The council, in turn, appoints a full-time city manager. At the time of our study, the city government included fourteen department directors and approximately five hundred employees, staffing the following city departments: Administrative Services, Communications, Community Development, Electrical, Fire, Garage, Inspection, Maintenance and Stores, HR, Police, Public Works, Recreation, Sanitation, and Water.

Olympia lies adjacent to the Spartan regional airport. The city has a major industrial section and several thousand residential units populated principally by middle-income citizens representative of both the white and black races. One of the first assignments given a new HR director was to develop and implement a classification and pay plan that would recognize differences in job worth by providing a rational, logical, and orderly assignment of jobs to pay grades.

The Classification and Pay System

Over the years the city of Olympia, like many governments, had, through various means, developed a classification and pay system. Their system had jobs assigned to classes, and the classes were, in turn, assigned to pay grades. There were nineteen grades and each pay grade had six steps. From the minimum to the maximum rate of pay in each pay grade, there was a spread of approximately 28 percent, with an approximate 5 percent difference between the third steps of adjacent pay grades. However, no one in the city government could justify or substantiate why any one job was in a particular pay grade. The indefensibility of the system was the result of years of mending, patching, and taking care of the "squeaking wheel."

After an initial review of the existing job classification and pay plan, the HR director recognized that improvements were needed and could be made in all phases of the plan. Some jobs had job descriptions; others had none. Descriptions of many jobs were out of date or did not adequately describe the responsibilities of the jobholder and the qualifications needed for job entry. No logical, orderly, and systematic approach for assigning jobs to pay grades existed, and the relationship of rates of pay to the pay grades had become distorted through across-the-board pay increases that had been implemented in recent years.

Human resource specialists from the Spartan Regional Commission (SRC) had at one time redesigned the classification and pay system, but Olympia city council members had revised it to such a degree that it bore little resemblance to the plan originally presented by the SRC.

Shortly after the human resources director assumed her duties, employees in various departments began to report dissatisfaction with their pay. There was significant concern over the inadequacy of pay, and many employees felt that the pay they received for the work they did was not equitable when compared to what others received. These pressures from employees concerning both the absolute amounts and the relative amounts of pay were also being felt by the mayor and city council who, in turn, had directed the city manager to do something about the problem. Recognizing inadequacies in the existing classification and pay plan, and responding to both employee and city council concerns, the city manager had placed a high priority on this project.

Developing an Acceptable System for Determining Job Worth

After becoming familiar with the Olympia classification and pay plan, the human resources director began analyzing the opportunities for improving it. In late November, she contacted Dr. Richard I. Henderson, then a professor in the Management Department at Georgia

State University, to discuss available alternatives for achieving the objectives set forth by the city manager. Dr. Henderson thus became the project consultant.

At that time, certain constraints were identified that would possibly limit types of methods and procedures for establishing an equitable pay system. The principal constraints were:

1. No funds were available to hire a consultant.
2. There was no staff, other than the human resources director, with experience in human resources management.
3. The results of the completed project were to be presented to the city manager by April 1.
4. The recommendations for assignment of jobs to (1) pay grades and (2) rates of pay were to be reviewed by the mayor and city council by May 1.

The impact these constraints would have on the methods and procedures available for establishing an internally equitable pay system were discussed. Major issues that required immediate attention were (1) determination of methods and procedures, (2) acquisition of human resources to assist in conducting the project, and (3) acquisition of funds to cover project costs.

When reviewing methods and procedures for classifying jobs and establishing a pay structure, the human resources director and the project consultant agreed on two guiding concepts. First, the method of job evaluation selected for the project would compare all jobs on the kinds and levels of responsibilities and duties, the knowledge and skills required, and the conditions within which the jobs are performed. Second, job descriptions would be developed and used for evaluation purposes. (Time and funding limitations eliminated the possibility of developing position descriptions, while class descriptions were far too broad and general for evaluation purposes.)

These two guidelines, in addition to the desire of the city manager that the system and its component parts be able to support a pay plan acceptable to the mayor and city council, limited the search for acceptable and useful methods of job evaluation.

Four major job evaluation methods were identified that could be used for this project. They were (1) whole-job ranking and allocation of jobs to specific pay grades, (2) the market-pricing guideline method, (3) the American Association of Industrial Management method, and (4) the Factor Evaluation System of Position Classification (FES). The following eight criteria were used to compare the four methods and to make a final selection:

1. Knowledge and skills required to analyze, describe, and evaluate jobs.
2. Time required to perform the analysis, description, and evaluation of jobs.
3. Ability of the system to establish an internally equitable ordering of jobs.
4. Opportunities for employee interaction.
5. Acceptability of system to policymakers and employees.
6. Potential of system for meeting validity and reliability criteria.
7. Relationship between internal ordering of jobs and final rates of pay set for each job.
8. Ability of the city to maintain the system, once implemented.

After reviewing all four methods relative to these eight selection criteria, the FES method of job evaluation was chosen. The selection process did not involve a quantitative analysis, but it did include a qualitative analysis. Being the most rigorous of the four methods, FES required more skills and consumed more time in the analysis of jobs and in the writing of job descriptions and job specifications but ranked low on criteria 1 and 2. It did, however, outweigh the other methods on criteria 3, 4, 5, 6, and 8. Much of the material in this book will identify from an after-the-fact and continuing research perspective the strength of FES relative to these criteria. As far as criterion 7 was concerned, the project team recognized that there would undoubtedly be differences between the internal ordering of jobs and the final rates of pay set for each job. They therefore decided that it was better to place all the cards on the table right from the beginning, as follows:

- Establish a rating of job worth compared with other jobs in the organization.
- Identify market information that provides "going-rate" pay data.
- Recognize an acceptable rate of pay, given traditional and political considerations.

Establishing Procedures

Both the human resources director and the project consultant had experience and were conversant with a number of different job analysis and job evaluation methods, including the FES. In the initial discussion of procedures, they decided that, if at all possible, the following activities would be implemented:

- Completion of a job analysis questionnaire by all employees.
- Audit of 40 to 60 percent of all questionnaires.
- Development of job descriptions.

- Use of a job evaluation method that permitted employee involvement.
- Opening of lines of communication to all city employees concerning purpose and design of all project activities.

The first step in determining the time required to complete a project having these five goals was to obtain a brief overview of the work being performed by the 470 employees in the city government. From this overview, it was concluded that there were approximately 90 different jobs being performed by city employees. (When the project was completed, 164 different jobs were eventually identified, described, and evaluated.)

Allowing one hour to review each of the 470 job analysis questionnaires, one hour to perform a bench or desk audit, one-half hour to review each questionnaire and assign it to a single job category, and one hour to complete a first draft of a job description added up to an estimated 1,030 hours for this phase of the project:

470 questionnaires x 1 hour	=	470 hours
235 audits x 1 hour	=	235
470 questionnaires assigned to job category x .5 hour	=	235
90 written job descriptions x 1 hour	=	90
Total		1,030 hours

Dividing the 1,030 total hours by eight resulted in approximately 129 days of analyst time; however, from January 3 until March 31 there were only 64 working days available. If the project were to be in the hands of the city manager by April 1, the job descriptions would have to be finished by March 10 at the latest to allow time to perform job evaluations and market surveys using current, accurate job information both for evaluation purposes and for identifying comparable jobs. This reduced by 15 the number of working days available for the analysis and evaluation phases of the project, leaving 49 days. Even if the human resources director and the project consultant worked full time on the project (which was not possible), they could not complete it on time.

Search for Additional Help

Recognizing the critical need for additional project staff, potential sources of HR that could be obtained at no cost to the city were identified. The human resources director initiated correspondence with the Spartan Regional Commission (SRC)—the local area planning and development commission. SRC agreed to provide two human resources specialists for technical assistance on a part-time basis. The Spartan regional office of the Office of Personnel Management was also contacted, and this office agreed to provide one staff member on a part-time basis.

At the same time, the project consultant requested funds through the Urban Life Institute of Georgia State University. The requested funds of $5,500 included $1,750 to pay the salaries of two graduate students, $750 for supplies (principally paper and printing services), and $3,000 for a one-course release for the project consultant. The request was approved.

Thus, a seven-member job-classification project team was assembled, including the human resources director and the project consultant, who also served as project leaders. The first meeting of the project team was held in January. Following the introduction of members, there was a discussion of the goals of the project and the methods and procedures to be used. It was decided at that time that each person would be responsible for auditing the questionnaires completed by a certain group of employees. After completing the audit, the project team members would write a job description for each job they identified and would also serve as members of job evaluation teams charged with evaluating specific jobs. All of the project team members, with the exception of the two Georgia State students, had prior job-classification experience. The two students were to receive assignments and workloads similar to those given to the other team members. The human resources director provided special training as well as personal direction as the students performed these assignments.

The final part of this meeting focused on the job analysis questionnaire to be used for the project and on the use of FES. A copy of the questionnaire and instructions on the use of FES were given to all team members. A second meeting was scheduled to review FES so that each person would be familiar with it and would be able to correlate their reviews of the completed job analysis questionnaires and the audits of their assigned positions with the information necessary to write an adequate FES job description.

A Possible Alternative to Team Development

Few organizations are able to acquire at no cost to themselves the part-time but very productive efforts of four compensation professionals plus two bright and willing students who provided invaluable job analyst services. Even with a lack of assistance, however, an organization need not turn to a consultant or consulting organization for these services.

A major reason for writing this book is to explain how the methods and procedures used in this project function and operate. An individual with some knowledge of the compensation area, and an interest and willingness to learn, can obtain sufficient information to implement a program such as the Olympia project in his or her own organization. The major requirements are the ability to read, a basic knowledge of the subject, a willingness to work and to accept the risk for program success, sufficient time to do the work, support from management, and the assignment of some temporary staff members to assist in performing the project.

This project need not, in fact, should not, be the exclusive domain of human resource specialists. Every manager in an organization has responsibilities for the efficient and effective use of human resources. What better opportunity is there for involving line employees in improved utilization of human resources than through learning (1) what jobs are all about, and (2) the methods and procedures used for determining job worth and job rates of pay?

FES is a particularly effective tool when used by an interdisciplinary and intra-organizational task force responsible for designing and implementing a classification and pay plan. In the Olympia project, the project leaders had to start from square one in teaching various Olympia employees (with absolutely no previous classification and pay experience) what FES is, what it provides, and how to use it. In the two major employee involvement stages, managers who were members of job evaluation committees and employees representing all types and levels of jobs who were appealing the classification of their jobs, or who sat as members of the formal classification appeals board, were trained in FES. Much was learned from these experiences, and areas were identified for improving the training of employees on the use of FES. These training programs will be discussed in detail in the chapters related to job evaluation and the appeal of classification.

Other Considerations

Two other areas considered extremely important by the team leaders were not addressed directly by the city manager or city council. These were issues relating to (1) the Equal Pay Act of 1963 and Title VII of the Civil Rights Act of 1964 and (2) employee rights at the workplace or, specifically, due process. In 1993, as the original effort is being revised, the Americans with Disabilities Act of 1990 (ADA) is creating similar kinds of concern for almost all organizations and will be discussed in appropriate sections throughout this book.

The 1930s witnessed the passage of the National Labor Relations Act of 1935 and the Fair Labor Standards Act of 1938. These two laws provided large numbers of workers with certain rights. The National Labor Relations Act granted employees the right of self-organization and the right to bargain collectively through representatives of their choice. Wages, hours, and other terms and conditions of employment became bargaining issues. In 1938, the Fair Labor Standards Act set minimum wages and overtime pay for the majority of American workers.

Initially, both of these laws had minimum impact on city, county, and state employees because governments were exempted from their provisions. This today is no longer true. Amendments to the FLSA have placed wage and hour requirements on government workers similar to those initially placed only on private sector employees. Indirectly, however, the impact of the laws significantly influenced the actions of city, county, and state governments before local and state government employees received protection under these laws. These bodies do not function within a vacuum; they must operate within a work environment established by all kinds of organizations—public and private, profit and nonprofit. Governments may not have been required to meet collective bargaining, minimum pay, and overtime standards as set forth by the federal government, but social pressures are an entirely different matter. These social pressures do not permit any government to treat its employees in a manner significantly different from that of other organizations in the same labor market.

From their enactment, the Equal Pay Act of 1963 and Title VII of the Civil Rights Act of 1964 were entirely different stories. All governments had to comply with the regulations set forth by these two laws. The Equal Pay Act of 1963 states that employees of one sex may not be paid wages at a rate lower than those paid to employees of the opposite sex if both are doing work requiring equal skill, effort, and responsibility that is performed under similar working conditions. The intent of Congress in passing this law was to ensure that female workers performing work similar to or equal to that of their male peers received equal pay.

Title VII of the Civil Rights Act of 1964 established the Equal Employment Opportunity Commission (EEOC). This act also made it unlawful to discriminate against any individual with respect to hiring; compensation; and terms, conditions, or privileges of employment because of race, sex, or national origin. Title VII prohibits limiting, segregating, or classifying employees in any way that would deprive them of employment opportunities, including initial hiring, promotions, layoffs, or termination.

Under the Equal Pay Act, discrimination and unfair and illegal action only transpire when males and females performing jobs of similar level in the same occupation are paid differently. However, the Equal Employment Opportunity Commission (EEOC) took a much broader view of the equal pay issue. EEOC became interested in gaining equality of pay for those working in jobs of comparable worth or of equal value. Their interest and subsequent investigations acquired even more significance when the EEOC took over enforcement of the Equal Pay Act on July 1, 1979. The thrust of the EEOC was to gain equal pay for those working in jobs of comparable worth or of equal value. This action changed the battle cry from one of "Equal Pay for Equal Work" to "Equal Pay for Jobs of Equal Worth."

The issue relating to comparable worth is far more complex than that of equal work. As long as the measurement relates to equal work, it is fairly simple to investigate the responsibilities, duties, tasks, and working conditions of one job and compare them with the responsibilities, duties, tasks, and working conditions of another job. When an analysis of job content provides documentable evidence that two jobholders are doing the same kind and level of work, equal pay for equal work becomes an issue.

On the other hand, a very difficult and complex problem arises when comparing the worth of dissimilar jobs. Comparing the worth of the job of a secretary to that of a maintenance mechanic is an example of the complexity of the "equal worth" problem. What can an organization do to compare the worth of the responsibilities, duties, and tasks of a secretary in an air-conditioned, relatively quiet office with the responsibilities, duties, and tasks of a maintenance mechanic repairing equipment on the production floor under conditions that may vary from extreme cold to heat, and where noise and fumes may not only be emotionally unacceptable but actually damaging to the health?

Both equal pay for equal work and equal pay for jobs of comparable worth were issues that placed an additional dimension on the Olympia Classification and Pay Study, and both project leaders felt that they must be addressed.

Another issue that began to gain major recognition during this period was that of due process. Due process at the workplace relates to the rights employees have concerning their jobs and the procedures for obtaining these rights. Although the human resources director was never given any charge to develop a classification and pay program that provided due process for Olympia employees, the program as it evolved moved human resources practices in that direction.

In selecting FES, the project leaders felt that this method of job evaluation and the procedures developed to support it would come extremely close to meeting the seven requirements of due process as identified by David W. Ewing.[1] FES relates closely to Ewing's main requirements for due process in that it is

- a procedure (must follow rules and not be arbitrary).
- visible (must be well known and potential violators of rights and victims of abuse must know it).
- predictably effective (employees must have confidence in the system).
- institutionalized (must be a permanent fixture).
- perceived as equitable (information and documentation supports conclusions).
- easy to use (relatively).
- applied to all employees (all entitled to the same treatment).

Establishing a Trusting Workplace Environment

One of the primary goals of the Olympia project was to involve employees in the job classification process. To achieve such a goal required that employees be provided with sufficient information to understand what job evaluation and classification is all about. They had to be taught (1) why internal equity is essential for a healthy work environment, (2) the difficulties involved in relating value judgments that establish job worth, (3) the relationship between job worth and job content, and (4) the major factors that identify and measure job worth, i.e., job knowledge and skill requirements, responsibilities that must be accepted and performed satisfactorily, and conditions under which work must be performed. Efforts of this kind help remove any aura of secrecy concerning how pay is set. The more open the information about pay, the less chance for uninformed or misinformed employees to make pay-related decisions that benefit neither themselves nor the organization.

Ability to understand the design of a pay system and its features does not require high levels of behavioral science education or quantitative analysis skills. Acceptance of a pay system, however, does require some basic understanding of the purpose, desired end results, and the tools and techniques to be used. Providing this type of information removes the mystical or magical qualities that frequently relate to efforts in the pay area. By opening channels of information regarding the entire area of job worth and assigned rates of pay, human resources specialists lose some influence in these vital areas. But, through widespread understanding, they develop credibility in the process.

An open classification and pay system is not something that can be established overnight. It is a slow process that requires taking one firm step at a time. Involvement develops as employees learn that they have an influence in describing the jobs they actually perform. They not only have a major input into the writing of their job descriptions, but they become the major link in keeping them current. Through involvement in the evaluation process, they recognize and understand the link between job content and job pay. Linking responsibility for accurate and valid descriptions of job requirements to changes in job pay rates permits important feedback from the jobholder to those responsible for pay administration. When employees see through demonstrated organizational behavior that they can have access to and can influence this vital aspect of their work lives, there is a greater likelihood that they will accept and buy into the pay system.

Employee understanding establishes a basis for an acceptable classification and pay system. With acceptance comes credibility, and credibility must be present before employees will trust any operation that has the impact their pay has on their lifestyles.

It is the belief of the authors that a well-designed, properly administered pay system is one of the most valuable tools any organization has at its command to modify or channel the behavior of its employees to benefit both the employees and the organization.

Endnote

1. David W. Ewing, *Freedom Inside the Organization: Bringing Civil Liberties to the Workplace* (New York: Dutton, 1977), 156.

Chapter 6

COLLECTING JOB CONTENT INFORMATION FOR OLYMPIA

Recognizing that the final success of the Olympia project depended directly on the quality of the collected job content information, one of the first decisions made after selecting FES was to use the questionnaire approach as the principal vehicle for collecting job information. This decision continued to be supported in the many follow-up applications of FES in a variety of organizations. Interviews and observations continued to be used to support, revise, and verify questionnaire-collected information. A typical job analysis schedule includes the following steps:

1. Design job analysis questionnaire (JAQ).
2. Field test first draft of questionnaire.
3. Review collected data and revise questionnaire. Once designed, a questionnaire is field-tested to ensure its adequacy and understandability. A small sample covering a wide range and level of jobs is selected, and incumbents in those jobs are asked to complete the questionnaire. These employees are instructed to comment specifically on any ambiguities or flaws perceived in the questionnaire. The questionnaires are then reviewed to ascertain whether or not the desired information has been provided. Finally, the comments are reviewed with respondees to identify and correct vague or unclear wording.

4. Form job analysis team. Include a job analyst from the HR department and four to six members to serve part-time who have good job knowledge of particular units within the organization and have interviewing, observation, and writing skills or are capable of and willing to develop such skills.
5. Meet with department heads; describe and discuss project. Train these individuals on how to complete a JAQ.
6. At group meetings, distribute job analysis questionnaires to all employees for completion. Train employees on how to complete JAQ.
7. Return completed questionnaires to human resource office.
8. Train job analysis team to review a questionnaire and perform a job audit. The training process includes an organization-developed video tape to provide a realistic, on-site example of one or more employees involved in the various steps of providing complete and valid job content information. This tape could be used in all job analysis training sessions. Training techniques are discussed in Part III.
9. Complete job audits. Job audits (personal interviews) are used by the analysts to clarify any vague or omitted questionnaire responses and to spot-check the reliability of the information supplied. Many of the audits include direct observation of the work performed and equipment utilized.

Human Resource Department Responsibilities

The Human Resource (HR) department is responsible for overall administration of the job collection phase of the project. They organize all group meetings and do as much informal groundwork as possible to gain acceptance of the project; their contacts range from elected or appointed officials and board members to entry-level, unskilled employees.

They distribute questionnaires, answer any questions that arise concerning completion of the questionnaires, follow through to ensure that all department directors return the completed questionnaires, and check each returned questionnaire to see that all portions are completed. The final step in this phase of the project is the distribution of completed questionnaires to the appropriate project team members for review, audit, and the writing of job descriptions.

Design of Job Analysis Questionnaire

No part of the pay determination process has received more attention and gone through more change than job content collection. Job analysis questionnaires (JAQs), in some manner, have been modified or even radically changed in almost every project. The discussions and examples of parts of a JAQ presented in this chapter are what we have found to be the most useful ways of designing a JAQ for collecting job content information. The JAQ includes the following:

- Employee Identification Section (Exhibit 6-1)
- Job Activity Identification Section (Exhibits 6-2 and 6-3)
- Knowledge, Skills, and Education Identification Section (Exhibit 6-5)
- Job Specification/Level of Factors Section (Exhibit 6-6)
- Additional Employee-Provided Information Section (Exhibit 6-8)
- Supervisor Review Section (Exhibit 6-9)

Employee Identification Section

This section (Exhibit 6-1) normally is a form the employee completes, providing such information as name, current job title, name and title of supervisor, assigned department title, tenure on job, length of service in organization. In recent years, this section has been transformed into a mini-organization chart. It is a good starting point for data collection because it requires the incumbent to think of his or her job as it relates to other jobs in the organization. (The analyst may be surprised to find that often the incumbent does not even know the identity of his or her immediate supervisor.)

Job Activity Identification Section

After completing the mini-organization chart, the incumbent is requested to think about his or her job and to identify job activities. The following form (Exhibit 6-2) was used in the Olympia project and in other early class and compensation studies. However, there were endless problems related to the employee-provided outputs to this form.

The more complex Activity Identification Section presented in Exhibit 6-3 is more commonly used by the authors, although the form described in Exhibit 6-2 was used in the Olympia study. In order to obtain the best use of this form, project leaders go to great lengths to teach supervisors and employees how to write an activity statement.

Writing An Activity Statement

The job activity identification section (Exhibit 6-3) is the "heart and guts" of a JAQ. Over the years, this section has taken many forms. The authors have also used various approaches to obtain job content information from employees requested to complete a JAQ. A major problem facing many employees is a lack of writing skills in using appropriate words and combining them in an organized manner to define job activities.

There can be no room in job analysis for misinterpretation or misunderstanding. Each word, each term must have a specific meaning and, in all cases, their use in any practice, method, process, or procedure must be consistent with this definition. It must also be noted that as computer-based applications assume a major role in the entire job analysis/job description writing process, specificity of determination will become even more critical.

Exhibit 6-1: Employee Identification Section

Part I—To The Employee. You are the best person to provide the information about your job. You know the exact tasks you perform and your responsibilities. Therefore, you are asked to fill in this job analysis questionnaire. You should answer every question. If the space provided for any particular item is not sufficient, please attach another sheet. (Be sure to show the number of any question answered on the sheet attached.)

You know the exact duties you perform and the responsibilities of YOUR POSITION. DO NOT COPY OTHER EMPLOYEES' ANSWERS, EVEN IF THEIR JOBS ARE SIMILAR TO YOURS. WE WANT YOUR OWN STATEMENT OF YOUR RESPONSIBILITIES AND DUTIES IN YOUR JOB.

You may ask your immediate supervisor to explain questions you do not understand, but use your own words in answering all questions.

After the questionnaires have been analyzed and preliminary job descriptions developed, an interview will be scheduled with you to be certain that the job description accurately reflects your position.

Drawing Your Job Picture

We plan to analyze all the component parts of your job and combine all of the essential parts into an accurate description of your work. We are counting on your honest and correct accounts of what you do while performing your job. Be as objective and informative as you can in completing all pages of this questionnaire. Our first request is for you to complete this chart. The completed chart gives us an understanding of where your job fits in the organizational structure.

(Continued on next page)

To assist employees and gain uniformity in defining activity statements, the authors have taken a strong position in defining words and terms that have a direct relationship to job analysis and organization design. The definitions of terms provided in Chapter 3 delineate our stand. Because there are many definitions related to these words and terms, we are not stating that these are the only acceptable meanings. We are stating, however, that this is how we define these words and terms, and we will use them in this context throughout all of our discussions.

Exhibit 6-1—*continued*

Name of your department

Your immediate supervisor's name

Your immediate supervisor's title

Your name

Your job title

Date of entry into current job

Date of hire into organization

Names of your subordinates:

Titles of your subordinates:

Our proposed way of writing an activity statement becomes the next critical covenant. This approach covers any job content activity such as a task, responsibility, duty, function, or behavior.

Like many other job analysis-related efforts, writing activity statements appears on the surface to be a fairly simple assignment. It is far from simple, however; it is a demanding and difficult challenge that faces all those involved in describing work content.

First and foremost, those responsible for writing job activity statements must describe precisely what they mean. Because of the many crucial organizational- and employee-related programs that are rooted in job content, considerable effort and discipline are required.

(Text continued on page 96)

Exhibit 6-2. Duties

List the various activities that you do on your job. NUMBER EACH ACTIV-ITY. Describe these activities so specifically that they will be clear, even to someone who is not familiar with your work. Give examples where appropriate. Please list each activity in order of importance, from most important to least important. ESTIMATE THE AMOUNT OF TIME THAT YOU SPEND ON EACH ACTIVITY. Although this may be difficult, you are better able to do it than anyone else. State the number of hours each day you spend on each activity. If you perform any of these activities on an irregular basis (weekly, monthly, quarterly, etc.) please note this and explain. If you perform duties of a supervisory nature, describe those duties specifically and in detail. Remember, if you need more space, use the back of this page.

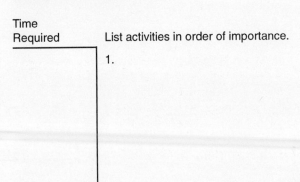

Time
Required   List activities in order of importance.

1.

Which activity or activities do you think are most difficult? (List the *numbers* only.)

Exhibit 6-3. Job Activity Identification Section (Page 1 of 3)

RESPONSIBILITIES AND DUTIES

Instructions: What are all the activities you perform on your job? By completing this job analysis questionnaire, you will help us update or write a job description for your job. We will be using two terms to help describe your job: *Responsibilities* and *Duties.*

Responsibilities: The major job activities you perform in completing your job assignment. Each of these is an umbrella statement that covers a segment of your job.

Duties: The specific, more detailed activities you perform when accomplishing each responsibility.

Look at the following examples:

Job: Secretary I

Responsibility: 1.0 Acts as a receptionist

Duties: 1.1 Answers telephone, relaying information or transferring calls to appropriate individuals.

1.2 Greets visitors, answering their questions and/or directing them to appropriate individual.

Responsibility: 2.0 Performs various administrative activities

2.1 Schedules appointments

2.2 Composes routine correspondence

2.3 Makes travel arrangements

2.4 Coordinates meetings by notifying participants of scheduled date and time, and by reserving meeting room

We would now like you to do the following:

1. On page 2 of this questionnaire (Responsibility Identification Form), write the identifying information at the top of the page. Then write all the responsibilities of your job. (As a general rule, most jobs can be described with 3 to 7 responsibility statements.)

2. Beginning with page 3 of the questionnaire, write the first responsibility you listed on page 2.

3. Now think of the more detailed activities you must perform to accomplish this responsibility. These are called duties. (Normally, 3 to 10 duties describe a Responsibility.)

4. On page 4 of the questionnaire, write the second responsibility you listed on page 2 and the duties related to it.

5. Continue writing one Responsibility and its associated duties on the remaining pages until you have covered all responsibilities identified on page 2.

(Continued on next page)

Exhibit 6-3—continued *(page 2 of 3)*

DEPARTMENT _____ YOUR NAME _____

JOB TITLE _____ DATE _____

RESPONSIBILITY IDENTIFICATION FORM

	(1) WHAT IS DONE? (Action Verb)	(2) TO WHAT IS IT DONE? (Object)	(3) MODIFYING PHRASE(S) (Further describes action)
RESPONSIBILITY #1			
RESPONSIBILITY #2			
RESPONSIBILITY #3			
RESPONSIBILITY #4			
RESPONSIBILITY #5			
	Types	Letters	From rough draft
Using word processor
For superintendent

Example:

Note: Responsibility column could be expanded to allow for the Identification of 7 to 9 Responsibilities.

Exhibit 6-3—*continued (page 3 of 3)*

Name of Employee _____

RESPONSIBILITY # _____

_____

DUTIES:

1. _____

_____

2. _____

_____

3. _____

_____

4. _____

_____

5. _____

_____

6. _____

_____

7. _____

_____

8. _____

_____

9. _____

_____

10. _____

_____

(Continue on back of page if necessary)

Note: Reproduce as often as necessary for inclusion within JAQ to ensure complete description of job. 5 to 7 Copies may be sufficient.

(Continued from page 92)

The data collection and description phase obtains details about the job. Processing job data into activity statements requires the writer first to think, "What do I want to say?" and, second, "How do I say what I want to say?" Because of the need for brevity and clarity, the suggested syntax of *action verb + object + why and how descriptive information* becomes the "control tower" syntax that establishes a measure of conciseness for those writing activity statements. thus,

action verb (word) + object of the verb + words or terms
that further describe action taken = the activity

The "control tower" approach exerts a degree of discipline in writing style. When the sentence begins with the action verb, third person, present tense, the resulting direct and vigorous writing style permits the verb to pull the rest of the words in the statement and make it truly action-oriented. In reality, the subject of the sentence is the job title. For example, in the job description of a *payroll clerk*, an activity statement reads: "Records daily hours worked." The full form of this statement would be *"Payroll clerk* records daily hours worked." (It is certainly acceptable to use first person, present tense. In that case, the subject of the activity statement is "I [the incumbent] do this or that.")

Certain requirements apply to the writing of all kinds of activity statements. These requirements may be met by taking the actions implied by the following questions:

1. *Is the verb selected the most descriptive verb possible?* If there is any question, continue to search for a better, more appropriate verb.

2. *Does the statement require the use of more than one verb?* If it does, check to see whether or not it is possible to find one verb that conveys the meaning or action transmitted by the compound verbs. When using compound verbs, be sure that they fit together into a natural, commonly occurring sequence of actions. If this is not the case, separate the verbs into two or more statements.

3. *Does the statement involve a sequential relationship of verb + object, verb + object, verb + object, etc., plus why and how information?* In this case, is it possible to use one verb and object that have a comprehensive meaning and combine with some common *why* and *how* modifiers? As in point 2 above, if this series of verbs and objects does not fit into a common and sequential series of actions, it is preferable to separate the verbs + objects into separate statements.

4. *Does the statement consist of a single verb + object with compound modifiers?* If it does, it may be useful to divide the single statement into two or more statements, each with its own *why* and *how* modifiers.

Selecting the most appropriate/applicable verb to describe the action taken is the secret to writing an accurate activity statement. In most cases, more than one verb can be used to open the sentence. Since many verbs have more than one meaning, care and attention should be given to the selection of the most suitable verb. For example, in clerical assignments related to working with forms, the verb "handles" frequently appears in the activity statement. Does "handle" mean review the data on the form for accuracy, enter data on the form, transcribe data to other forms, or transfer the form to other individuals? Or, possibly even more important, does it mean that the incumbent is reviewing what is on the form and making decisions and taking actions in response to those data?

Verb selection requires an effort to identify the word that best describes the activity. This kind of effort will be invaluable in reducing vagueness or ambiguity in a major product of the job analysis—the job description. The right verb will tell the reader exactly what is happening on the job. The right verb—the most appropriate verb—must be one the person performing the job and those reviewing the job recognize and understand. In other words, a commonly used word will, in most cases, be the best word.

Adding to the confusion is the subjectivity problem, which has its roots in the meanings of the action verbs. Verbs are words; words are not nearly as precise and uniformly understood as numbers. A certain amount of ambiguity or vagueness is present in many verbs. Verbs may have a variety of meanings as to level or degree of action. These differences in meaning can easily result in significant variations in interpretation of the work to be performed and the expected outcome.

Also, beware of jargon—that is, words used by specific occupational groups. Those outside the field may be unable to recognize the intended meaning of the verb, and thus may wrongly interpret the description. Jargon may be used as long as the words are widely and clearly understood.

The final, edited copy of accurate and precise activity (task, responsibility, or duty) statements cannot be left to amateurs—not even incumbents or immediate supervisors. Many managers, even human resources specialists, make the mistake of requesting the incumbent or an immediate supervisor to write a description of the job under study and then expect to receive an acceptable and final draft. The writing of clear, precise, and concise activity statements requires the efforts of highly skilled professionals.

Attention must also focus on the use of every word in the activity statement. When selecting words, be consistent in their use. Establish a meaning for a word and stick to it. Try to avoid ambiguous words. Use quantitative words when possible ("makes 20 customer contacts daily," not "makes many customer contacts daily"). Avoid making conclusions ("performs work requiring the lifting of 94-pound bags of concrete," instead of "performs strenuous work").

Using A Task Identification Card (TIC). In a classification and compensation pay study for the Marathon County Public School System, the TIC (Exhibit 6-4) was developed and used instead of the different forms presented in the Job Activity Identification Section of Exhibit 6-3.

The TIC is printed on 5" x 8" index cards. A separate task is entered on each card. The stiffness of the index cards, compared to paper, permits the individual completing the cards, and the analysts auditing them, to easily transpose and organize the entries, as opposed to organizing and reviewing tasks presented in a long list on one sheet of paper. Another benefit of TICs is the ease in identifying statements using different words and terms that mean the same thing—that describe the same activity. It is relatively easy to group completed cards together to form a major area of work or responsibility. It may be possible to identify one of the tasks as a good cover statement for all grouped together TICs or to write a separate statement that can be used as a responsibility statement with other related TICs used as duty statements. Finally, using the frequency and criticality responses, it again is relatively easy to order the duty statements from most to least important.

When using TICs to collect job content information, the collection of knowledge, skill, and education information can be part of Phase II in the JAQ process. At this time, the employee can review the editing completed by the job analyst. He or she can make any revisions necessary and then identify knowledge, skills, and abilities required of a new hire as well as those required of a fully proficient employee. See the next section for an extended discussion of knowledge, skills, and abilities (KSAs).

In the Marathon School System project, each involved employee was initially given 50 cards. Some employees used less than 15, and some used more than 100 cards to define their jobs. The mini-organization chart was also placed on a card and was the first card to be completed by the employee. (See mini-organization chart in Exhibit 6-1, Employee Identification Section.)

Exhibit 6-4: Task Identification Card

1.	Name:

2.	List only one of your tasks in this space.

3.	How often do you perform this duty? Please circle the appropriate response.

Daily	Weekly	Bi-monthly	Monthly	Quarterly	Anually
3 or more times a week	1 or 2 times a week	at least twice a month	at least once a month	at least 4 times a year	at least once a year

4.	How critical is this task in the overall successful performance of your total job? Please circle the appropriate response.

Not very critical	Somewhat critical	Critical	Very critical

Knowledge, Skills, and Education Section

Like other presentations in this chapter, there is a need to start this section with our definitions of knowledge (K), skills (S), and abilities (A)—KSAs.

Knowledge—Extent of information and facts that a worker must possess and understand to perform job assignments, including the application of kinds and levels of skills required. It is a familiarity, awareness, or understanding acquired genetically or through learning.

Skill—The degree of mastery of a technique or proficiency required of an employee to accomplish a job-required activity.

Ability—The quality of being able to do something. A natural or acquired talent.

Some experts have historically differentiated skills and abilities by defining skill as a physical capability, while an ability relates to an intellectual capability. This archaic definition is *not* the way we differentiate skill and ability. From a HR, job content application, a level of a skill can be identified through job performance. A kind and level of an ability can be established through some kind of test. Because HR professionals working in the area of employee selection have little opportunity to investigate and measure demonstrated on-the-job skills, the focus is most often on an applicant's abilities. However, those involved in pay determination want to know the skills required of a jobholder, and these skill requirements play an important role in determining job worth and establishing job rates of pay. Very simply, from our perspective, *a skill is an on-the-job demonstrated ability.*

The knowledge, skill, and education form (Exhibit 6-5) requests the employee to identify knowledge and skills required in the performance of each identified duty. In addition, the employee is further asked to identify how the knowledge and skills were acquired—through some level of formal education or some kind of experience. The employee is asked to identify whether a person must have the knowledge or skills before being placed on the job or if they can be acquired after being assigned to the job. This is critical in determining minimum knowledge and skill requirements.

ADA Requirements. This section can be expanded to meet the Americans with Disabilities Act (ADA) requirements. An employee can also be requested to identify which duties must be performed without assistance from any other employee and the duties the employee could ex-

---

Exhibit 6-5. Knowledge, Skills, and Education Section

KNOWLEDGE AND SKILLS

Instructions:

1.　Please review the **RESPONSIBILITIES** and Duties you have just listed. Then think about the knowledge and skills you must have to perform each **RESPONSIBILITY.** List below all the knowledge and skills you can think of that relate to each **RESPONSIBILITY.** (Examples: Knowledge of laws and ordinances regarding building codes; knowledge of supervisory techniques; skill in delegating and directing work to others, skill in communicating orally and in writing).

2.　Review your knowledge list, thinking about how you acquired each one (that is, where you learned it). In the column labeled "How Knowledge Acquired", write a number using the code below which describes how you acquired each knowledge.

1. = In grammar school	5. = In graduate school
2. = In high school	6. = In specialized training sessions
3. = In junior (2-year) college	7. = Through on-the-job experience
4. = In college	8. = Other

(Continued on next page)

pect assistance with from other employees. This information can be used in the job description to identify the physical, sensory, and mental abilities necessary to perform the essential duties of the job. Although the authors do not use the term *Essential Job Function* in describing or defining responsibilities and duties, the ranking and rating of responsibilities and duties can be a very critical step in establishing essential job functions.

Exhibit 6-5—*continued*

3.   After you have completed Instruction 2, write an asterisk (*) to the left of those knowledge and skills that you think a person should have before being hired for your job.

	Knowledge	How Knowledge Acquired	Skills
Responsibility #1			
Responsibility #2			
Responsibility #3			
Responsibility #4			
Responsibility #5			
Responsibility #6			
Responsibility #7			

Examples of kinds of knowledge an employee may be requested to provide or a job analyst may be expected to identify:

Knowledge of policies, practices, and procedures of the organization and job.

Knowledge of concepts required for effective performance of job assignments (job responsibilities and duties).

Knowledge of grammar, punctuation, and spelling.

Knowledge of equipment, tools, and work aids used in the performance of job assignments.

Kinds of knowledge gained through academic programs.

Knowledge of computer systems and operations.

Examples of skills and abilities required in the performance of job assignments:

Skill/ability to interact with and influence others.

Skill/ability to direct the work of others.

Skill/ability to solve problems.

Skill/ability to perform mathematical computations.

Skill/ability to make effective oral presentations.

Skill/ability to produce useful written documents.

Skill/ability to compile, analyze, and organize data and information.

Skill/ability to interact with computer-driven system.

Skill/ability to repair, maintain, and operate equipment and machinery.

Job Specification/Level of Factors Section

This part of a JAQ obtains information regarding the demands the job makes on the jobholder. If a Knowledge and Skills section is not a separate part of a JAQ, this section will include a request for Knowledge and Skill/Abilities information. If an organization is using a specific kind of point-factor job evaluation method, questions can be asked in this section that relate to specific factors in the method. The questions in Exhibit 6-6 have commonly been used in this part of a JAQ.

If the JAQ specification section is to include questions related to specific factors of the job evaluation plan, checklist questions are relatively easy for a jobholder to answer and may prove to be very useful information during the actual job evaluation process. Developing information that substantiates and justifies a level of a compensable factor may be critical in the correct evaluation of a job and in justifying the selection of anyone who wants to know why a certain level was selected. The Patterns of Concepts developed by the designers of FES provide splendid assistance here.

Exhibit 6-6. Knowledge and Skill/Abilities Information

---

1. If you were hiring someone to replace you in your present position, what is the lowest educational level you would require them to have? (check one)

    _____ completion of a high school education
    _____ graduation from a technical or junior (2-year) college
    _____ graduation from a 4-year college or university
    _____ possession of a master's degree or equivalent
    _____ possession of a doctorate

2. If you were hiring someone to replace you in your present position, how many years of relevant work-related experience would you require them to have? (i.e., minimum experience requirement)

3. What licenses, registrations, or certificates are legally required to perform your job? (please list)

4. Are you required to either participate in any additional training in order to maintain your licensures, registrations, or certification? If yes, please list them below:

5. Are there any other jobs an applicant should have performed before entering this job? If yes, please list the job titles below:

6. List any tools, equipment, vehicles, and machines you use while performing your work.

7. What specific laws or ordinances do you use or follow in your work? (Laws or ordinances that you must have knowledge of and use as a reference to perform your job)

(Continued on next page)

Exhibit 6-6—*Continued*

8. Describe the physical demands of your job. (Example: work is generally sedentary; requires long periods of standing or walking; recurring bending or stooping)

9. Describe the normal and usual conditions of your work. (Example: work is performed in an office; in a very noisy place; around much dust, dirt, grease, etc.; around smoke fumes, irritating chemicals or toxic conditions, outdoors; on call 24 hours/day)

10. Describe working conditions that cause you to feel stress when performing your job activities.

11. Please list below the number of the most difficult responsibility you perform. (The one that is hardest for you) Why is this responsibility difficult?

Most of the nine FES evaluation factors have two or more parts (underlying concepts or subfactors) that are identified in the Patterns of Concepts. A careful study of each factor and a review of the Patterns of Concepts yields sufficient information to develop a series of statements that describe various levels of the quality of the factor. A similar series of statements, or a factor-level checklist describing various levels of a factor, were included in the Olympia job analysis questionnaire. This checklist permitted the incumbent to select the statement that best described the level of the factor required in the performance of the job. These statements reduced the need for an incumbent to conceptualize responses that described specific qualities or features of the job and also reduced the amount of writing required to describe these features. The checklist statements did, however, significantly increase the length of the questionnaire. Each checklist always concluded with an open-ended question requesting the incumbent to provide additional information if the statements relating to a specific factor did not adequately describe that part of the incumbent's job. (Very few employees, however, used this opportunity to provide additional job information.)

There are both advantages and disadvantages to using a series of factor-level checklists. Some of the advantages are (1) it is easier for a respondee to answer and facilitate completion of the questionnaire and (2) it provides information directly related to a factor in terms that assists in writing the substantiating or job-related factor statement. The disadvantages are (1) some employees misinterpret a statement and select one or more that do not relate to their jobs, (2) the employee recognizes that the selection has an impact on the evaluation of the job and selects the statement that appears to provide the highest evaluation, and—possibly most important—(3) none of the statements in the checklist accurately or adequately describe the level of the factor required in the performance of the job, but the employee does not spend the time or effort to describe the level adequately.

Employees frequently do not check any statement, and, as already mentioned, do not provide information more appropriate to the work performed. Often, when employees respond to open-ended questions, their answers are extremely brief or are difficult to understand. Occasionally, an employee is so verbose that it takes hours to comprehend and reduce all the information to useful form. This is also true in listing job activities. The following checklist questions in Exhibit 6-7 relate to Factors 2-9 of FES.

(Text continued on page 109)

Exhibit 6-7. Factor Checklist

Factor 2

SUPERVISORY CONTROLS

a. List the responsibility numbers (from the Job Activity Identification section) that you do repeatedly without receiving new instructions from your supervisor. These instructions will be referred to as standing or continuing instructions.

What is the nature of the standing or continuing instructions you have been given regarding these tasks? (check one)

_____ The instructions are detailed, specific and cover all aspects
of the work.
_____ The instructions are somewhat general; many aspects of the work
are covered specifically, but I must also use some judgment.
_____ The instructions are general, requiring me to use judgment.
_____ The instructions are very general, requiring me to use much judgment.
_____ The instructions are in terms of goals and objectives.
_____ Other (describe fully)

(Continued on next page)

Exhibit 6-7—*continued*

b. List the responsibility numbers (from the Job Activity Identification section) for which you do not have standing or continuing instructions.

   What is the nature of the instructions your supervisor gives you when assigning new or one-time duties? (check one)

   _____ The instructions are detailed, specific and cover all aspects of the work.

   _____ The instructions are somewhat general; many aspects of the work are covered specifically, but I must also use some judgment.

   _____ The instructions are general, requiring me to use judgment.

   _____ The instructions are very general, requiring me to use much judgment.

   _____ The instructions are in terms of goals and objectives.

   _____ Other (describe fully)

c. How does your immediate supervisor review your work? (check all that apply)

   _____ My supervisor reviews most or all of my work while I am doing it.

   _____ My supervisor spot-checks my work as I am doing it.

   _____ My supervisor reviews most or all of my completed work.

   _____ My supervisor spot-checks my completed work.

   _____ My supervisor does not review my work.

   _____ Other (describe fully)

d. When your supervisor reviews your work, what is the purpose of the review? (check all that apply)

   _____ My compliance with detailed and specific instructions.

   _____ My compliance with established procedures.

   _____ The accuracy of my work.

   _____ The nature and propriety of the final results of my work.

   _____ Other (describe fully)

Factor 3

GUIDELINES

a. What written guidelines or procedures (e.g., laws, building codes, rules and regulations) do you use in your work?

b. Do the guidelines you use in your work require interpretation or are they clear and specific?

(Continued on next page)

Exhibit 6-7—*continued*

c. Do you ever have to determine which guideline to apply in a specific situation? ____ If so, when? Please give an example.

Factor 4
COMPLEXITY

a. Describe what makes your work routine, complicated, unusual or difficult to perform. What obstacles are there in the work itself that make it difficult to accomplish?

Factor 5
SCOPE AND EFFECT

a. What is the purpose of your assignment?

b. What is the effect of the work you produce within your department?

c. What impact does your work have beyond your immediate department?

d. How does your work affect outside organizations?

e. What is the effect of errors you may make within your department? Within other departments?

f. Does your work affect the reliability, accuracy or dependability of other work processes? If so, how?

Factor 6
PERSONAL CONTACTS

Describe the occupations of people with whom you deal in carrying out your work (e.g., co-workers, workers in related support units, recipients of direct services, members of the general public, or representatives of other organizations). Do not include contacts with your supervisor since supervisory contacts are described under previous questions.

(Continued on next page)

Exhibit 6-7—*continued*

Factor 7
PURPOSE OF CONTACTS

Describe the purpose of the above contacts, for example: to give or exchange information; to resolve problems; to provide services; to motivate, influence, or interrogate persons; or to justify, defend, negotiate or settle matters, etc.

Factor 8
PHYSICAL DEMANDS

Describe the physical demands of your job by checking as many of the following that apply.

_____ Typically sitting at a desk or table
_____ Intermittently sitting, standing or stooping
_____ Typically standing or walking
_____ Typically bending, crouching or stooping
_____ Occasionally lifting light objects (less than 24 pounds)
_____ Frequently lifting light objects
_____ Occasionally lifting heavy objects (25 or more pounds)
_____ Frequently lifting heavy objects (25 or more pounds)
_____ Climbing ladders
_____ Using tools or equipment requiring a high degree of dexterity
_____ Distinguishing between shades of color
_____ Other (please specify)

Factor 9
WORK ENVIRONMENT

Describe the normal or usual conditions where your work is performed by checking as many of the following that apply.

_____ Work is performed in an office, library or computer room.
_____ Work is performed in a stockroom or warehouse.
_____ Work is performed in a very noisy place.
_____ Work exposes me to much dust, dirt, grease, etc.
_____ Work exposes me to machinery with moving parts.
_____ Work exposes me to contagious or infectious diseases, or irritating chemicals.
_____ Work is performed outdoors and occasionally in cold or inclement weather.
_____ Work requires use of protective devices such as masks, goggles, gloves, etc.
_____ Other (please specify)

(Continued from page 105)

Additional Employee-Provided Information Section

The final three questions (Exhibit 6-8) permit the incumbent to provide additional information pertaining to the job. Finally, the incumbent is requested to sign and date the questionnaire. The completed job analysis questionnaire is the official source of content data for job evaluation. It is the foundation on which the job description is built. It also may serve as a starting point in a future appeals procedure or as a base to aid in identifying future changes in job content. For these reasons, it is important that the questionnaire be signed and dated. It is a basic document for establishing employee job obligations.

Exhibit 6-8. Additional Employee-Provided Information Section

---

ADDITIONAL INFORMATION

1.   Are there any job activities that you are not performing now that you should be? If so, please list them below.

2.   Are there any job activities that you are now performing that you should not be? If so, please list them below. Use numbers assigned to relevant responsibilities and duties (Example: 2.01, 2.06.)

3.   Is there any additional information that you would like to tell us about your job that you feel we should know?

IF YOU HAVE ANY PROBLEMS COMPLETING THIS FORM, PLEASE CONTACT:

_____

_____

CERTIFICATION

I certify that the above information is accurate and complete.

Signature of Employee _____ Date _____

Supervisor's Review Section

Questionnaires completed by incumbents must be reviewed for accuracy and adequacy by their immediate supervisors (Exhibit 6-9). This is not a mere rubber-stamp function. The supervisory review is critical for identifying inadequacies. Next to the incumbent, the immediate supervisor knows the most about the job.

Supervisors are requested to certify the accuracy of the statements made by the employee, noting any exceptions and providing any additional relevant information not fully covered in the questionnaire. The supervisors are also asked to list and number what they think to be the most important activities performed by jobholders. This provides a critical check with the information given by the jobholders.

Exhibit 6-9: Job Analysis Questionnaire—Supervisor's Review Sheet

---

Name of Employee_____   Date_____

Job Title_____   Department _____

Part II—To the Immediate Supervisor. Review this employee's questionnaire carefully to see that it is accurate and complete. Then fill out Items A through D. Do not fill in these items unless you supervise the employee directly. If you direct this employee through a subordinate supervisor, have that supervisor complete Part II.

Your certification in Item D means that you accept responsibility for the accuracy and completeness with which the entire questionnaire describes the duties and responsibilities of the job. If Part I does not express your view of the duties and responsibilities that you have assigned the employee, it will be necessary for you to use Part II to qualify or elaborate on the description.

There are two essential cautions you should observe:

1. Under no circumstances should you change or alter the employee's entries in Part I.

2. Do not make any statements or comments about the employee's work performance, competence or qualifications. This questionnaire will be used to evaluate the duties that constitute the position, not the performance or qualifications of the employee.

Sign and date the certificate showing that you consider the entire questionnaire to be accurate and complete.

(Continued on next page)

Completion of the Questionnaire

The most important part of a classification and pay project is the completion of the JAQ. It is no simple matter to entice employees to fill out these admittedly lengthy documents and to get supervisors to ensure that the questionnaires are adequately completed in a timely manner. Valid and adequate reasons must be presented to all employees and their supervisors explaining why it is in their best interests to complete the questionnaires. Many employees are unable to see that their efforts to complete the questionnaire have a direct effect on how their jobs are evaluated and, ultimately, on how much they will be paid. This is particularly relevant in large departments and in job classes encompassing a large number of employees. Some feel threatened by

---

Exhibit 6-9—*continued*

A. Describe briefly the employee's position as you see it. Show how it relates to the functions of the department.

B. List the duties assigned to this employee that are most important (use the responsibility numbers).

C. State any additions or exceptions to the statements made by the employee in Part I.

D. I certify that the above information is accurate and complete.

Signature of
Immediate Supervisor _____

Name (please print) _____

Date_____ Department_____

E. Comments by department head:

F. I certify that the above information is accurate and complete.

Signature of
Department Head _____

Name (please print) _____

Date_____ Department_____

the questionnaire because they do know the effect it could have, and they are afraid of the possible unfavorable outcomes—especially of a relative reduction in the rate of pay for their jobs in comparison to that paid for other jobs. Thorough explanations at every step in the process are critical to success.

Job Analyst Training

From the Olympia project to the present, it has been both useful and necessary to implement a training program for members of the project task force/team responsible for analyzing jobs and writing the job descriptions. To ensure a uniform approach for analyzing and validating JAQ-provided information, for gathering additional job content information, and then for writing uniform, complete, and accurate job descriptions, training programs ranging from a half-day to a full day should be implemented.

Prior to the meeting, each task force member is assigned specific organizational groups or specific kinds of jobs. (The project consultant or project director is frequently assigned to analyze all department manager jobs.) The procedures followed by all project members take this form:

1. Read and carefully review all assigned questionnaires.
2. Note any areas that are unclear and require additional information.
3. Identify inconsistencies or statements that appear to be inaccurate.
4. Specifically check identified activities against statements checked in the specification section.
5. Schedule appointments through department managers for on-site desk or bench audits. (If the supervisor cannot be reached, contact the HR department for assistance in making appointments.)
6. Audit all single-job classes.
7. Audit all secretarial positions.
8. Audit any completed questionnaire that appears to relate to a job different from that being described in other questionnaires with the same job title.

The training program focuses primarily on editing collected job content information and providing information that will assist in establishing levels of the nine FES compensable factors.

Editing Session

The editing part of the training program focuses on the following seven issues:

1. Are there sufficient responsibilities to cover all major areas of the job?
2. Do the identified duties fit within the assigned responsibility?
3. Does it appear that there may be missing duties?
4. Are the responsibility and duty statements too vague or too specific?
5. Are there an excessive number of responsibility statements (more than seven) and duty statements (more than ten)?
6. Is it possible to combine responsibility or duty statements, or should any responsibility or duty statement be further subdivided?
7. Review the action verbs. Are they appropriate? Is one verb used too often? Could it be replaced with a more descriptive verb? Remember, the verbs actually draw a job picture. The more and better the verbs used to define work activities, the more descriptive the definition. The challenge to any writer of responsibility and duty statements is not only to use the most descriptive action verb possible, but to start each duty statement with a verb that is different from the verb used to originate the responsibility statement. Using the same verb in the duty statement and in the responsibility statement is like defining a word with the same word.

The team members are told that some of these questions may not be answerable without returning and asking more specific and detailed questions of the incumbent or higher levels of management. Frequently, the incumbent and even the immediate supervisor are so close to the job that they fail to recognize everything that is going on or they assume that others recognize activities being performed, when in reality they are undetected.

Clarifying Deviations

Before completing a first draft job definition, it may be necessary to clarify issues arising from the completed Responsibility and Duty Identification Forms. In the review process, the analyst may sense, from having reviewed other completed questionnaires or from learning work unit operations, that an activity is missing or that an activity is poorly described. In this case, the analyst must verify the problem areas with someone— normally the incumbent or that individual's supervisor—to get a more accurate description of the job. A form requiring verification should be so noted. One procedure is to place a "V" at the top of the completed form, indicating the need to review and verify that particular job.

It is not unusual to find employees who have had insufficient instruction or training and who are doing things they should not be doing.

However, deviations between what the employee *is* doing and *should be* doing do not necessarily arise from faulty effort or work knowledge. There may be valid reasons for deviations. For example, the employee may have developed unique improvements and found a better way of doing the job, or some of the tasks may have been assigned permanently or temporarily to another employee. Other reasons may involve different production requirements, the availability of equipment, revised or new technology, or the array of knowledge among members of the work group. Thus, a complete analysis may require more detailed information.

These deviations may arise because past job descriptions included obsolete duties that continue to be considered part of the job or duties of minimal importance. Maintaining such inaccuracies may ensure an unwarranted high pay for the incumbent or may assist managers in building "empires" by making jobs appear to be more important than they actually are. Unwarranted or unimportant duties also assist in the development of artificial employment barriers.

Because the job analysis touches so many areas fundamental to effective and efficient working relationships, both the worker performing the job and the immediate supervisor must have the opportunity to review the analyst's editing efforts. This review provides an excellent opportunity to determine if the edited copy is (1) factually correct, (2) easily understood, and (3) complete. The report may also require a review by others performing the same job.

This review procedure is a major step in gaining employee acceptance of the entire compensation program. Involvement at this stage provides employees with the opportunity to gain some insight into the way the organization views their jobs and vice versa. It also enables the employees to take a good look at themselves in their jobs and to inform the organization about their contributions and the work they actually perform.

Using the FES Audit Worksheet

The FES Audit Worksheet (Exhibit 6-10) was developed by the federal government to assist analysts in writing job descriptions. This worksheet comes directly from the Pattern of Concepts developed by the designers of the FES. Usually, this worksheet is completed by the job analyst.

By completing the audit worksheet, the analyst recognizes the kind and degree of missing information. The intent of the worksheet is to assist the analyst in describing the levels of the nine FES factors. When completing the FES Audit Worksheet from information provided by the JAQ or collected in subsequent observations and interviews, the analyst focuses on describing work activities that illustrate or identify the use of the factor in the specific job rather than on simply paraphrasing a factor statement in the primary or class-series standards. The very heart of the FES lies in the translation of job content information into terms that identify or relate to the nine FES compensable factors.

It may be possible to provide the form to the jobholder when returning a first draft of the job definition for review and approval. At this time, the jobholder would be requested to provide the information necessary for completing the worksheet. Having this information from each incumbent would be extremely useful and valuable for those involved in the job evaluation part of a classification and pay study.

Obtaining Line Personnel Assistance

From the beginning of a classification and compensation project, if accurate and complete job descriptions are to be written, the incumbents must be the prime source of job information. The HR department must coordinate all data collection activities. All work must pass through the department, and its personnel must check for schedule maintenance and process and collect any information needed by the analysts. The HR department also does a final editing of the job descriptions written by all project members. This ensures sufficient job content information and consistency of format. Changes or corrections are made where necessary.

In the Olympia project, the analysts reviewed the questionnaires, performed any additional bench or desk audits, collected missing information, and wrote the job descriptions. From a detailed analysis of the work done by the analysts, it is conceivable that line personnel in each unit could have performed these assignments. With time permitting, well-designed training programs that divided each segment of the job analysis-job description phases into workable segments could have been developed. These programs would have explained in understandable terms how to analyze a questionnaire, how to write responsibility and duty statements, and how to write factor statements. This approach would have freed the project members and the HR specialists to review, edit, and do a final rewrite when necessary to ensure uniformity, consistency, and validity of the job information provided. Even more important, it would have brought line personnel into direct contact with these important functions and assisted in improving incumbent-supervisor communications regarding what the incumbent's job is and what it is not.

Exhibit 6-10: FES Audit Worksheet

Title _____ Incumbent _____

Factor 1: Knowledge Required by the Position

a. Kind of Knowledge and Skill Used   b. How Used in Doing Work

_____   _____

_____   _____

_____   _____

_____   _____

Factor 2: Supervisory Controls

a. How Work Assigned: _____

_____

_____

b. Employee Responsibility for Carrying Out Work: _____

_____

_____

c. How Work Reviewed:_____

_____

_____

Factor 3: Guidelines

a. Guidelines for Performing Work: _____

_____

_____

b. Judgment Required to Apply Guidelines: _____

_____

_____

Factor 4: Complexity

a. Nature of Assignment: _____

_____

_____

(Continued on next page)

Exhibit 6-10—*continued*

b. Difficulty in Identifying What Needs To Be Done: _____

_____

_____

c. Difficulty & Originality Involved In Performing Work: _____

_____

_____

Factor 5: Scope and Effect

a. Purpose of Work: _____

_____

_____

b. Impact of Work Product or Service: _____

_____

_____

Factor 6: Personal Contacts

a. People and Conditions Within Which Contacts are Made: _____

_____

_____

Factor 7: Purpose of Contacts

a. Reasons for Contacts in Factor 6; Interpersonal Skills Required: _____

_____

_____

Factor 8: Physical Demands

a. Nature, Frequency, and Intensity of Physical Activity: _____

_____

_____

Factor 9: Work Environment

a. Risks and Discomforts Imposed by Physical Surroundings; Safety Precautions Required: _____

_____

OTHER IMPORTANT JOB INFORMATION:

Chapter 7

WRITING JOB DESCRIPTIONS FOR OLYMPIA

Although this and the previous chapter focus on traditional ways of collecting job information and converting it into job descriptions, part of this chapter provides information on how computer-based processing will significantly improve these activities from both a content and cost perspective. Before reviewing computer-based opportunities, we will review traditional processes, methods, and procedures used to convert collected job analysis information into useful job descriptions.

Even today, many of the same criticisms discussed in Chapters 2 and 3 regarding job analysis and the writing and use of job descriptions continue to surface. If job descriptions are to provide meaningful rebuttals to criticisms previously identified as well as to some of the following criticisms, these descriptions must describe jobs honestly, accurately, and completely. The following statements are often made to support claims that job descriptions are expensive and worthless documents:

- Job descriptions are frequently obsolete and do not describe what the jobholder is actually doing.
- Job descriptions are frequently too general; they provide insufficient job information, limiting their usefulness.
- Too much time is required in identifying verbs, emphasizing descriptive phrases, and searching for subtle and insignificant distinctions.

- The use of words and terms is inconsistent.
- Most people dislike writing job descriptions.
- Many people are unable to write a description of their own jobs.
- Some people use job descriptions for their own personal gain, and this can be harmful to organizational performance, for example, (1) obtaining a higher rate of pay than one earned by the job requirements or (2) adding personnel to a particular work unit.

Recognizing a certain amount of truth in these complaints makes it imperative that the job analysis-job description process be accomplished in a fully satisfactory manner. To achieve this goal, one of the first steps is to establish an operating plan and schedule of activities. The following is the schedule for the Olympia project and follow-up projects:

1. Develop an acceptable and approved format for the job descriptions.
2. Train a job analysis team to write job descriptions.
3. Perform job audits and write job descriptions.
4. Transmit job description information to administrative support/ word processing.
5. Have the HR director review all job descriptions for consistency.
6. Have appropriate manager for each department review all job descriptions.
7. Send each job description to the respective employee for review and comment.
8. Have HR director review returned job descriptions for final approval.
9. Return all edited and approved job descriptions to administrative support/word processing for final copy.
10. Send final job descriptions to each employee with the established rate of pay for the job and the procedure for appealing classifications. (This step is accomplished after all jobs have been evaluated and classified and a pay system has been designed and approved.)

It must be recognized that the writing of good and useful job descriptions requires significant attention from all involved individuals. Review, revision, and modification are common time-consuming events. It is seldom that any job description is accepted after a first draft. Review and editing are ways of life in the job description writing process.

Class, Job, Position Descriptions

Most class and compensation studies done to date have primarily produced class or job descriptions. Where jobs have only one incumbent, a position description is used. Usually, job descriptions are sufficiently precise and accurate to describe the work of each involved employee. In cases where the work requirements of various incumbents are sufficiently similar and historical precedents and political pressures are strong, class descriptions are produced. In this book, the term *job description* covers class, job, and position descriptions.

Occupations where class descriptions are almost always found are in public safety—police, fire, and emergency rescue—and in labor-trades. In the administrative support occupations such as clerks, typists, and secretaries, job descriptions are replacing typical class descriptions. In the administrative support area, it is not uncommon to find that one job description covers jobs held by various incumbents whose jobs have different titles. In these cases, a list of working titles frequently follows the official job title.

Formatting Job Descriptions

The format used to produce job descriptions includes the following sections: (1) job identification, (2) job summary, (3) job definition, and (4) job specifications.

Identification Section

The identification section may include only the title of the class, job, or position. However, in more and more job descriptions, this section includes job status, job code, title of immediate supervisor, division/department/section where job is located, pay grade assigned to job, and the date the description was written.

Title. The identification section always includes the title of the class, job, or position being described. When using a class description, the title may include working titles of specific jobs or positions. A title that correctly and precisely identifies the job is of value (1) for the jobholder's information and self-esteem, (2) for purposes of job relationships, and (3) for comparison with similar jobs in other organizations.

The title should lend some prestige to the job and should contribute to the personal satisfaction of the jobholder. Every effort must be made to establish a legitimate and realistic title that provides the maximum possible amount of dignity and status to the incumbent. The title should not allude to gender or age requirements. The title is the first step in defining the job and establishing a ranking order with other jobs. It is valuable as an outline to department, division, or functional groupings, a guide for promotions or transfers, and an indicator of training and development requirements.

The title indicates to anyone reviewing the description, and specifically to the jobholder, the particular field of activity of the job, its relationship to that field, and its professional standing. However, caution should be used in selecting a title that tends to *inflate* job importance or value. This could lead to higher expectations of pay among incumbents, inappropriate (higher) job matches when performing market surveys, and even the development of dysfunctional empires by managers.

The job title is especially important when one is attempting to compare the job with similar jobs in other organizations, a process critical in developing pay surveys and recruiting employees. For this reason, every effort should be made to use titles commonly found in the marketplace. It is possible to use a double title with the generic (common) title first, followed by the organizational identifier, such as, Executive Secretary-Finance; Senior Clerk-Accounting.

Like the job description, job titles must be kept current. Jobs with similar duties and similar requirements should have the same title. The *Dictionary of Occupational Titles* (DOT), produced by the U.S. Department of Labor, Employment and Training Administration, is extremely valuable for this purpose.

Job Status. The job status section of a job description permits quick and easy identification of the exempt or nonexempt status of the job relative to its compliance with the Fair Labor Standards Act. Exemption status is becoming more important in the public sector. Organizations must know precisely what they can and cannot do relative to hours worked and work requirements.

Job Code. the job code permits easy and rapid referencing of all jobs. It may consist of letters or numbers in any combination. Each code must have sufficient characters to identify all the jobs in the organization. The code can be a four-character alphanumeric code (B 735) or even a six-digit numeric code (007.167), as used by the U.S. Department of Labor, Employment and Training Administration in the DOT. Any other suitable combination of numbers or letters will serve, but brevity is vital.

A brief review of the manner in which the DOT uses its six-character code will aid any organization that develops its own code or that uses the DOT code. An example follows:

007.167

007	—The first three digits signify occupational group arrangement.
0	—Professional, technical, and managerial occupations.
0	—Occupations in architecture and engineering.
007	—Mechanical engineering.
.167	—The second three digits represent worker trait arrangement: respectively, data, people, things (see Exhibit 7-1). For example, 167 specifically relates to engineering, scientific, and technical operations— 1—Coordinating data; 6—Speaking-signaling to people; 7—Handling things.

Title of Immediate Supervisor. This space is self-explanatory.

Division/Department/Section. This space provides for the precise location of the job.

Grade. This space is for the grade of the job if there is such a category.

Date. The date on the job description refers to the date that it was actually written. Although seldom appearing on a job description, this piece of data can at times be extremely valuable. As frequently mentioned, job

---

Exhibit 7-1: Descriptive Verbs for Work Functions

Verbs used to describe work functions within the Data, People, and Things categories developed by the U.S. Department of Labor are:

D_ata_	_People_	_Things_
0 Synthesising	0 Mentoring	0 Setting up
1 Coordinating	1 Negotiating	1 Precision working
2 Analyzing	2 Instructing	2 Operating–Controlling
3 Compiling	3 Supervising	3 Driving–Operating
4 Computing	4 Diverting	4 Manipulating
5 Copying	5 Persuading	5 Tending
6 Comparing	6 Speaking-Signalling	6 Feeding-Offbearing
	7 Serving	7 Handling
	8 Taking instructions and helping	

---

duties—even responsibilities—change. When reading a job description that identifies the date written, a reader can recognize whether or not the descriptive material is current and accurate. The person responsible for updating the description will know when it is time to review the job and make any necessary modifications and revisions.

Job Summary

The job summary is normally a word picture of the job that delineates its general characteristics, listing only major functions or activities. Through precise ordering and careful selection of words, it indicates clearly and specifically what the jobholder must do. This section of the job description provides enough information to identify and differentiate the major functions and activities of the job from those of others. It is especially valuable to the individual who wants a quick overview of the job. The summary is often used in job matching when participating in a pay survey.

Although job summaries often include code words for describing various aspects of the job ("under close supervision," "general supervision," "considerable," "unusual"), care should be taken in the use of these words. As organizations grow and more and different employees take on the responsibility of collecting and analyzing job data and writing job descriptions, it becomes difficult to achieve total understanding of the meaning of such code words, especially among employees who have some of the job activities defined by these words. Additionally, these words may give supervisors and even incumbents an opportunity to try to gain unwarranted higher ratings for jobs under review. Using behavioral examples to anchor or further describe code words minimizes misinterpretation.

When such words are used, however, they should be defined as precisely as possible and their definitions made available to all employees. The following code words for *kind and frequency of direction received in the performance of a job* are often found in the summary section of a job description. In fact, these terms are often the first words used in the summary section.

- *Under Immediate Direction*—Within this job, the incumbent normally performs the duty assignment after receiving detailed instructions as to methods, procedures, and desired end results. These detailed instructions normally allow little room for deviation. The immediate supervisor may, at times, provide close and constant review while work is under way and when the assignment is completed.

- *Under General Direction*—Within this job, the incumbent normally performs the duty assignment after receiving general instructions as to methods, procedures, and desired end results. The incumbent has some opportunity for discretion when making selections among a few, easily identifiable choices. The assignment is usually reviewed upon completion.
- *Under Direction*—Within this job, the incumbent normally performs the duty assignment according to his or her own judgment, requesting supervisory assistance only when necessary. The assignment is frequently reviewed upon completion.
- *Under Administrative Direction*—Within this job, the incumbent normally performs the duty assignment within broad parameters defined by general organizational requirements and accepted practices. Total end results determine effectiveness of job performance.
- *Under Guidelines Set by Policy*—Within this job, the incumbent normally performs the duty assignment at his or her discretion and is limited only by policies set by administrative or legislative authority. Total end results determine effectiveness of job performance.

Job Definition

The job definition section includes the responsibilities and duties of the job. Responsibilities identify the primary reasons for the existence of the job. These are the major or broad categories of work activities that, in total, define the scope of the work assignments. A responsibility is of sufficient importance that *not* carrying out the duties within it or performing them below a minimally established standard will critically affect the required results and demand remedial actions by management. Unacceptable performance of a responsibility may result in one or more of the following:

- Removal from current job that could include lateral transfer, demotion, or even termination
- Prohibition of receipt of performance-based rewards
- Provision of training and other developmental services

With the establishment of responsibilities, the job becomes subdivided into specific categories or component parts.

After the responsibility statements are completed, each statement should be analyzed separately, and a list of duties should be developed for each responsibility. The definition process is continuous, from the broad and relatively vague to the narrow and precise.

Duties further describe a responsibility. Duties explain in more detail what actually occurs in the performance of a responsibility, and thus provide more individuality and uniqueness to the job description. Duties establish the foundation of performance standards and, when necessary, the procedures to be followed in performing them. Each responsibility and its assigned duties becomes a module of work, or a responsibility module.

Job Specifications

The job specifications section provides information on the requirements or demands the job makes on the jobholder. This section describes knowledge and skills the incumbent must possess. It identifies physical and environmental conditions under which the incumbent must work. The job specification section may take a form that closely relates to the factors of a job evaluation plan, or it may consist of employment standards or job qualifications. (Here again, the DOT can be of assistance as it provides detailed information on reasoning, language, and mathematical requirements for many occupations.) This section could also include physical requirements and any licenses, certifications, or registrations that the jobholder must possess. An additional statement to comply with the ADA is included. "Requirements may be subject to modification in order to reasonably accommodate individuals with disabilities who are otherwise qualified to perform the essential duties of the job."

Computer-based Assistance

As previously mentioned, a variety of computer-based support services are now available or soon will be available to assist all parties in the writing of complete, current, and valid job descriptions. Although much work has been done on the development of Occupational Task Inventories, their widespread use by HR practitioners has yet to arrive. The next section introduces you to task inventories and their potential value in writing job descriptions.

Occupational-Task Inventories

Some years ago, the Training Command of the U.S. Air Force developed extensive task inventories of Air Force specialties (occupations). This work is known as the **Comprehensive Occupational Data Analysis Program** (CODAP). A second generation addition to CODAP is the approximately 150 catalogs (task inventories of specific occupations) produced by the **Vocational-Technical Education Consortium of States** (V-TECS), which is a part of the Southern Association of Colleges and

Schools. Both CODAP and its direct descendant, V-TECS, use the words *duty* and *task* to define action word work statements. Their word *duty* is similar to the word *responsibility* as presented in this book, and their word *task* is similar to the word *duty* as used in this book. The authors use the word *task* as a more generic term relative to an activity used to define a specific job.

Through the use of occupational specific inventories placed on disks or into permanently stored computer data bases, (1) incumbents can identify and select statements that define their work and even modify the statements to reflect more precisely what they do; (2) analysts and other SMEs can review, revise, edit, and write job statements; and (3) administrative support personnel can enter, revise, and produce final copy more easily. In addition to task statements, computer-stored inventories include lists of related knowledge, skills, and abilities, and, potentially, performance standards. Glossaries provide occupational-related definitions of all verbs used in the activity statements.

Recent advancements in optical scanning permit rapid and relatively inexpensive entry of large amounts of job information into computer-based storage. This further reduces the data-entry cost. This inventory can be modified and revised with ease. Additional responsibilities and duties can be added as they are identified. Each verb used in this inventory can be defined and placed in a readily available computer-based glossary.

Job Description Formatting. A second valuable use of computer-based word processing is the development of a format that permits quick and inexpensive production of job descriptions. Exhibit 7-2 is an example of computer-based job description format.

Exhibit 7-2: Job Description for Nancy Horn's Job

Number: 201.362

Title: Department Secretary

Responsible to: Title of immediate supervisor

Responsible For: Titles(s) of reporting subordinates

Exemption Status: Exempt

Qualifications:

Knowledge: Standard secretarial office support

Skill: Resolving people-related problems

Experience: Minimum 5 years office secretarial work

Licenses: Driver's license

Center Manager
Title of Immediate Supervisor

Department Secretary
Position Title

Office Clerks
Title of Immediate Subordinates

Summary:

Under direction. Provides administrative support services for office manager and other center personnel. Performs routine secretarial services. Operates word processing equipment and other standard office equipment. Trains new hires and assists employees. Resolves novel or unique problems. Reviews and rates performance of clerical staff, making promotion and pay adjustment recommendations. Must be thoroughly familiar with all operating practices and procedures in the center.

Definition—Responsibilities and Duties:

1.0 Provides Administrative Support Services

   1.1 Maintains appointment calendar for employer.

   1.2 Places and receives phone calls for employer, screening incoming calls as necessary.

   1.3 Prepares employer's trip itinerary, making travel arrangements, including airline, rental car, lodging, and entertainment reservations.

   1.4 Prepares travel vouchers for employer, keeping employer's travel expense records.

   1.5 Coordinates meetings and conferences, reserving facilities and equipment and making arrangements for entertainment, receptions, and dinners.

(Continued on next page)

Exhibit 7-2, *continued*

1.6 Ensures availability or presence of equipment, supplies, and services for meetings.

1.7 Coordinates or prepares agenda items for meetings and conferences.

1.8 Notifies participants of pending meetings, reminding them of required actions.

1.9 Obtains and compiles data and information required for preparation of summary reports, studies, and guides.

1.10 Greets guests, providing appropriate information.

1.11 Records messages for unavailable recipient.

1.12 Contacts individuals by telephone to resolve problems or obtain information.

2.0 Performs Secretarial Assignments

2.1 Types correspondence, reports, and other documents using typewriter and electronic word-processing equipment.

2.2 Takes dictation, transcribing from shorthand, speedwriting, or stenotype machine into usable documents.

2.3 Composes correspondence and reports.

2.4 Reviews and edits correspondence and reports, ensuring neatness and proper form, proper grammar, and accuracy.

2.5 Attaches pertinent correspondence to incoming mail for employer, writing notes as appropriate.

2.6 Determines priority of action required in response to incoming correspondence.

3.0 Performs clerical assignments.

3.1 Opens, sorts, and prioritizes mail and packages requiring different processing actions.

3.2 Processes outgoing mail, including signing documents as prescribed, addressing mail, forwarding mail, posting registered and certified mail.

3.3 Transmits documents, using fax and electronic mailing system.

3.4 Files documents and correspondence, checking for completeness and accuracy.

3.5 Retrieves documents and correspondence from files.

3.6 Transfers records to inactive files.

3.7 Maintains clipping file, marking articles to be clipped.

3.8 Prepares and maintains personnel files on office staff.

3.9 Assembles and staples duplicated material.

3.10 Cross-references materials, correspondence, and files.

(Continued on next page)

Exhibit 7-2, *continued*

3.11 Sorts and routes multiple copies of forms and other documents, determining number of copies needed to meet routing requirements.

3.12 Prepares new file folders.

3.13 Sends standard letters or other literature and materials on a regular schedule or upon request.

4.0 Directs Work Activities of Clerical Staff

4.1 Schedules and prioritizes work assignments, distributing work load as required.

4.2 Schedules clerical staff vacations.

4.3 Schedules employees for training.

4.4 Monitors and reviews performance of clerical staff, recommending changes as necessary.

4.5 Guides and assists employees in work activities.

4.6 Resolves workplace problems, including complaints and difficult and complex situations.

4.7 Updates office manuals and procedures handbooks.

Mission:

Ensure smooth operation of all office administrative support services.

Chapter 8

IMPLEMENTING JOB EVALUATION FOR OLYMPIA

One of the primary reasons any organization expends the energy and costs to perform detailed job analysis and then summarizes the information in well-written job descriptions is to establish the basis for determining comparable worth among jobs. A systematic method commonly used for determining comparable worth is job evaluation. [1] Through job valuation, organizations obtain information that allows decisions regarding equality and equity. Equality with regard to pay occurs when jobs that require a comparable mix of knowledge, skills, and effort, have responsibilities with similar complexity and scope, and are performed under similar working conditions receive the same pay. Paying different amounts to jobs requiring different amounts of these factors establishes an equitable pay relationship.

Before selecting the federal government's Factor Evaluation System (FES) for evaluating jobs at Olympia, a number of criticisms had to be addressed. These included:

1. Employees have no opportunity for interaction in the design of the job evaluation method.
2. The point-factor method is extremely complex, too technical, and too statistically or quantitatively oriented.

---

[1] The "Development of Occupational Standards" section of this chapter and Occupational Standards appearing in the Appendix were written by Louis Little, Project Researcher.

3. Point-factor job evaluation methods promote an aura of authenticity through precise statistical calculations that are not justified.
4. There is reverence and sanctity for the point-factor job evaluation method because of the scoring process (the method becomes an end in itself and not the means).
5. Compensable factors are described in abstract terms.
6. Excessive time is required to train a job evaluation committee.
7. Excessive time is required to evaluate jobs.
8. Management has difficulty communicating procedures and employees have difficulty understanding the process.

By selecting a predesigned job evaluation method—FES—and agreeing to follow it as faithfully as possible, there was no opportunity for interaction in design of the method. The very strength of FES lies in the design of the factors themselves. It is not by chance that the same factors keep appearing over and over again in practically all factor-related job evaluation methods designed in the past sixty years. Empirical investigations rationally underscore the fact that the jobs differ according to such factors as knowledge, supervision received and given, interpersonal contacts, scope and complexity, physical demands, and environmental conditions.

To state that the factors, the weight of the factors, and the factor levels are not subject to verification nor validated empirically would fail to recognize the time, expert judgment, and mathematical procedures used in the development of FES. To minimize any chance of factors being selected or weighted in an arbitrary manner, hundreds of qualified specialists reviewed and ranked hundreds of jobs. They reviewed and ranked both the jobs as a whole and the nine FES factors as to their importance and value in evaluating the jobs under study. From this analysis, it was possible to develop interval scale values that represented job values relative to each other.

The statistical research for developing the interval scale values used a modified paired-comparison technique employing multiple-rank orders. The accuracy of this type of scaling procedure became apparent when job factors and subfactors were multiple-correlated with the criterion measure, which was the arc sine scale values derived from the multiple rank-order probabilities. Although those involved in the Olympia project did no additional research relative to the validation of the factors and weights of the factors in FES, an investigation of the validation procedures used by the federal government appeared to be more than sufficient to allow the Olympia investigators to accept the FES methodology at face value.

The involved selection procedure and the use of sophisticated statistical techniques open FES to both criticisms numbers 2 and 3, but the alternatives are seat-of-the-pants determinations that allow job evaluation to be even more severely and validly criticized.

The project leaders felt the remaining criticisms could be answered by involving as many Olympia employees as possible in the entire job evaluation process. Those in charge of the project also believed that meaningful participation would be a key to successful implementation of the job evaluation part of the project.

Participation in Job Evaluation

A critical decision when using any point-factor job evaluation method is to determine who will make the evaluation ratings. A number of alternatives are available. The job evaluation decision maker may be a HR specialist, a department head, a team consisting of both management and nonmanagement employees, or a team of HR specialists. These alternatives have both positive and negative aspects.

The most expedient method is to assign the task to a HR specialist skilled in job evaluation. This takes the least amount of time, has the advantage of using someone with expertise and experience, and involves the least amount of conflict. A critical weakness of this choice, however, is that it permits only a single point of view. A team of skilled HR specialists would bring a broader approach to the deliberations. This view, however, would be from a staff perspective only. A department manager would have an in-depth knowledge of the jobs in his or her operations, but, like the HR specialist, would be prone to present a very narrow viewpoint. A team composed of employees from an operating department would also tend to have a narrow perspective. Although this kind of a group would have an excellent knowledge of the jobs in their units, they might also overrate the worth of their jobs to the organization.

A team composed of both staff and line employees offers the benefits of technical expertise and in-depth job knowledge as well as the advantages of both staff and operational points of view. These different points of view, however, may provide a greater opportunity for conflict. Although the presence of conflict may be considered a negative aspect, a good team (where mutual trust, support, and genuine communication are well established) accepts it as an asset. Natural and healthy conflicts provide an impetus for growth and innovation.

Perhaps the most significant feature of an integrated and participative approach is that the employees learn about the system and are a part of the job evaluation process. Job evaluation no longer is a mysterious procedure developed behind closed doors but is open to employee participation. In this way employees "buy into" the system. While they may not always agree with the outcome, they now have an understanding of the procedure. This can play a significant role in the acceptance of the pay system within the organization. It bears out the old saying that "the person in the lifeboat with you never bores a hole in it. "

The attitudes and perceptions of people are a primary cause of the successes and failures of systems that have a direct influence on employee work and lifestyle. When a number of employees are involved in the process, these people can share their understanding and experience with their peers, thus spreading information throughout the organization about how the system really works.

Job evaluation is not a science. It is a systematic application of judgment in the measurement of both concrete and intangible facts that involves using judgment to make many decisions. In implementing job evaluation, there must be a willingness to bring the system to light as it exists, imperfections included. One must be prepared to share the decision making with employees, even though responsibility for the final project can never be delegated. In both of these areas, as well as in the process of working through conflict, there is an element of risk. While all of this can be disconcerting, there is little doubt that the benefits of a team approach far outweigh its disadvantages.

The success of participation is directly related to ensuring that certain essential conditions are met. Some of these conditions relate to the participants; others, to the environment. There are six major prerequisites for effective participation. They are:

1. There must be time to participate before action is required. (With proper planning, this condition can be met.)
2. The financial cost of participation should not exceed the value derived from it. (Training employees for participation and the time taken by evaluation meetings both involve cost. It is unlikely this cost would exceed the value resulting from employee input, understanding, and acceptance of the system. These things, however, are difficult to measure in a quantitative way.)
3. The reason for participation must be relevant to the participant's organization or something in which he or she is interested. Otherwise, the participant will look upon it merely as busywork. (Without doubt, participants will recognize the relevancy of the job evaluation process to their organization. There are few employees who would not be interested in a process that has direct impact on their pay.)

4. The participant should have the intelligence and knowledge to participate. (The project leader can select appropriate employees to meet the first aspect of this condition and can ensure that training is provided to give participants a knowledge of the entire procedure.)

5. The participants must be able to mutually communicate—to talk each other's language—in order to be able to exchange ideas. (The fact that all participants are part of the same organization, although not members of the same division or department, should give a common ground for communication. Any specialized or technical areas of job evaluation must be covered in the training process in order to facilitate an unrestrained exchange of ideas.)

6. None of the participants should feel that their positions are threatened. When workers think their status will be adversely affected, they will not participate. If managers feel that their authority is threatened they will refuse to participate or will become defensive. (It is important to be particularly aware of this area, which can present problems. A climate of mutual trust needs to be established; with the support of top management this can be facilitated with training and can be significantly influenced by the role of the team leader.)

Scheduling Job Evaluation Activities

In choosing a job evaluation strategy for Olympia, the decision was made to use a team approach in order to have the pooled judgment of several people rather than that of one individual. This same approach has been used with success in many follow-on projects. The following steps were taken:

1. Evaluation of all jobs by the project team.
2. Evaluation of department jobs by a job evaluation committee consisting of two project team members, the department director, and one member of the department selected by the department director.
3. Review of all evaluation factors by level of each factor for each job by (1) jobs in a class-series or family, (2) jobs within a department, and (3) jobs having similar responsibilities (for example, department directors).
4. Review of all evaluations by the HR director and the city manager.
5. Addition of tenth factor, supervisory accountability, to the FES.

Evaluating Jobs Using FES

This section presents the material as if the FES of job evaluation is being implemented for the first time.

Step One—Introduce FES. In this first step, the evaluator becomes familiar with the nine factors and recognizes which aspect of the job can be associated with each specific factor. At this initial step, the evaluator also learns to differentiate the factors.

Step Two—Review Job Facts. Now, the evaluator becomes as familiar as possible with job content, job specifications or requirements, expected performance level of a fully qualified incumbent, fit of the job within the assigned work unit and organization, and environmental factors that influence incumbent performance.

Step Three—Rate Factor 1—Knowledge Required by the Position. This begins the actual rating process. This is not only the first step, but possibly the most important step. In FES, knowledge receives a 41 percent weighting. (Note: The highest point score available for knowledge is 1,850 points, which is 41. 3% of the total available FES points of 4,480.) This factor has the most significant influence on the final rating of the job and also on the pay received by a jobholder. Most job evaluation plans heavily weight the knowledge, know-how, or skill factor. Some plans, like FES and the Hay Plan, provide certain patterns that restrict, or at least "red flag" other factor ratings relative to the selected rating of the knowledge factor. In this factor, even when not specified, the reviewer must make inferences from job duties regarding the level of education and the amount of prior job-related experience and training demanded of an incumbent.

Step Four—Rate Factor 2—Supervisory Controls. The rating of this factor requires the evaluator to recognize direct and indirect controls exercised by the supervisor (read introductory section to Supervisory Controls in Appendix A). The important issue is that the supervisor does not have to be directly behind the employee to maintain close controls. The kind of work and the structured nature of the work establish the degree of controls exercised by a supervisor. A supervisor may not actually observe an employee for weeks, even months, yet, in some manner, by checking finished work, the supervisor can exercise strict to loose controls.

Step Five—Rate Factor 3—Guidelines. Confusion can arise in differentiating the rating of this factor from factor 2, Supervisory Controls. Of significance here is the amount of judgment the incumbent is permitted to use in performing job assignments. Here, procedures, standing orders, policy manuals, and other reference materials establish the guidelines within which the job is performed and the amount of judgment required of the employee. The guidelines factor does not rate the knowledge required but, rather, the constraints imposed on the use of knowledge.

Step Six—Rate Factor 4—Complexity. This factor recognizes the nature, number, variety, and intricacies of the interactions required in getting the job done. Difficulty of assignments and originality in work performed are recognized and valued.

Step Seven—Rate Factor 5—Scope and Effect. The purpose, breadth, and scope of work are recognized by Factor 5. In addition, the factor recognizes the impact the job has on the work of others. A question that must be answered is: How does the assignment of this job affect the work output of others or the delivery of quality services?

Step Eight—Rate Factor 6—Personal Contacts. This factor recognizes who the incumbent must contact in performing job assignments and the degree of structure relative to these contacts.

Step Nine—Rate Factor 7—Purpose of Contacts. Now, the evaluator identifies the reasons for the contacts that were rated in Factor 6. In this factor, the complexity of the situation and the reasons for the contacts must be explained.

Step Ten—Rate Factor 8—Physical Demands. This factor recognizes the frequency and intensity of various kinds of physical demands placed on an incumbent in performing job assignments.

Step Eleven—Rate Factor 9—Work Environment. This factor recognizes unpleasantness, discomfort, and risks encountered by an incumbent on the job.

Step Twelve—Rating a Set of Benchmark Jobs. Steps Two through Eleven are repeated for a set of benchmark jobs. (Benchmark jobs cover the full range of jobs—from lowest to highest paid in different occupational settings.) The major reason for rating a set of benchmark jobs is to establish an accepted interpretation between kinds and levels of job facts and a specific factor rating. In fact, after a sufficient number of jobs has been evaluated at different levels and in different occupations, the jobs themselves become factor-level benchmarks. The extensive use of the Factor-Level Analysis Matrix—see Exhibit 8-1—stresses the importance of combining the factor-comparison process with the point-factor method presented by FES. Combining these two methodologies significantly strengthens the entire evaluation process.

What must be recognized now is that the benchmark jobs carry with them an organizational-related meaning to a specific level (degree) of a factor. It is *always* possible for anyone to argue about the assign-

Exhibit 8-1: Factor-Level Analysis Matrix

Job Description Title	Factor 1	Factor 2	Factor 3	Factor 4	Factor 5	Factor 6	Factor 7	Factor 8	Factor 9	Total Points

ment of a particular level of a factor relative to a specific job (again, the problems related to ambiguity and inference-making). However, the argument becomes much more difficult to prove when the arguer is asked to compare the job and factors in question with already-accepted ratings of benchmark jobs. The rebuttal takes this route—"John, do you believe the job of secretary in the Purchasing Department is more complex than the librarian job in the Computer Center?" Once established jobs are evaluated and their evaluations have been accepted, they then supplement the rating material provided in the primary standards, series standards, or the FES-provided benchmark jobs. This factor-comparison addition holds true and is useful for any point-factor job evaluation methodology.

Evaluating A Sample Job

A job description for a lead programmer-analyst is provided in Exhibit 8-2. A Factor Evaluation System Position Evaluation Statement for the lead programmer-analyst is shown in Exhibit 8-3. The form is completed by an evaluator, following Steps Three through Eleven of the preceding section.

Step One—Become familiar with the nine FES factors and the levels within each factor.

Step Two—Review job description of lead programmer-analyst.

Step Three—Rate Factor 1—Knowledge Required by the Position. When involved in a point-factor evaluation process, an evaluator must become skilled in the "field artillery" method of pinpointing a target. In the process of centering in on a target, those who control the sighting of the gun will often find that, after firing the projectile, it is either short or long of the target. The firing officer then goes back and forth over the target until the exact range is determined and the target is hit.

In targeting the most appropriate knowledge level for the lead programmer-analyst, an evaluator can quickly skim over levels 1 through 4, recognizing that they are inadequate and inappropriate. At level 5, the knowledge level begins to make sense. The incumbent must have knowledge of a discipline that is of a professional level, and he or she is involved in performing projects requiring the use of specialized, complicated techniques.

Moving on to level 6, an evaluator also is able to make comparisons between statements in level 6 and job requirements. The incumbent must have thorough knowledge of languages used for applications programming, be familiar with embedded computer systems programming specifications, be able to predict the influence that new applica-

---

Exhibit 8-2: Job Description of a Lead Programmer-Analyst

Identification

Job code: 007.167

Job title: Lead Programmer-Analyst

Status: Exempt

Date: April 10, 1992

Written by: Arthur Allen

Approved by: Juanita Montgomery

Title of Immediate Supervisor: Programming and Analysis Supervisor

Plant/Division: Olympia, Inc.—Main Office

Department/Section: Data Processing Information Systems

Grade: 17   **Points:** 1960   32,818-49,227

Summary

Under direction. Performs studies, develops and maintains program concerned with employee benefits, focusing specifically on life, medical and hospitalization, accident and disability, and retirement insurance for all divisions of Olympia.

Responsibilities and Duties

1.0 Serves as a lead member of the employee benefits team of programmers.
    1.1 Updates, modifies, and designs new applications in such areas as enrollment, premium costs, premium collections.
    1.2 Maintains existing programs constituting employee health and retirement benefits program for employees of Olympia.
    1.3 Develops reports on the status of existing program for which responsible.

2.0 Recommends needed redesign studies.
    2.1 Reviews proposed changes in legislation.
    2.2 Consults with user representatives on proposed changes in existing benefits programs, constraints, and potentially relevant developments.
    2.3 Discusses with other programmers and software specialists use of most suitable applica- tion programming technology.
    2.4 Identifies impact of program changes on existing computer programs.
    2.5 Advises supervisor of changes to be made in applicable software.

3.0 Carries out study projects.
    3.1 Investigates feasibility of alternate design approaches with a view to determining best so- lution within constraints set by available resources and future demands.
    3.2 Explores desirability of various possible outputs, considering both EDP and non-EDP costs, benefits, and trade-offs.
    3.3 Identifies types and designation of inputs needed, system interrelationships, processing logic involved.
    3.4 Develops programming specifications.
    3.5 Informs supervisor of progress, unusual problems, and resources required.

(Continued on next page)

Exhibit 8-2—*continued*

4.0 Designs internal program structure of files and records.
    4.1 Determines detailed sequences of actions in program logic, reviewing operations.
    4.2 Codes, tests, debugs, and documents programs.
    4.3 Writes and maintains computer operator instructions for assigned programs.
    4.4 Monitors existing programs to ensure operation as required.
    4.5 Responds to problems by diagnosing and correcting errors of logic and coding.
5.0 Coordinates efforts of other DP professionals.
    5.1 Assigns and schedules work as required.
    5.2 Reviews the work of other DP professionals.
    5.3 Interprets user requirements for other DP professionals.
    5.4 Assists other DP professionals obtain full user cooperation.

All identified duties are essential.

---

tions will have on applications already in the system, and, certainly, be familiar with user requirements.

Level 7 is also a possibility for the job, but there is a good likelihood that an incumbent would not need to know many of the concepts, principles, and practices described at this level.

After a review of level 8, the evaluator notes that there is no relationship between the job and level 8. Now, the evaluator must make adjustments between levels 5 through 7. After an in-depth review of the job and its requirements, level 6 appears to be a good match and provide a solid rating for the job.

Step Four—Rate Factor 2—Supervisory Controls. In a review of the five levels of Supervisory Controls, the "bracketing" approach focuses on levels 2, 3, and 4. In this job, the supervisor assigns a particular project and is available for consultation when difficult problems arise. Programming specifications and project directions define the goals and deadlines. The employee plans his or her own assignments and makes necessary day-to-day decisions, resolving problems in accordance with established practices. The employee provides written and oral reports at specific times and upon completion of the project. Completed work is reviewed and rated for timeliness and adequate accomplishment of specifications and compatibility with other programs. Because the employee is on his or her own, using knowledge gained through prior training, level 2 was rejected. Since the job does not require interpreting policy and establishing objectives and other high-level controls as described in level 4, it also was rejected. It appears that there is a strong match between job requirements and level 3.

Exhibit 8-3: Factor Evaluation System Position Evaluation Statement

Accountabilities

1. Completion of projects on assigned schedule.
2. Development of programs that best use resources of organization.
3. Prompt recognition of program defects or shortcomings.

Specifications

Factor	Substantiating Data	Level	Points
Knowledge Required	Knowledge of operation and capabilities of computers of Olympia. Detailed knowledge of processes and rules governing programming to carry out assignments. Knowledge of relevant employer and employee benefits program of Olympia.	6	950
Supervisory Controls	Assigned responsibility for development and operation of several programs. Consults with supervisor on target dates, unanticipated problems and conflicts that arise with other work units of Olympia. Projects reviewed in terms of effectiveness in meeting requirements.	3	275
Guidelines	Published subject-matter procedures, programming standards; modification of existing documentation frequently required. Judgment required in gathering information and developing programs that meet system and client demands.	3	275
Complexity	Wide variety of programs requiring changes to meet exceptions and new technology, changes in benefit designs; must anticipate future changes.	4	225
Scope and Effect	Formulate project recommendations; analyze technical problems; establish specifications.	3	150
Personal Contacts	Representatives of users in other work units, other programmers, and computer operations personnel.	2	25
Purpose of Contacts	Determine program and system requirements; monitor production to correct errors; answer questions; relay instructions; assist other programmers in solving their problems.	2	50
Physical Demands	Work is sedentary. Some travel to office of clients.	1	5
Work Environment	Work is performed in typical office setting.	1	5
	Total points		1960

Step Five—Rate Factor 3—Guidelines. After quickly rejecting level 1, level 2 appears to describe the guidelines and judgment used by the incumbent. Moving on, level 3 also has some applicability because this lead programmer-analyst must work where there are gaps in specificity and must use judgment in interpreting and adapting guidelines.

Level 4 discusses initiative and resourcefulness in deviating from traditional methods and in developing new methods and criteria. Level 5 does not apply. The evaluator must make a decision between levels 2 and 3. The incumbent must meet programming specifications and department standards and also must use some judgment in interpreting guidelines and in developing logic. A careful review of the job requirements and levels 2 and 3 results in a selection of level 3.

Step Six—Rate Factor 4—Complexity. Moving through the six levels of complexity, level 1 is quickly eliminated. Level 2 is also eliminated after reading such statements as "related steps, processes . . . " and "requiring the employee to recognize the existence of differences among a few easily recognizable situations. " Level 3 may be appropriate—the work does involve different and unrelated processes—i. e. , writing application programs, reviewing requirements with users, explaining software and hardware constraints to users, ensuring that new applications interface properly with existing applications, etc. Level 4 appears to be appropriate. The work does involve different and unrelated processes. It requires the interpretation of considerable data. Level 4 is a possibility. Level 5 identifies a degree of complexity beyond that found in the job.

Returning to levels 3 and 4, the evaluator selects level 4. This level was selected because each project required different programming applications and configurations. Each new application must integrate with programs currently in use. The incumbent must be able to advise users on significant aspects of application design and programming specifications. This individual must also explain user requirements to other Information Systems personnel.

Step Seven—Rate Factor 5—Scope and Effect. Once again, level 1 is quickly eliminated. Level 2 may be appropriate because the work involves the execution of specific rules and regulations and affects the reliability of other services. Level 3 also appears to be a possible match. The work treats conventional problems and affects the operation of systems, programs, etc. At level 4, concepts appear that do not relate to the job being evaluated. The work at this level does not involve the establishment of criteria or the formulation of projects. Once again, the choice is between levels 2 and 3. Because the work of the incumbent affects all employees and influences a number of different internal units and external organizations such as insurance companies and various government agencies, level 3 was selected rather than level 2.

Step Eight—Rate Factor 6—Personal Contacts. A review of the four levels of this factor quickly eliminates level 1, but level 2 looks like a good choice. The incumbent works with individuals in the Information Systems department and with personnel specialists, possibly finance and accounting personnel, and also various providers of insurance and other benefits. The settings are rather structured. Level 3 may be a possibility—the contacts are made in a moderately unstructured setting. Level 4 is not appropriate.

Level 2 was selected rather than level 3, recognizing that even when the incumbent meets with other people in a moderately unstructured setting, both parties know rather precisely why they are meeting and what facts they wish to exchange.

Step 9—Rate Factor 7—Purpose of Contacts. A review of the four levels of this factor focuses on level 2. Although many contacts of this job relate to obtaining, clarifying, or giving facts (level 1), the employee must also plan, coordinate, and advise on work efforts to resolve operating problems, making the 2 level a better choice. Level 3 was rejected because the employee is not required to work with skeptical, uncooperative individuals in a dangerous situation.

Step 10—Rate Factor 8—Physical Demands. A scan of the three levels of this factor take the evaluator back to level 1. The job is primarily sedentary in nature.

Step 11—Rate Factor 9—Work Environment. With most of the work of this job performed in an office setting, a review of the three levels of this factor also result in the selection of level 1.

After each individual committee member completes the rating as described in Steps Three through Eleven, the committee as a whole reviews the individual evaluations factor by factor and comes to an agreement on a selected factor. Here, each committee member defends his or her rating, explaining why a specific level was selected. If individual committee members cannot adequately respond to questions pertinent to the selection of a specific level of a factor, calls are made to the incumbent, the supervisor, or to other appropriate job experts to answer any questions. It may even be necessary for the committee or a selected member to revisit the job and collect the necessary job data.

This example may begin to provide some view as to the amount of time consumed in evaluating jobs. It is impossible to overstate the importance of multiple and consensus judgment in the job evaluation process. A certain amount of subjectivity may always be found in *any* form of job evaluation. The committee process—using the intellect of committed and knowledgeable individuals to seek the most accurate rating—will minimize the negative aspects of subjectivity.

Evaluation Levels

Because the city of Olympia was using FES for the first time, the jobs were evaluated three times. First, the individual responsible for analyzing the job and writing the job description completed the Position Evaluation Statement (Exhibit 8-3) and, in doing this work, evaluated the job.

Next, all seven members of the project team sat as a job evaluation committee and went through the process. It was crucial that these seven individuals be thoroughly familiar with the FES primary standards and their application to the jobs being evaluated. Even though team members had become familiar with the nine factors and their respective levels, major differences existed in the interpretations of the primary standards. By working through the evaluation process with a number of jobs, an understanding and consensus evolved among the seven members of the team. It was agreed that the standards must be strictly applied and that individual interpretation had to be limited. In developing consensus, the team rated approximately one-third of the jobs.

This training session permitted the team members to become familiar with the evaluation process. In this job evaluation session, the person who wrote the job description and first evaluated the job had to justify the level he or she assigned to it. Those who disagreed gave their reasons for other ratings. Finally, agreement was reached on an acceptable evaluation. The exercise proved to be invaluable. In this session, each member completed and signed a Position Evaluation Statement. These forms have been retained as part of the permanent job evaluation records.

The remaining two-thirds of the jobs were rated by the two individual team members assigned to the formal job evaluation team. After all jobs were evaluated and the Position Evaluation Statements were given to the HR department, a Factor-Level Analysis Matrix was completed for all jobs in each department. The project leaders then reviewed the matrixes to identify any factor levels that appeared to be out of line in relation to other jobs in the respective departments. These matrixes proved extremely valuable for quickly identifying an incorrect factor-level selection because an out-of-place factor-level selection stuck out like a sore thumb. In fact, the matrixes are extremely useful as "sore-thumb" indicators.

"Sore-thumbing" the Ratings

After all jobs have been evaluated, printouts (this phase of the evaluation process makes excellent use of readily available computer spreadsheet programs) can be developed that rank all jobs from highest- to lowest-rated point score and include the points (or levels) assigned to each factor. This analysis can be done in many ways. (Once again, computer technology can be extremely helpful. By entering a job code, job title, and evaluation score for each factor into a data base, desired combinations can be quickly reproduced and changes can easily be made with regard to any factor rating.)

High to low job evaluation spreadsheets can be developed for all jobs in the organization, or all jobs in a specific unit or location, or by such major job groupings as (1) all managers, (2) all professionals, (3) all technicians, (4) all administrative support (including clerical), (5) all exempt, and (6) all nonexempt. Reviewing ratings using these kinds of spreadsheets assists in identifying factor ratings that don't make sense—that stick out like "sore thumbs. " Exhibit 8-4 is a completed Factor-Level Analysis Matrix (spreadsheet) for jobs in the Information Systems Occupations.

Several years ago, Paul Krumsiek and Thelma Nixon analyzed 506 FES evaluated benchmark jobs within the U. S. Customs Services. From an analysis of their review, one of the authors has developed an FES Knowledge Level Convention (see Exhibit 8-5). Using the data from the report by Krumsiek and Nixon, a percentage relationship was developed between the rating level of Knowledge and the occurrence of the rating levels of all the other eight factors. Not surprisingly, there is a direct relationship between the selected level of the Knowledge factor and the selected levels of all other factors. It is highly unlikely that a job requiring a low level of knowledge (e. g. , level 1 or 2—possibly level 3) would require an incumbent to work in an unstructured setting with minimal supervision or that the job would be as complex or broad in scope or have as critical an influence on the success of the organization as a job requiring a higher level of knowledge. Conversely, a job requiring a high level of knowledge would not be simple in nature, would not require close supervision, and would have minimal impact on the performance of the organization. As discussed earlier in this chapter, the knowledge or skill requirements of a job drive the evaluation rating, while other compensable factors provide additional information to "fine tune" the final rating.

Since the percentages provided in Exhibit 8-5 come from a study of a major agency of the federal government, the percentage relationship may not relate exactly to another government or even to a private-

(Text continued on page 150)

Exhibit 8-4: Factor-Level Analysis Matrix

Job Description Title	Factor 1	Factor 2	Factor 3	Factor 4	Factor 5	Factor 6	Factor 7	Factor 8	Factor 9	Total Points
Sr. Systems Programmer	8 / 1550	5 / 650	5 / 650	5 / 325	5 / 325	3 / 60	4 / 220	1 / 5	1 / 5	3790
Sr. Programmer Analyst	7 / 1250	4 / 450	4 / 450	5 / 325	4 / 225	3 / 60	2 / 50	1 / 5	1 / 5	2820
Systems Programmer	7 / 1250	4 / 450	3 / 275	4 / 225	3 / 150	3 / 60	2 / 50	1 / 5	1 / 5	2470
Programmer Analyst	6 / 950	3 / 275	3 / 275	4 / 225	3 / 150	2 / 25	2 / 50	1 / 5	1 / 5	1960
Senior Programmer	6 / 950	3 / 275	3 / 275	3 / 150	3 / 150	2 / 25	1 / 20	1 / 5	1 / 5	1855
Programmer Analyst	6 / 950	2 / 125	3 / 275	3 / 150	2 / 75	2 / 25	1 / 20	1 / 5	1 / 5	1630
Associate Programmer	5 / 750	2 / 125	2 / 125	2 / 75	2 / 75	1 / 10	1 / 20	1 / 5	1 / 5	1190
Secretary	3 / 350	3 / 275	2 / 125	2 / 75	2 / 75	2 / 25	2 / 50	1 / 5	1 / 5	985
Sr. Computer Operator	3 / 350	2 / 125	2 / 125	3 / 150	2 / 75	2 / 25	1 / 20	2 / 20	1 / 5	895
Programmer (Trainee)	3 / 350	2 / 125	2 / 125	3 / 150	2 / 75	1 / 10	1 / 20	1 / 5	1 / 5	865
Sr. Computer Clerk	3 / 350	2 / 125	2 / 125	2 / 75	2 / 75	2 / 75	1 / 20	2 / 20	1 / 5	870
Assoc. Computer Oper.	2 / 200	2 / 125	2 / 125	2 / 75	2 / 75	2 / 25	1 / 20	2 / 20	1 / 5	670
Assoc. Computer Clerk	2 / 200	2 / 125	1 / 25	2 / 75	2 / 75	1 / 10	1 / 20	2 / 20	1 / 5	555
Data Entry Clerk	2 / 200	2 / 125	1 / 25	2 / 75	2 / 75	1 / 10	1 / 20	2 / 20	1 / 5	555
Computer Clerk	2 / 200	2 / 125	1 / 25	1 / 25	1 / 25	1 / 10	1 / 20	2 / 20	1 / 5	455

Exhibit 8-5: FES Knowledge Conventions

Knowledge Level Selected	Factor Level Selected	2 Super	3 Guide	4 Compl	5 Scpef	6 Perco	7 Purco	8 Phyde	9 Woren
					Other FES Factors				
		Percent of time factor level selected with given knowledge level							
1	1	70	100	100	100	75	100	85	75
	2	30	—	—	—	25	—	15	25
	Dominant Level	1	1	1	1	1	1	1	1
2	1	15	70	70	100	80	100	70	65
	2	85	30	30	—	20	—	30	35
	Dominant Level	2	1	1	1	1	1	1	1
3	1	7	4	—	—	11	41	41	63
	2	67	92	63	97	86	52	52	26
	3	26	4	37	3	3	7	7	11
	Dominant Level	2	2	2	2	2	2	2	1
4	1	—	—	—	—	10	25	65	65
	2	40	75	20	60	75	75	33	33
	3	60	25	80	40	15	—	2	2
	Dominant Level	3	2	3	2	2	2	1	1
5	1	—	—	—	—	15	25	67	70
	2	20	30	15	50	70	75	33	30
	3	65	70	70	50	15	—	—	—
	4	15	—	15	—	—	—	—	—
	Dominant Level(s)	3	3	3	2/3	2	2	1	1

	1	2	3	4	5	6	7	8
6								
1	—	—	—	—	—	—	100	100
2	—	—	—	50	60	100	—	—
3	50	100	50	50	40	—	—	—
4	50	—	50	—	—	—	—	—
Dominant Level(s)	3/4	3	3/4	2/3	2	2	1	1
7								
1	—	—	—	—	—	2	3	43
2	—	—	—	—	25	40	60	49
3	28	85	2	85	73	58	37	8
4	72	15	92	15	2	—	—	—
5	—	—	6	—	—	—	—	—
Dominant Level	4	3	4	3	3	3	2	2
8								
1	—	—	—	—	—	—	75	75
2	—	—	—	—	—	—	20	20
3	—	—	—	—	85	75	5	5
4	35	50	—	30	15	25	—	—
5	65	50	85	60	—	—	—	—
6	—	—	15	10	—	—	—	—
Dominant Level	5	4/5	5	5	3	3	1	1
9								
1	—	—	—	—	—	—	100	100
3	—	—	—	—	25	—	—	—
4	—	—	—	—	75	100	—	—
5	100	100	—	20	—	—	—	—
6	—	—	100	80	—	—	—	—
Dominant Level	5	5	6	6	4	4	1	1

(Text continued from page 146)

sector organization. However, the convention provides a pattern of relationships that permits a quick review of all ratings, so when a rating falls outside the range provided in the FES convention, it should be an immediate warning that either the factor should be reevaluated or, possibly, that an inappropriate knowledge level was selected. Again, because the convention comes from the work of only one federal agency, it should be used only as a guide. For example, a study in a particular organization may find a job receives a knowledge level rating of 5 and a guidelines rating of 4. The convention says this level of guidelines should not occur. After close review, however, it may be that in this organization the job under study requires the incumbent to deviate from traditional methods and use resources, initiatives, and judgment based on experience, resulting in a level higher than that normally expected to occur.

Evaluation Teams

In Olympia the formal job evaluation teams were developed differently from the normal approach. Instead of one large job evaluation committee of from seven to nine members, there were fourteen minicommittees. Each mini-committee consisted of the department director, a second member of the department selected by the department director, the team member who wrote most of the job descriptions for the department, and either the HR director or project consultant. All jobs within a department were rated with the exception of the department director position. Another team composed of the project leaders and the city manager evaluated those jobs.

The composition of these teams worked well. The departmental personnel brought an in-depth understanding of the job that could not have been gained just through a job analysis. This understanding, in addition to the project team members' expertise in the area of job evaluation and their familiarity with all of the jobs in the city, made the mini-committee more knowledgeable. It was also recognized that a balance in numbers on each "side" would be important. Although the relationship between the two groups was not adversarial, it was not unusual or unlikely that viewpoints depended on the perspective of the individual evaluator. During a number of meetings, arguments over the specific level to be assigned to a job reached an impasse. Although frustration, anger, and hostility began to appear, serious conflict was prevented because of the earlier decision that final resolution would be left to the city manager, who would act as an arbitrator.

The two department representatives on the job evaluation mini-committees did not receive the training in evaluating jobs with FES that the project team members had received. If those members had been given the same opportunity to learn how FES worked, the formal evaluation process at Olympia would have been significantly improved. All things considered, however, the fourteen departmental evaluation meetings went smoothly. Depending on the number of jobs to be rated and the ability to proceed through the process without necessary delays, these meetings lasted from two to sixteen hours.

The project team participated on an equal basis with the departmental representatives. The previous ratings, determined solely by the project members, were not revealed at these meetings but were kept as a check of the process, although in no way were they used to predetermine the final results of the formal mini-committees. The differences between the results of the project-team-member job evaluation committee and the mini-committees were negligible.

The participants were told at the beginning of the procedure that the goal was to reach a group consensus. This was usually possible, but when an impasse was reached, this was recorded along with the opposing views. Again, the Position Evaluation Statements were completed by each member of the mini-committee. The "comment" section became particularly relevant and very important when there was a major disagreement. All problems normally encountered by a job evaluation committee were also faced by the mini-committees.

One lesson learned here was that, although the mini-committees worked well, the second non-HR member should be from a department other than that of the department director. By having the line committee members represent different organizational units, a broader perspective of job requirements can be presented.

The pitfalls encountered were basically the two extremes—the department members who overrated almost every job, and those who underrated almost all jobs. Some department directors would overrate every job and then question and argue over any suggestion to lower the rating. The major impetus behind overrating was the thought that higher job evaluation ratings would lead to the eventual attainment of higher rates of pay for department members. The underrating of jobs was the result of two situations: Some department heads believed that all jobs in their units deserved very low ratings because they were not as important as their own jobs; the other was an attempt to sabotage the entire project by underrating jobs in order to cast doubts on the credibility of the system. Although this situation was not the most aggravating, it was certainly the most dangerous. The danger inherent in the underrating approach is that HR specialists and consultants representing management typically have to battle with line managers and employees who want to inflate factor ratings or overevaluate their jobs to gain higher levels of pay. It thus becomes very easy for management representatives on a job evaluation committee to accept unreasonably lower levels of factor ratings. If, by chance, this condition occurred in critical jobs—for example, jobs already low-paid and occupied by minorities or women—the subsequent and justifiable criticisms of the job ratings developed by the groups could destroy the validity and success of the entire program.

Point Rating

The next step was the development of matrixes for all jobs in each department and for jobs that were similar but in different departments (clerks, secretaries, inspectors, supervisors, maintenance workers). These matrixes provided an easy and accurate way to identify factor levels that were out of line and insured consistent application of factor-level treatment to all jobs. (Once an absolute point score is assigned to a job, the next and equally important issue is the relationship of the levels and total point score assigned to one job as compared to others.)

The final procedure in the point-rating process was a review of all jobs in the city and a reconciliation of any differences. This was done by the city manager and the HR director. The Position Evaluation Statements and matrixes proved most beneficial in facilitating any necessary adjustments. By using the matrixes, the city manager was able to review all job evaluations for comparability with different departments, different occupations, and jobs within class series. When this was completed, the final points were recorded on departmental matrixes. The same procedure was followed for the department director jobs.

Supervisory Accountability

The FES was followed faithfully at Olympia, with one major change—the addition of a tenth compensable factor, Supervisory Accountability. FES was developed by the Office of Personnel Management of the U. S. Government to evaluate nonsupervisory jobs. The city of Olympia planned to use the system to evaluate all jobs in the city, including those with supervisory responsibilities. A number of approaches for measuring this type of responsibility were considered.

Some thought was given to adding credit for supervisory responsibility within each factor. This idea was rejected because it would add subjectivity to the application of the standards. It was decided that it would be better to add a factor for the sole purpose of giving appropriate credit for supervisory accountability. After reviewing the elements of a job that are changed by the responsibility for supervising the work of others, it was decided that two basic areas were missing from the other nine factors and should be added to the system for properly evaluating those in a supervisory capacity. These two elements were (1) the number of people supervised and (2) the level of work that is done by the subordinates (identified by the FES score earned by each job). Thus Supervisory Accountability was credited in the following way: for each supervisory job, all jobs for which the supervisor was held accountable were identified and the number of incumbents in each of these jobs were noted. The FES score for each job was multiplied by the total number of incumbents in each of these jobs. The scores for all incumbent jobs were then added together to determine a total number of accumulated subordinated points for each supervisor's job. (For example, the fire chief is held accountable for all jobs in the fire department. The assistant fire chief is accountable for all jobs except those of the fire chief and any assistants who report directly to the fire chief.)

Three hundred points were assigned to the tenth factor, Supervisory Accountability, and the factor was given six levels. The relationship between the total subordinate point scores, multiplied by the number of incumbents and the factor level, was determined by natural breaks or clusters when all the FES subordinate point scores earned by each supervisor were reviewed. The accumulated subordinate rating scores and the corresponding levels of factor 10 were:

Accumulated Subordinate Point Score	Factor Level	Factor Level Points
500 – 1,995	1	50
2,000 – 4,895	2	100
4,900 – 6,995	3	150
7,000 – 12,995	4	200
13,000 – 74,995	5	250
75,000 and higher	6	300

This is the final step in evaluating the factors and cannot be completed until all nonsupervisory jobs have been evaluated. The information is retained on the Supervisory Accountability form (Exhibit 8-6), which was used to determine the appropriate factor level for each supervisor's job.

Another change in the factor levels that was contemplated but never implemented was the addition of a fourth level in both factors 8 (Physical Demands) and 9 (Work Environment) with an assignment of 100 points to the fourth level. The level would be available for jobs that require an incumbent to be exposed to (1) excessive physical demands, (2) extremely unsatisfactory environmental conditions, or (3) very hazardous conditions. This would apply to some members of the public-safety units and to employees in certain blue-collar type jobs. (Factors 1 and 4 do, to some degree, recognize these conditions by providing higher levels for knowledge and skills required to cope with emergency conditions.)

Development of Occupational Standards

When the Olympia project was implemented, there were only about six FES occupational standards written, so all evaluation was done using the Primary Standards. Approximately 70 Occupational Standards were developed, although OPM has written no new standards since the early 1980s. After appropriate Factor-Level Descriptions (occupational standards) became available, they were used for checking the evaluation developed by the job evaluation committees. Thus, when it was possible to evaluate jobs using occupational standards that used words, terms, and examples that related directly to the jobs being evaluated, the understandability and acceptability of the process by all involved were increased dramatically.

Exhibit 8-6: City of Olympia Supervisory Accountability

Department: _____ Position:_____

Position Supervised	A Number of Incumbents	B Position Points	A x B = C C Supervisory Points
	Total Supervisory Points		

Occupational standards redefine the Primary Standards in terms more specific to the occupation in which the job being studied is categorized. These standards do not change the essential meaning of the Primary Standard, but merely make the classification and evaluation process easier. A project was implemented to develop standards that would relate specifically to the occupations found in the city of Olympia.

An occupational analysis of the jobs at Olympia led to the establishment of the following eight distinct groups:

Occupation	_Number of Jobs_
Clerical	28
Engineering	1
Inspection	7
Labor and Trades	53
Public Safety	23
Recreation	4
Staff/Administrative	22
Technician	12

The single-job occupational category (Engineering) was omitted from any further effort because of a lack of a sufficient data base. Many of the jobs were substantially the same (for example, each secretarial position was listed as a different job), further limiting the available data base.

Identifying Factor Levels

Jobs in each of the remaining seven occupational categories were then arranged in matrix format, giving the level of each factor that was assigned during the classification project. Within the occupational category, jobs were placed in decreasing order, according to point totals from the nine job content factors. Factors 1 and 2, Knowledge Required by the Position and Supervisory Controls, were weighted much heavier than the other seven factors. These two factors also tended to appear in decreasing order.

Factor-level evaluations for each job were reviewed for any obvious errors that may have been made. Questions concerning possible errors were directed to the city manager, to the project leaders, and to a representative of the Office of Personnel Management (OPM). Because of the limited data base available for the writing of these occupational standards, it was critical that any evaluation error and unacceptable discrepancies and distortions of the factor-levels be identified and corrected.

The factor-levels identified in the jobs within each occupation established the initial range of levels within each factor to be included in the occupational standards. These ranges were then reviewed to ensure that they would adequately represent the occupation. After discussion with the project leaders and the city manager, factor-levels were added or deleted where necessary.

The primary reason for additions (accounting for 90 percent of the total number of changes made) was to provide factor-level ranges that would cover lower-level jobs not included in the classification study; these jobs either were part-time (for which ample job content information was available) or did not exist in Olympia at the time. The occupational standards for the Recreation series accounted for the majority (53 percent) of these additions; existing part-time positions were evaluated by the HR director and a project researcher to provide the desired data. Two additions to the upper end of initial ranges were made to allow for possible errors made in the evaluation process.

Two deletions of factor-levels from initial ranges, both at the upper end, were determined to be appropriate. In one case, the position had been incorrectly evaluated; in the other, the position included duties other than those associated with the occupation, which allowed evaluation at the higher level. In both cases, it was felt that these factor-levels were not needed to fully represent positions in the occupation and would probably not be found in a local government the size of Olympia.

Writing Factor-Level Descriptions

The project team requested reference material concerning the writing of occupational standards using FES from the Standards Development Center of the U. S. OPM. Six FES position-classification standards, either proposed or already in use by the federal government, were reviewed to develop an understanding for the kinds of occupational information that had been used in translating the concepts embodied in the Primary Standards into occupational terms. In writing the factor-level descriptions for the occupational standards at Olympia, close attention was paid to the Primary Standards, which serve as the "standard for standards. " This was especially true where factor levels were added and no substantial or supporting job-related data were available.

The first draft of the Labor and Trades series was reviewed by the project leaders, a representative of OPM, and the Olympia city manager, who made minor changes. A few other area classification specialists with knowledge of FES agreed to review and comment on the initial draft. A representative of the county Bureau of Personnel Operations raised several questions concerning some of the examples used in Factor 1, Knowledge Required by the Position, to illustrate the use of knowledge and skills. The questions basically dealt with reservations about the level at which some of the examples appeared as well as vagueness in wording of the examples. While one could debate the level evaluation of these examples, the comments were well-taken because illustrative examples included in factor-level descriptions are supposed to be definitive and unambiguous; they are not supposed to raise questions concerning the propriety of their inclusion in a particular level. However, the limited data base provided by the jobs found in the Olympia city government and the fact that the OPM does not use FES for blue-collar jobs, left little on which to proceed. (OPM is responsible for General Schedule (GS) jobs; other sections of the federal government, including the Department of Labor and the Department of Defense, have responsibility for classifying and establishing rates of pay for Federal Wage Grade—blue-collar—jobs.)

To identify a set of clear, unambiguous examples to use in factor-level descriptions for the Labor and Trades Series, it was decided to prepare a list of activities or duties performed in positions covered by that group. Accompanying this list was a copy of the Primary Standard descriptions for the four levels of Factor 1, Knowledge Required by the Position, which were thought to include the blue-collar jobs found in Olympia city government. These two components were used to survey fifteen HR specialists in the county who had a working knowledge of FES, ten of whom responded. The results of the survey indicate that there was some difficulty in reaching a group consensus on many of the examples. This was expected for two reasons:

First, there still existed a degree of vagueness in the wording of some of the examples. This could have been at least partially eliminated by adding explanatory statements to qualify the information already given. Certainly, in the formal evaluation process, the participants do not suffer from this lack of job information. But what was desired were examples of activities or duties (not complete job descriptions) that, without going into a lengthy description and detracting from the underlying concepts found in the Primary Standard, would establish a common understanding of that particular factor level. Therefore, some examples consisted of a single activity statement; others combined closely related activities.

Second, respondents understandably associated the activities in the examples with the "whole job" performed by individuals having such activities as part of their work. Whether borrowing this information from positions existing in their jurisdiction or from some other experience, this association tended to cause disagreement in evaluating the levels of the examples. At this point, it may be helpful to note that a "whole job"—the universe of responsibilities that comprise an employee's work—may consist of individual activities that relate to different levels within a specific compensable factor.

This kind of problem is one of the most serious issues facing any evaluator using a point-factor job evaluation method. When identifying a level of a compensable factor through an analysis of job activities or duties, it is quite possible that the different activities or duties will relate to more than one level of a factor. If this occurs, the problem is to determine which level of the factor best represents the whole job. One extremely helpful approach when facing this problem is to have the incumbent identify differences among activities such as importance, frequency of occurrence, time consumed, difficulty, complexity, and so forth, by rating them on a scale from 1 to 10.

This information may have already been used to identify responsibilities and duties in order to establish a hierarchical ordering among them. This information is also useful in determining which level of the factor predominates among the activities/duties of the job or best represents the job.

After analyzing various bits of information provided for developing the levels of factor 1 (Knowledge Required by the Position) for the Labor and Trades categories, a revised draft was developed. This draft was reviewed and approved by the project leaders. Similar problems were not encountered when writing occupational standards for the other eight factors, so there was no need to use the survey of county HR specialists. These occupational standards were completed without further incidence. A complete copy of the occupational standards for Olympia, including the Labor Trades, Public Safety, Technician, Inspection, Clerical, Staff/ Administrative, and Recreation Series may be found in Appendix C.

The occupational standards cover practically all of the jobs found in the city of Olympia. They will assist in the maintenance of the recently implemented classification system. Other local governments will be able to transfer much of the Olympia system for their own use.

Because smaller jurisdictions have limited personnel resources, the HR director suggested the use of borrowed personnel, or temporary transfers, from other areas within the organization. The ability of these people to learn FES was demonstrated in the Olympia project.

The main benefit of acceptance of FES by other jurisdictions is the establishment of a common system that allows meaningful interaction between jurisdictions in the area of job classification and compensation.

Joint projects are possible, and such effort would permit a synergistic reduction in the resources otherwise necessary if the projects are carried out separately. Joint projects can also provide a much larger comparable job content and job evaluation data base than that which is available to most local governments that independently perform their own classification and compensation studies.

Chapter 9
Establishing a Pay Structure for Olympia

Over the years, no part of the classification and compensation process has witnessed more change than the design of the pay structure/pay plan. A major reason is the widely diverse views regarding the design of a pay plan. These views range from following a course of action that gives little thought to the relationship between job worth and job rates of pay to designing a pay structure that attempts to integrate such conflicting requirements as internal equity, market rates of pay, and squeaking wheel demands. In the public sector, just as in the private sector, the noisiest "squeaking wheels" sometimes occur when negotiating rates of pay with representative unions. The more powerful the union, the greater its influence on rates of pay for the jobs it represents.

The major part of this chapter is a historical review of actions taken in the design of the pay plan for the city of Olympia. A primary reason for this review is that similar situations continue to exist today that influence pay structure design decisions. These influences may not always be in the best long-term interest of the organization, but they are facts of life.

The final section of the chapter discusses the development of an expanding or fan-type pay structure. Because of the authors' concerns regarding the Olympia pay plan, significant thought and effort went into the design of subsequent pay plans. In particular, classification and compensation projects for other cities permitted the Olympia project consultant to develop an expanding pay structure that minimized political influences in the final design of the pay plan and made full use of the pay plan for all employees from those assigned to the lowest pay grade to directors and top administrators assigned to the highest pay grade.

A History of Olympia's Pay Structure

The city of Olympia had a pay structure commonly found in many public sector organizations. Exhibit 9-1 shows the original existing pay structure. The pay structure began with pay grade 18 because, over the years, instead of adjusting the entire structure upward to meet changing economic pressures, grades were added to the top of the structure, while grades at the bottom were eliminated; then all jobs were upgraded by the number of pay grades that related closest to the approved percent increase in pay. When an across-the-board pay increase was approved, each step in each pay grade was adjusted upward by that across-the-board increase. After a number of years, the two part-time jobs in pay grades 18 and 19 had been eliminated, so for all practical purposes, the pay structure began with pay grade 21 and ended with pay grade 39.

Adding and Eliminating Pay Grades

Adding and eliminating pay grades as a procedure for changing the pay structure works in this manner:

1. City council decides to provide all employees with a 5 percent increase in base pay.

2. Checking the existing pay structure and multiplying a number of Step III's (or any step) in any pay grade by 5 percent provides these results:

    Grade 23 Step III $312.76 \times 1.05 = \$328.40$
    Grade 29 Step III $415.76 \times 1.05 = \$436.55$
    Grade 38 Step III $623.80 \times 1.05 = \$654.99$

3. A comparison of the results with the existing pay structure reveals:

Existing Grade Step Times 1.05	*Current Grade and Step*
23/III ⟶ \$328.40	\$327.60 ⟵ 24/III
28/III ⟶ \$436.55	\$436.22 ⟵ 30/III
38/III ⟶ \$654.99	\$655.35 ⟵ 39/III

4. A relatively simple procedure for adjusting the pay structure up by approximately 5 percent is to eliminate pay grade 21, move all jobs up one pay grade, develop a new pay grade 40, and the system now grants all employees a 5 percent pay increase.

The problem with this approach is that pay grade designation becomes meaningless and weakens the establishment of a rational, logical approach to the ordering or classification of jobs.

Movement Through the Pay Plan

Movement from Step I to Step IV in the pay structure required six years of service. An employee who performed acceptably during the year was eligible for the annual step increase. It was not possible at the time of the study to identify a single eligible person who did not receive the annual in-grade step increase since eligibility related strictly to time-in-grade. In addition, employees who had advanced to the top of the pay scale, usually beginning with their seventh year of service, were eligible to receive an additional 1 percent seniority bonus for each additional year of service until reaching a maximum allowed bonus of 10 percent.

Designing a New Structure for Olympia

Before assigning rates of pay using the FES method to establish internal equity, it was necessary to design a new pay structure that would meet current demands and also have sufficient flexibility to meet future requirements. The problems to be faced and the questions raised related to the following critical issues:
1. What would be the lowest and highest rates of pay provided city employees?
2. How many pay grades would be in the pay structure?
3. Would there be clearly defined steps in the pay grade? If so, how many, and how would they relate to each other?
4. What would be the relationship between pay grades?
5. How would the assignment of jobs to pay grades relate to internal equity (worth as determined by job-content analysis—FES point output)?
6. What influence will the "market" and other considerations, such as historical relationships and political pressures, have on the final assignment of jobs to pay grades?
7. What kinds and degrees of changes in pay relationships are acceptable to the city council (the makers and approvers of compensation policy)?

(Text continued on page 167)

Exhibit 9-1: Existing Pay Structure

Salary Schedule

1977-78 (Amended effective October 3, 1977)

Grade	Classification	Step I	Step II	Step III	Step IV	Step V	Step VI
18	School Crossing Guard (Part Time)	$ 80.85	$ 87.59	$ 94.34	$ 101.06		
19	Cook (Part Time)	214.23 5,570.00	224.92 5,848.00	236.54 6,150.00	248.12 6,451.00	$ 260.65 6,777.00	$ 274.04 7,125.00
20	None	224.92 5,848.00	236.54 6,150.00	248.12 6,451.00	260.65 6,777.00	274.04 7,125.00	287.47 7,473.00
21	Switchboard Operator	259.84 6,756.00	271.87 7,069.00	284.91 7,408.00	298.84 7,770.00	312.76 8,132.00	327.60 8,518.00
22	Accounting Clerk I, Auto Serviceman, Car Pool Attendant, Refuse Collector, Laborer	271.87 7,069.00	284.91 7,408.00	298.84 7,770.00	312.76 8,132.00	327.60 8,518.00	343.37 8,928.00
23	Accounting Clerk II, Clerk Typist, Stock Clerk, Key Punch Operator, Laborer II, Equipment Operator I, Painter I, Custodian, Meter Reader, Lineman Helper	284.91 7,408.00	298.84 7,770.00	312.76 8,132.00	327.60 8,518.00	343.37 8,928.00	360.07 9,362.00
24	Secretary, Engineer's Aide, Laborer III, Recreation Assistant	298.84 7,770.00	312.76 8,132.00	327.60 8,518.00	343.37 8,928.00	360.07 9,362.00	379.07 9,856.00
25	Laborer Foreman I, Equipment Operator II, Painter II, Tree Trimmer, Water Works Foreman I, Meter Repairman	312.76 8,132.00	327.60 8,518.00	343.37 8,928.00	360.07 9,362.00	379.07 9,856.00	396.26 10,303.00

Grade	Positions	Step 1	Step 2	Step 3	Step 4	Step 5	Step 6
26	Auto Mechanic I, Recreation Leader	327.60 / 8,518.00	343.37 / 8,928.00	360.07 / 9,362.00	379.07 / 9,856.00	396.26 / 10,303.00	415.76 / 10,810.00
27	Accounting Clerk III, Draftsman, Laborer Foreman II, Equipment Operator III, Tree Trimmer Foreman, Meter Foreman, Water Works Foreman II	343.37 / 8,928.00	360.07 / 9,362.00	379.07 / 9,856.00	396.26 / 10,303.00	415.76 / 10,810.00	436.22 / 11,342.00
28	Executive Secretary, Dispatcher	360.07 / 9,362.00	379.07 / 9,856.00	396.26 / 10,303.00	415.76 / 10,810.00	436.22 / 11,342.00	457.57 / 11,897.00
29	License Inspector, Cartographer, Auto Mechanic II, Lineman 1, Filter Plant Operator, Pump Station Superintendent, Patrolman, Firefighter, Reservoir Superintendent	379.07 / 9,856.00	396.26 / 10,303.00	415.76 / 10,810.00	436.22 / 11,342.00	457.57 / 11,897.00	479.84 / 12,476.00
30	Water Works Mechanic, Laboratory Technician, Recreation Superintendent, Garage Foreman	396.26 / 10,303.00	415.76 / 10,810.00	436.22 / 11,342.00	457.57 / 11,897.00	479.84 / 12,476.00	503.05 / 13,079.00
31	Operator in Charge, Fire Analyst, Fire Sergeant, Filter Plant Superintendent Assistant, Police Sergeant, Lineman II, Signal Engineer	415.76 / 10,810.00	436.22 / 11,342.00	457.57 / 11,897.00	479.84 / 12,476.00	503.05 / 13,079.00	527.17 / 13,706.00
32	Housing Code Inspector, Building Inspector, Electrical Inspector, Plumbing and Heating Inspector, Electrical Coordinator, Assistant Director Buildings and Grounds, Line Maintenance Foreman, Filter Plant Supervisor, Assistant Recreation Director	436.22 / 11,342.00	457.57 / 11,897.00	479.84 / 12,476.00	503.05 / 13,079.00	527.17 / 13,706.00	552.31 / 14,360.00

(Continued on next page)

Exhibit 9-1, Continued

Grade	Classification	Step I	Step II	Step III	Step IV	Step V	Step VI
33	City Clerk, Assistant Director of Inspection, Laborer Foreman III, Senior Operator, Line Maintenance Foreman, Lieutenant Fire, Lieutenant Police, Water Works Foreman	457.57 11,897.00	479.84 12,476.00	503.05 13,079.00	527.17 13,706.00	552.31 14,360.00	580.08 15,082.00
34	Fire Analyst II, Captain Fire, Captain Police	479.84 12,476.00	503.05 13,079.00	527.17 13,706.00	552.31 14,360.00	580.08 15,082.00	607.93 15,806.00
35	Purchasing Agent, Fire Training Officer	489.19 12,719.00	513.30 13,346.00	538.46 14,000.00	566.23 14,722.00	594.07 15,446.00	623.80 16,219.00
36	Assistant Fire Chief, Assistant Police Chief, Civil Engineer, Assistant Director Sanitation, City Treasurer	513.30 13,346.00	538.46 14,000.00	566.23 14,722.00	594.07 15,446.00	623.80 16,219.00	655.35 17,039.00
37	None	538.46 14,000.00	566.23 14,722.00	594.07 15,446.00	623.80 16,219.00	655.35 17,039.00	687.88 17,885.00
38	Superintendent Buildings and Grounds, Community Development Director, Director of Inspection, Director Vehicle Maintenance, Director Sanitation, Director Recreation, Director Tax, Director Business License, Director Personnel, Director Communications	566.23 14,722.00	594.07 15,446.00	623.80 16,219.00	655.35 17,039.00	687.88 17,885.00	722.15 18,776.00
39	Director Water Works, Director Electric Services, Police Chief, Fire Chief, Director Public Works	594.07 15,446.00	623.80 16,219.00	655.35 17,039.00	687.88 17,885.00	722.15 18,776.00	758.39 19,718.00

Note: With the exception of Grade 18, the first row is a biweekly rate of pay, and the second row is an annual rate of pay. Grade 18 shows only a biweekly rate of pay.

(Text continued from page 163)

Lowest and Highest Pay Rates

A first rational step in developing a pay structure is to identify what would be acceptable to the policymakers as the lowest and highest rates of pay. The approach taken for developing a lowest rate of pay included these considerations:

1. Lowest hourly rate of pay (March 1978)—$3.25 for jobs in Grade 21, Step I.
2. Minimum hourly rate of pay as established by the Fair Labor Standards Act—$2.65 (1978).
3. Bureau of Labor Statistics adjusted poverty level income for a family of four (April 1978) was $6,200, or approximately $2.98 per hour.
4. Bureau of Labor Statistics report on an austere income for a family of four was $9,222 per year, or $4.43 per hour for a family with one wage earner (April 1977).
5. A Gallup Poll survey of what Americans themselves believed was necessary for a family of four to make ends meet indicated the median estimate in the South was $10,400 per year, or approximately $5.00 per hour (February 1978).

Bureau of Labor Statistics and Gallup Poll figures were very useful in assisting Olympia compensation policymakers to identify the lowest rate of pay they wanted any employee to receive. After reviewing these figures and other labor-market information for types of jobs normally assigned the lowest pay grades, Olympia officials set $6,892 per year, or $3.31 per hour, as the lowest, rate of pay to be offered any employee. This was eventually increased to $7,069 per year, or $3.52 per hour.

The setting of the highest rate of pay was not determined through such clearly identified pieces of information, but after much review, the very top pay the council felt should be provided to any employee was in the vicinity of $25,000 per year. This amount was arrived at after an analysis of the jobs normally assigned to the highest pay grade, current rate of pay assigned those jobs, market considerations, and other council member personal considerations. For structure development purposes, $7,000 per year and $25,000 per year were set as the lower and upper limits.

Number of Pay Grades. At the start of this project, 19 pay grades existed and this number of pay grades was adequate for differentiating pay among Olympia jobs. Since the FES was being used for job evaluation, the procedure used by the federal government for converting FES job points to General Schedule grades was investigated. A review of the initial points assigned to the lowest and highest evaluated jobs would relate to GS grades 1 through 12.

Since no Olympia jobs required the levels of knowledge and skills, scope, and complexity of responsibilities of highly rated General Schedule (GS) federal jobs, it was possible to divide the points in half for each of the first 12 GS pay grades and have a 24-grade pay structure for Olympia.

Exhibit 9-2 shows (1) the federal Factor Evaluation System (FES) Grade Conversion Table and (2) the Olympia Modified Grade Conversion Table.

An underlying consideration for this pay structure was to have it follow as closely as possible the approach used by the federal government in relating FES scores to GS pay grades. By using the same approach, it was thought that future federal actions with FES would be useful and directly applicable by Olympia officials.

An alternative approach for the design of the pay structure was also developed. It could have been used if the modified federal government FES conversion table had not been used. This second approach did, in fact, provide information to check the value of the procedure selected.

Exhibit 9-2: The Federal Government General Schedule and the Olympia Pay Structure

(1)Federal government General Schedule (GS)		(2) Olympia (O) pay structure			
GS Grade	Point range	O Grade	Point range	O Grade	Point range
1	190- 250	1	190- 220	2	225- 250
2	255- 450	3	255- 350	4	355- 450
3	455- 650	5	455- 550	6	555- 650
4	655- 850	7	655- 750	8	755- 850
5	855-1100	9	855- 975	10	980-1100
6	1105-1350	11	1105-1225	12	1230-1350
7	1355-1600	13	1355-1475	14	1480-1600
8	1605-1850	15	1605-1725	16	1730-1850
9	1855-2100	17	1855-1975	18	1980-2100
10	2105-2350	19	2105-2225	20	2230-2350
11	2355-2750	21	2355-2550	22	2555-2750
12	2755-3150	23	2755-2950	24	2955-3150
13	3155-3600				
14	3605-4050				
15	4055- up				

The optional approach first arrayed all jobs by FES point score from lowest to highest evaluated rating. Scores were grouped into clusters and separated where natural breaks occurred. A lower and upper FES point limit was set for each cluster. The clusters were then matched against the twenty-four intervals set by using the FES conversion table. The major difference between the clustering approach and the FES conversion table was that more pay grades resulted from using the conversion table, allowing for a closer relationship between evaluated score and assigned rate of pay. This clustering approach became a critical concept in the design of the expanding pay structure discussed later in this chapter.

Internal Grade Design. Following the determination of the number of pay grades and the setting of an upper and lower limit of FES points for each pay grade, the next decisions regarded the internal design of a specific pay grade.

The theory underlying advancement through the six steps of the existing pay grades was that an in-grade step increase would recognize meritorious performance. The problem was that Olympia had an extremely poor performance appraisal program, and advancement through the steps related almost totally to seniority.

After a number of lengthy meetings, the city manager and the project leaders decided on a pay structure with three steps in each pay grade. The maximum in each grade closely relates to what may be a market or "going rate" for the jobs in that pay grade. The three steps are:

I. *Entry Step* (Employee is in a probationary status.)

II. *Interim Step* (Employee has demonstrated the ability to perform the job in a creditable manner and is no longer in probation. Procedures were to be developed for determining demonstrated job competency. Lacking such procedures, an arbitrary figure of one year was set for advancement from entry to interim.)

III. *Job Rate Step* (Employee performs assignments in a fully proficient manner, meeting all standards and requiring minimum amounts of direction. Procedures were to be developed for determining fully acceptable job proficiency. Lacking such guidelines, an arbitrary figure of one year was set for advancement from interim to job rate.)

The difference between entry and interim was set at 5 percent and between interim and job rate, 10 percent. This 15 percent movement between Step I and Step III would be significantly different from the approximately 26 percent difference between Steps I and VI of the prior six-step, 19-grade pay structure.

Merit Pay. Although there is no provision in the plan for merit pay, the idea underlying the three-step pay grade was that, at some future time, a merit plan could be designed that would recognize superior quality performance by granting employees a certain percentage increase beyond the established maximum.

Pay Grade Relationship

The next step in the design of the pay structure was the determination of an acceptable difference between adjacent pay grades. Recognizing the narrow band of point difference between adjacent pay grades and amount of comparability in knowledge, skills, and responsibilities in jobs assigned to adjacent pay grades, a 5 percent difference between pay grades was established, resulting in an approximate 69 percent pay overlap between jobs in adjacent pay grades. This relates closely to the comparability in knowledge, skills, and assigned responsibilities and the duties of jobs in these pay grades. For example:

$$\text{Overlap} = \frac{\$8,165 - \$7,422}{\$8,165 - \$7,069} =$$

$$= \frac{\$743}{\$1,096} = 68\%$$

$8,165 — Grade 2 — $7,422

$7,069 — Grade 1

Identifying Relevant Market Data

Although the city of Olympia had slightly less than 500 employees, they performed in more than 160 different types of jobs. In some jobs the relevant labor market included other city and county governments. In other cases, however, the relevant labor market was highly specialized, focusing on the type of work performed or the specialization related to the geographic area closely adjacent to the work site.

The HR director, in prior work activities, had very close contact with the other public-sector governments and had in her possession current pay schedules and job descriptions from four city governments and one county government. The administrative design features of the pay schedules for these governments were similar to the one existing in the city of Olympia, so for this part of the study the most important bit of pay data was the current minimum and maximum rates of pay for comparable jobs. The telephone was used to collect missing information or to check on information where matching appeared to be weak or inconclusive.

Since the city had its own electrical distribution system, information for developing comparable pay data was collected from the major electrical utility and from three public-sector governments that had their own electrical distribution systems.

Local automobile repair shops were used to collect pay data on mechanics and other jobs included in the garage (vehicle maintenance). Most of the clerical workers resided within a few miles of their work sites and, for this reason, the survey of clerical pay related to what employers paid in the local labor market. Additional pay data for clerical and secretarial jobs were obtained from other governments in the Spartan region.

The major purpose of the survey was to provide the city council with information indicating what comparable jobholders in relevant labor markets were currently receiving, so that the council members could understand and appreciate the recommendations resulting from the classification and pay study.

Establishing Dollar Value for Pay Grades

With the setting of the lowest rate of pay and the identification of pay-grade features (twenty-four pay grades, with three steps in a pay grade, a 5 percent difference between the entry and interim steps, a 10 percent difference between interim and job rate steps, and a 5 percent difference between pay grades), the remaining calculations were mathematically determined. When all final adjustments had been made, the lowest pay rate was set and the pay grade structure evolved as listed in Exhibit 9-3.

Assigning Jobs to Pay Grades

The assignment of jobs to a pay grade would appear to be a very mechanical process. This type of a rational decision would logically consider the time and effort that went into analyzing job content and describing job responsibilities, duties, and specifications; the large expenditures of funds; and the time of the many experts that went into the design and use of the job evaluation method. But even after all of these efforts, other factors may have influenced the final placement of a job in a specific pay grade. As mentioned in earlier chapters, market rates of pay, traditional pay practices, union influences (whether any group of employees are represented through a collective bargaining process), and political considerations all have an influence on the final assignment of a job to a pay grade.

Before the actual assignment process began, the city manager, the HR director, and the project consultant had a meeting in which the major topic of discussion was the relevance and importance of market pay data. At this meeting, the project consultant presented the information that follows to assist in analyzing and understanding the importance of the market and job evaluations in establishing rates of pay.

A basic employer-employee exchange process recognizes that for various employer-provided rewards, employees offer availability, capability, and various levels of performance. Employer-provided rewards are almost limitless, but one way to further understand them is to divide them into compensation rewards and noncompensation rewards. Noncompensation rewards are almost infinite in variety, but compensation rewards are much easier to identify and define, although they are far more extensive than base pay. Every organization provides a different package of rewards to its members. In addition, the unique qualities that affect the decision processes of each individual vary the worth of each reward component and the value of the entire reward package. Also, in providing compensation rewards, every organization is governed by the monetary limit of what it can afford.

Exhibit 9-3: Revised Olympia Pay Grade Structure

			Steps
Grade Number	Entry	Interim	Job Rate
1	$ 7,069	$ 7,422	$ 8,165
2	7,422	7,793	8,573
3	7,793	8,182	9,002
4	8,182	8,591	9,452
5	8,591	9,021	9,924
6	9,021	9,472	10,420
7	9,472	9,945	10,941
8	9,945	10,442	11,488
9	10,442	10,964	12,063
10	10,964	11,521	12,666
11	11,521	12,087	13,299
12	12,087	12,691	13,964
13	12,691	13,326	14,663
14	13,326	13,992	15,596
15	13,992	14,692	16,166
16	14,692	15,427	16,974
17	15,427	16,198	17,823
18	16,198	17,008	18,714
19	17,008	17,858	19,650
20	17,858	18,751	20,632
21	18,751	19,689	21,664
22	19,689	20,673	22,747
23	20,673	21,707	23,884
24	21,707	22,792	25,071

Recognizing that many variables are part of a reward system and that the quality and quantity of each reward component in some manner affect the value of the quantity and quality of all other reward components, it is both shortsighted and naive to allow the market to be the sole determinant for setting rates of pay. The reality is that most jobs have differences in job content, even though titles may be identical and—from their summaries—appear to be the same. Therefore, surveys provide a weak mechanism for determining pay rates or for establishing an internal ordering of jobs in an organization.

The rate of pay is the most visible compensation component, and it is the component most people will initially measure and relate to. The final take-home pay of an employee has its roots in the base pay established for the job. Take-home pay also determines the standard of living for most employees and their families.

However, these facts do not require an employer to meet market job rates or to pay 10 percent over the market, or even 5 percent under the market, to obtain the quantity and kind of employees necessary to perform the work required by an organization. This fact may have been less true in the past, but with increasingly sophisticated employee understanding of total compensation practices, base pay in itself is diminishing in importance for attraction or retention purposes.

As benefit components increase in cost and value and as taxable income and the sheltering of income become more widespread considerations, concern for total compensation becomes increasingly important. From a total reward perspective, good management and a high quality of work life also have decreased the importance of base pay as the critical determinant of employee behavior.

An understanding of these considerations influenced the final allocation of jobs to pay grades. An overall review of the 172 jobs and 470 incumbents identified 40 incumbents in 29 jobs whose proposed pay was higher than that identified by market information. Of these, 16 jobs and 22 incumbents were in the clerical-secretarial job family; 8 jobs and 12 incumbents in the public safety area; and 5 jobs and 6 incumbents in labor-trades and craft-worker occupations. Except for 4 public safety jobs that were lowered two pay grades, all other jobs were lowered by one pay grade. Even with this reduction, most clerical and secretarial jobholders were scheduled to receive annual pay increases in excess of $1,000.

There were also 84 incumbents in 12 jobs that had their FES assigned grades advanced because of market, traditional, and political considerations. The major job to be upgraded was that of firefighter (51 incumbents). The survey indicated that the assigned pay grade was slightly under market, and it was felt that Olympia had certain traditional parity relationships between police and fire personnel that should be maintained at the entry level. The upgrading also recognized that firefighters work fifty-six hours a week, while police officers work forty hours a week. (It was also recognized that firefighters were on a monthly schedule, working a 24-hour shift slightly more than two days per week.) The remaining 11 jobs and 33 incumbents were distributed within the public safety, communications, and labor, trades, and craft groups.

Placing Department Director Jobs

A major problem requiring review was the assignment of department directors to their respective pay grades. The job evaluation plan produced some major changes in the pay relationship among department director jobs. After a series of discussions between the mayor, the city council, and the city manager, it was decided to design a separate pay structure for all department directors.

A strategy developed by the city manager, the HR director, and the project consultant was to request each council member to rank the department director jobs and compare them with their FES ratings. The final results of the evaluation of department director jobs and the setting of pay for these jobs follow (Exhibit 9-4):

Exhibit 9-4: Final Pay Grades for Department Director Job

Department	Council Ranking	Team Ranking FES Scoring	Final Pay Grade Assigned
Police	1	1	A
Fire	2	2	A
Administrative Services	3	3	B
Water	4	9	C
Public Works	5	4	B
Communication	6	10	C
Electrical	7	8	C
Sanitation	8	13	C
Buildings and Grounds	9	12	C
Garage	10	14	C
Personnel	11	7	D
Recreation	12	11	C
Inspection	13	5	C
Community Development	14	6	C

Although the department director rankings assigned by the council members were significantly different from those obtained through FES ratings, many of the differences were minimized when the council members assigned the jobs to pay grades. The rating differences were never resolved to the satisfaction of everyone, but use of the paired-comparison method provided a means for arriving at a consensus.

The first step in designing a pay structure for department directors was the establishment of a minimum and maximum rate of pay. The council members set $16,800 as the lowest amount to be paid any department director and $21,392 as the maximum. They first decided that the fourteen department directors could fit into five natural pay groupings or grades, but in a subsequent meeting this was changed to four grades.

The final department director pay structure took this form (Exhibit 9-5):

Exhibit 9-5: Final Department Director Pay Structure

Grade	Entry	Interim	Job Rate
D	$16,800	$17,556	$18,480
C	17,640	18,433	19,404
B	18,522	19,355	20,374
A	19,448	20,322	21,392

The department director pay structure has a 4.5 percent increase between the entry and interim steps and a 5.3 percent increase between the interim and job rate steps. There is a 5 percent difference between similar steps in adjacent pay grades. Each step overlaps the next step by 50 percent.

With the removal of the department director jobs from the basic pay structure, it was only necessary to use pay grades 1-19. Grades 17, 18, and 19 overlapped all grades in the department director pay structure to some degree.

The Expanding or Fan-type Pay Structure

In classification and compensation projects that followed Olympia and were directly related to the Olympia effort, the project consultant had the opportunity to make some significant changes in the design of the pay structure. In later projects, the project consultant and highly supportive HR professionals in other local governments developed some innovative strategies that resulted in an expanding pay structure. This kind of pay structure has witnessed a wide variety of configurations and has permitted the involved organizations to develop pay plans that meet organizational compensation policy and recognized marketplace pay relationships. The critical design features that permit flexibility in design are (1) changes in midpoint-to-midpoint differences and (2) changes in ranges for pay grades.

Early expanding pay structure designs had pay sectors that had midpoint-to-midpoint differences that started at 5 percent (similar to that used at Olympia) and increased by one-half percent for each adjoining sector. Later plans started at 6 percent with a 2 percent increase for each additional sector. In early pay plans, the pay grades in Sector I were assigned a range of 20 percent and an increase in range of 5 percent for pay grades in each adjoining sector. Later plan designs seldom had a starting range of less than 30 percent, and some plans had a 10 percent increase in pay ranges for each adjoining sector, although a 5 percent increase is by far the most common design feature. Some plans had a uniform range. When this occurred, the range was 50 percent for all pay grades. The need to match or meet market rates of pay is the primary reason for changes in midpoint to midpoint and pay range features.

Another major design considered was the widespread use of a 9-step pay grade design. By dividing a pay grade into 9 steps, it is then possible to separate an incumbent's rate of pay into an apprentice set, journeyman set, and masters set. Steps 1, 2, and 3 reflect an employee relatively new to the job who is still acquiring all of the knowledge and skills required to perform in a fully proficient manner. Steps 4, 5, and 6 are journeymen steps that recognize the employee's capability of performing the job in a proficient manner. In addition, Step 5, the midpoint of the pay grade, reflects either (1) the market rate of pay for the job or (2) the organization's policy-established rate of pay for the job. Steps 7, 8, and 9 are the master level rates of pay for the job. Employees being paid these rates of pay should be recognized as individuals capable of performing job assignments at the mastery level.

The expanding pay structure presented here can include jobs from those requiring minimal levels of knowledge and skills to those requiring extensive knowledge and skills for successfully accomplishing the most difficult and complex assignments of the organization.

Expanding Pay Structure Architecture

Five critical data points control the design of an expanding pay structure:

1. Lowest rate of pay the organization wishes to pay any employee. This, in turn, will be the minimum or lowest rate of pay for Pay Grade 1 or the first pay grade in the pay structure.

2. Percentage range of pay for each pay grade or group of pay grades.
3. Midpoint-to-midpoint differences between pay grades.
4. Points (if using a point-factor job evaluation method) that establish the horizontal width of each pay grade.
5. If desired, dividing each pay grade into a series of steps.

Pay Sectors. An essential part of an expanding pay structure is the role of pay sectors. Pay sectors are groups of pay grades having identical or very similar pay structure characteristics, for example, identical percentage ranges and midpoint-to-midpoint differences and identical or very similar point-range widths. Each pay sector in an expanding pay structure is in reality a different pay structure. A pay sector relates closely to a "band" where different jobs are grouped together, a process called *broadbanding*. In the example provided in Exhibit 9-6, the seven linear pay structures developed through the seven pay sectors simulate a curved line. This simulation demonstrates that as job worth increases linearly, rates of pay for these jobs of increasing worth increase geometrically.

Jobs within pay grades of an assigned pay sector have similar knowledge and skill requirements and similar levels of responsibilities. These jobs may also have differences in the level of required knowledge and skills, in the scope and complexity of responsibilities, and in working conditions. The organization may wish to recognize these differences through assignment to different pay grades.

Midpoint-to-Midpoint Differences. The most critical pay data in an expanding pay structure is the midpoint of each pay grade. If an organization has established within its compensation policy the desire to meet the market, the midpoint of each pay grade should compare favorably (± 5 percent) with market survey midpoints of benchmark jobs assigned to each pay grade or OF benchmark jobs in a select sample of pay grades in each pay sector.

If an organization wishes to pay above or below the market, it first must recognize market rates of pay, then perform the necessary calculations to establish midpoint rates of pay that match compensation policy requirements. Note that initial steps in designing an expanding pay structure are quite mechanical; however, once a first draft pay structure is designed, it must then meet market-related pay criteria to establish the validity of the plan.

Pay Grade Widths. Since most point-factor job evaluations plans have a linear design relationship to levels or degrees of a factor, the width of a pay grade will depend on the job evaluation method. However, in mov-

Exhibit 9-6: Expanding Pay Structure Design Characteristics for Organization Using FES.

Pay Sector	Pay Grades	FES Point Range Per Pay Grade	Percent Spread of the Range	Midpoint to Midpoint Difference
I	1-4	50, 55	30	6.0
II	5-9	100,110	35	6.5
III	10-13	125	40	7.0
IV	14-17	145	45	7.5
V	18-21	185	50	8.0
VI	22-25	220	55	8.5
VII	26-27	355,360	60	9.0

ENTER PAY GRADE 1, STEP #5 12558

Pay Sectors	FES Point Width Min	Max	Range Spread%	Mid Point%	Pay Grade	Step #1	Step #2	Step #3	Step #4	Step #5	Step #6	Step #7	Step #8	Step #9
I	190	240	30	6.0	1	10920	11330	11739	12149	12558	12968	13377	13787	14196
I	245	300	30	6.0	2	11575	12009	12443	12877	13311	13746	14180	14614	15048
I	350	360	30	6.0	3	12270	12730	13190	13650	14110	14570	15030	15491	15951
I	365	420	30	6.0	4	13006	13494	13981	14469	14957	15444	15932	16420	16908
II	425	525	35	6.5	5	13557	14150	14743	15336	15929	16522	17115	17708	18300
II	530	630	35	6.5	6	14438	15069	15701	16333	16964	17596	18228	18859	19490
II	635	745	35	6.5	7	15376	16049	16722	17394	18067	18740	19412	20085	20758
II	850	860	35	6.5	8	16376	17092	17809	18525	19241	19958	20674	21391	22107
II	865	975	35	6.5	9	17440	18203	18966	19729	20492	21255	22018	22781	23544

III	980	1105	40	7.0	10	18272	19186	20099	21013	21927	22840	23754	24667	25580
III	1110	1235	40	7.0	11	19551	20529	21506	22484	23461	24439	25417	26394	27372
III	1240	1365	40	7.0	12	20920	21966	23012	24058	25104	26150	27196	28242	29280
III	1370	1495	40	7.0	13	22384	23503	24623	25742	26861	27980	29099	30219	31338
IV	1500	1645	45	7.5	14	23572	24898	26224	27550	28876	30201	31527	32853	34179
IV	1650	1795	45	7.5	15	25340	26765	28190	29616	31041	32467	33892	35317	36743
IV	1800	1945	45	7.5	16	27240	28772	30305	31837	33369	34902	36434	37966	39498
IV	1950	2095	45	7.5	17	29283	30930	32578	34225	35872	37519	39166	40814	42461
V	2100	2285	50	8.0	18	30993	32930	34868	36805	38742	40679	42616	44553	46490
V	2290	2475	50	8.0	19	33473	35565	37657	39749	41841	43933	46025	48117	50209
V	2480	2665	50	8.0	20	36151	38410	40670	42929	45188	47448	49707	51967	54226
V	2670	2855	50	8.0	21	39043	41483	43923	46363	48803	51244	53684	56124	58564
VI	2860	3080	55	8.5	22	41531	44386	47241	50096	52952	55807	58662	61517	64373
VI	3085	3305	55	8.5	23	45061	48159	51257	54355	57453	60551	63648	66746	69844
VI	3310	3530	55	8.5	24	48891	52252	56614	58975	62336	65697	69059	72420	75781
VI	3535	3755	55	8.5	25	53047	56694	60341	63988	67635	71282	74929	78576	82222
VII	3760	4115	60	9.0	26	56709	60962	65215	69469	73722	77975	82228	86481	90734
VII	4120	4480	60	9.0	27	61813	66449	71085	75721	80357	84993	89629	94265	98901

ing from pay grades in one sector to pay grades in the adjacent sector, the point length of the pay grade will normally increase. The height of the pay grade depends on whether an organization prefers different rates of pay for jobs with barely perceptible differences or for those with significantly perceptible differences. An increasing width of the pay grade permits the assignment of jobs with increasing linear differences in point scores to the same pay grades. Here again, the pay structure designers are recognizing that job value changes are a geometric perception, not a linear one. The clustering process discussed earlier in the section titled "Number of Pay Grades" was used in establishing a first-cut for point breaks in what resulted in a 27-grade pay plan. Fine-tuning was then performed to establish uniform or very similar point widths for pay grades with a common pay sector.

Single vs. Multiple Pay Schedules

Possibly the most powerful advantage of integrating FES with the expanding pay structure design concept is that it permits an organization to place almost all personnel (those being paid from minimum wage to approximately $150,000 per year) on a single pay schedule. (This applies equally to any valid point-factor job evaluation plan that relates to jobs of different values, i.e., janitor to top administrator.)

Through the use of increasing midpoint-to-midpoint differences and ranges between pay grade sectors, an organization can recognize market differences among jobs where variations in knowledge, skills, and responsibilities differ significantly, and pay differences among these jobs increase geometrically and not linearly. The expanding pay structure provides a more open, democratic process for administering pay. Organizations that use multiple pay schedules may actually be guilty of acquiescing to political influences of very powerful groups such as unions or associations and through the use of separate pay schedules may compensate jobs represented by these groups with wages that are much higher than an internally equitable pay system would recognize or provide.

Architectural Design Hints

PG 1 Minimum Rate of Pay. As previously discussed, use state or federal minimum wage mandates, poverty level income data, or a rate of pay that meets compensation policy requirements of the organization. In 1992, critical pieces of data for design consideration were the Fair Labor Standards Act, which set the minimum wage at $4.25 per hour, and the federal government-established poverty level income for a family of four of $13,354, or the equivalent of $6.42 per hour.

Midpoint of PG 1. Using the policy-established minimum rate of pay for PG 1 and the range for the pay grade, it is possible to establish the midpoint for the pay grade. All following midpoints in the expanding pay structure are built upon this midpoint.

Midpoints for All Remaining Pay Grades. All remaining midpoint calculations depend on the established midpoint-to-midpoint differences. In many cases, midpoint-to-midpoint differences can vary from 5 to 15 percent. However, in most cases, differences of from 6 to 10 percent will satisfy the needs of most designers. Usually, a 0.5 percent step-up from one sector to the next provides sufficient difference in rates of pay for jobs in each pay grade to meet market or organization-related demands. In organizations that have large numbers of employees performing jobs requiring significantly different knowledge and skills, a 1 or 2 percent midpoint-to-midpoint difference produces needed rates of pay for each pay grade. A possible example of an organization that may require 1 to 2 percent increases in midpoint-to-midpoint differences between adjacent pay sectors could be a hospital, or possibly a hospital specializing in research or performing state-of-the art surgical procedures. These institutions hire relatively low-skilled janitorial, laundry, and food service workers, moderately skilled nursing aides and LPNs, skilled technicians and nurses, and highly-skilled nursing specialists, researchers, and doctors. To include all of these kinds of jobs within one pay structure requires that an organization pay some employees close to government-required minimum wages and other employees in excess of $100,000 per year. The increase in pay between sectors can be significant, requiring more than a 0.5 to 1.0 percent increase from midpoint to midpoint.

Pay Grade Range. For jobs requiring unskilled and semiskilled workers, a range of 30 percent will usually be adequate. (A range less than 30 percent will often fail to provide rates of pay high enough for senior employees who have 10 or more years of service in these lower-level jobs.) Where jobs require relatively higher rates of pay—rates of pay in excess of $50,000 per year, it will be necessary to have ranges of 50 percent and greater when the upper limits of the pay grades exceed $75,000 per year.

Steps Within A Pay Grade. An option available to pay grade designers is to establish steps within a pay grade. Two primary approaches are available for determining a rate of pay for each step in a pay grade. Depending on the number of steps (n) desired, the difference between the maximum and minimum can be divided by $n - 1$ and this amount added successively to each previous step until reaching the maximum. For example, PG 1 minimum is $10,920 and PG 1 maximum is $14,196. $14,196 – $10,920 = $3,276 ÷ 8 = $409.50.

Step 1	*Step 2*	*Step 3*
10,920	11,329.50	11,739

Step 4	*Step 5*	*Step 6*
12,148.50	12,558	12,967.50

Step 7	*Step 8*	*Step 9*
13,777	13,786.50	14,196

If a constant percentage increase is desired, divide the range percent by the number of desired steps. Using the previous example of a range of 30 percent divided by 9 steps which equals 3.333%, start by multiplying 10,920 by 1.03333 (1 for the initial value and .03333 for the increase).

PG 1	*PG 2*	*PG 3*
10,920	11,284	11,660

PG 4	*PG 5*	*PG 6*
13,049	12,450	12,865

PG 7	*PG 8*	*PG 9*
13,294	13,737	14,195

Pay Sectors and Levels of Education, Experience, and Training

When developing pay sectors, an education/experience criterion may be most valuable for grouping pay grades within one sector. After evaluating all jobs, it is useful to review the education, experience, and training requirements for jobs within each pay grade. A first hint for grouping pay grades within a sector may follow this route:

Pay Sector	Education, Experience, Training
I	Less than high school education; no prior experience to a maximum of 2 years in related kinds of work; little or no formal training.
II	High school diploma, some prior experience in related work—minimum of one year; some formal training in technology related to job requirements.
III	Completion of associate degree program or at least 3 years experience in related field of work; formal training in field or possession of appropriate registrations, certificates, or licenses.

IV   Completion of baccalaureate program or extensive experience (5 to 10 years) in related fields of work. Must hold or be capable of acquiring required certificates or licenses.

V   Completion of masters program or extensive experience (10 or more years) in jobs within related fields of work. Must hold required certificates or licenses.

VI   Knowledge gained through formal education and work experience that exceeds levels acquired through a masters program. Must hold required certificates or licenses.

VII   Knowledge gained through formal education and job experience that establishes jobholders as masters of a professional field of work.

Spreadsheet Software

In many cases, the initial selection of midpoint-to-midpoint differences and pay ranges does not meet compensation policy demands and labor market-identified rates of pay. To meet these demands, designers of expanding pay structures will have to adjust their ranges (set for each pay sector) and the midpoint-to-midpoint differences for each sector. As previously discussed, designers have a wide latitude of options in varying these two areas of pay structure architecture. The expanding pay structure concept provides an ideal application for basic spreadsheet software.

The expanding pay structure developed in the exhibit uses 21 rows and 13 columns. The actual number of rows and columns required to design a pay structure depends on the number of pay grades to be included within the structure (rows) and the steps within each pay grade (columns).

After establishing the range-spread percentage and the midpoint-to-midpoint percentage in columns 2 and 3, enter the midpoint rate of pay for paygrade one (see line 5 "ENTER PAY GRADE 1, step 5). When the designer wishes to modify the proposed pay structure, all that must be done is to revise the range column (Col. 2) and midpoint-to-midpoint differences (Col. 3) or possibly reset the minimum pay for PG 1. With each revision, the program will recalculate a revised pay structure. Within a very short period of time and with minimal effort, the designer can perform several "what-ifs" by changing the different variables of the pay structure. These revised pay structures can then be compared with pay data from market surveys and subsequently used to facilitate calculation of payroll costs. One-half percent midpoint-to-midpoint difference and 5 percent variation in range can provide significant pay grade differences. Spreadsheet software simplifies the administrative support work required to produce expanding pay structures. It is possible that no configuration will satisfy organization requirements.

A Review of the Process

Pay-structure design is neither a highly scientific procedure nor a mystical one. A number of personal considerations and various external forces influence the design. Currently, and for the near future, the actual and final rates of pay for jobs will be based on rational considerations using an amalgam of information that includes:

- An internally equitable ordering of jobs
- Market rates of pay for comparable jobs
- Ability of an organization to pay
- Traditional relationships among jobs in the organization
- Political considerations and personal influences of jobholders

The Olympia project had many barriers to overcome. Possibly the most difficult barrier was a highly charged political environment where the elected officials had a significant voice in the pay determination process for all employees. Some of the elected officials had grave concerns that the classification and compensation project would reduce their influence over the operation of the city government. The HR director, a woman, was the first professional director of HR for the city.

A major reason for the success gained through the Olympia project was the extent of employee participation in all phases of the process. Participation by the work force took two distinct paths at Olympia. Some senior employees with strong political ties attempted to use their influence to scrap the entire process. The major impetus for scrapping the plan was to maintain (1) status quo on existing pay plan designs and (2) influence on future pay adjustments. Other senior employees and large numbers of employees in the work force who desired some type of a systematic, documented system that minimized favoritism and the influence of certain interest groups lobbied for acceptance of the plan. Here again, the more knowledge the employees have, the greater the likelihood they will lobby for a plan that maximizes a fair and just treatment for all members.

The final allocation of jobs to pay is possibly as sensitive as any issue facing management. A major union official once stated, "the most sensitive artery in the human body is the one that goes from the pocketbook to the heart." This certainly was a fact of life in Olympia.

Recognizing the need for an orderly, just, and explainable process for determining rates of pay was a primary reason for final acceptance of the pay plan. However, it is important to recognize that neither job evaluation nor market survey data were the ultimate, only, or final determinants of pay rates.

Some of the concepts developed at Olympia proved to be unworkable—for example, the 3-step pay grade concept—but Olympia was an outstanding learning process, and everyone involved, including the employees and citizens of Olympia benefited from the project.

PART III

SOLVING HUMAN PROBLEMS

Before a pay system can be fully implemented, two major barriers must be overcome: (1) acceptance by top management and (2) acceptance by employees of the organization. It is obvious that the plan must have top management's approval before it can be completely implemented. A more recent phenomenon is the need for employee acceptance. Gone are the days when organizations could ignore employee feedback. The link between employee involvement and the quality of work and service delivered has been clearly established. Employee participation is widely recognized as good, sound business. The concluding chapters outline the benefits of involving everyone in the organization, from top to bottom, in the process of developing and implementing a pay system.

Chapter 10

SELLING THE PLAN TO
TOP MANAGEMENT

The bottom line of any job evaluation and pay plan is its acceptance by the top management of the organization. Without the approval of this group even the best of plans is worthless and all effort is a waste of time. In local government, top management consists of elected officials who are responsible for policies related to employee compensation.

The following steps (I-VI) which occurred in the Olympia project spanned an eight-month time period. These steps, from introduction to adoption, provide lessons in both the process and the pitfalls involved in gaining acceptance by top management.

I. Initial presentation to the mayor and council to explain the basic design of the project and the selection of FES for job evaluation.

II. Detailed presentation to the mayor and council of the classification process. This included a detailed explanation of FES, review of the job analysis questionnaire, description of the audit process and the involvement of department directors and employees. The primary purpose of this step was to build a foundation of confidence in the system, through an understanding of the design and purpose of FES and the involvement of employees throughout the process.

III. Presentation of the final proposal to the mayor and council.

The city manager reviewed past plans used by the city, the current plan and problems with it, and the council's request for a new system. The benefits provided by FES were summarized:

- Enables employees and department directors to be involved in the process.
- Is less subjective than any system previously used in Olympia.
- Documentation allows for improved legal defense, if challenged.
- Possible to administer and maintain in-house.
- Understandable to most employees.
- Is research based.
- Establishes a fair, logical, equitable basis for assigning jobs to pay grades.

The city manager outlined the three issues on which agreement was needed from the mayor and council. The first, acceptance of an FES-based job evaluation plan, was agreed upon after much discussion.

The second issue was the design of a pay schedule using a three-step pay plan. It was pointed out to the elected officials that this plan would enable the city to compete more effectively with other employers in the area by paying higher entry-level salaries. Also employees would reach top pay sooner because of a significant (10 percent) increase over the interim rate of pay. The other advantage was that a pay-for-performance system could be added easily to this plan, with the job rate becoming the midpoint of the pay range. There were several meetings and discussions before this was accepted.

The third issue was the assignment of jobs to specific pay grades. The mayor and council were provided with the following items for study prior to making this decision:

1. Proposed pay schedule with jobs assigned to each pay grade.
2. Employee list for each department giving name, current job title, current pay grade and step, current base pay, proposed title, proposed grade and step, proposed base pay, dollar difference, percentage difference.
3. Comparable pay data from other jurisdictions and businesses in the area.
4. Breakdown, by department, with number of jobs receiving increases at initial implementation, as follows: $100-$500, $501-$1,000, $1,001-$1,500, $1,501-$2,000, $2,001-$2,500, $2,501-$3,000, $3,001-$3,500.
5. List of all employees receiving no increase, and comparable salary data for the jobs held by these employees.

6. List of all employees who would receive no initial increase, but who would receive an increase during the fiscal year when they moved from an entry to an interim step or from interim to a job-rate step in the pay grade.

Not surprisingly, the item that generated the most interest was (2), which contained information regarding individual pay rates. From this issue there were several problems to be resolved:

- *Amount of individual increases.* Some of the council members expressed concern that individual employees would receive as much as $3,000 or more in an annual increase. They wondered (a) whether or not the employee was "worth" this much money and (b) what the public would think when they learned the size of some individual increases. They decided to place a limit of $1,200 on the amount of increase to be granted to any one individual during the fiscal year. The guidelines for administering this limit were included in the Guidelines for Administration of Pay Plan (Exhibit 10-1).

- *Classification of department directors.* Traditionally, Olympia department directors have been very politically oriented. For many years, the pay for all department directors, regardless of responsibilities, was the same. In the last few years, the department directors had been assigned to one of two pay grades. Thus, the job-evaluation plan produced some major changes in the pay relationship among these department directors. The council seemed primarily concerned with personalities, rather than with job responsibilities. They felt that because emotions ran very high and could jeopardize the entire plan it would be appropriate to deviate from the Factor Evaluation System and pull the department director positions out entirely.

To expedite decision making by the council on the appropriate pay ranges for department directors, the HR director used the paired-comparison method to arrive at a consensus. She gave each council member a set of fourteen 3" x 5" index cards with each department designation written on a separate card. She then asked the council members to review the deck and hand her the card with the job title of the department director job that they felt to be the most important or most valuable to the city of Olympia. The members made this decision individually with no discussion of the responsibilities or competence of the individuals in question. After collecting a card from each person, she clipped them together and marked that group with a number 1. She then asked each person to give

her a card with the job title of the job they considered to be the least important among the remaining thirteen departments. These cards were clipped
and marked number 14. This process continued with the selection of cards
numbers 2 and 13, again identifying the most and least important of the
remaining jobs, and so on, until all jobs had been ranked by the council.

The HR director then went to a flip chart that listed the fourteen
departments in vertical rows, with a column for the ratings of the council members. She filled in the column with the appropriate scores and
then tallied them. The results compared with the ranking provided by
FES are shown in Exhibit 10-2.

At the end of this process, there was much disagreement among
the council members as to the appropriateness of the results. Approximately two weeks after this meeting, the council decided that the FES
ranking of the department directors was more appropriate than their own
and asked that FES be used instead.

Exhibit 10-1: Guidelines for Administration of Pay Plan

---

1. Employees outside of pay range will continue at present rate of pay.

2. Employees will be placed at the Entry, Interim, or Job-rate levels according to the
    following:

    a.   Those with 0-1 year completed in the job will be placed at the
    Entry level.

    b.   Those with 1-2 years completed in the job will be placed at the
    Interim level.

    c.   Those with more than 2 years completed in the job will be placed
    at the Job-rate level.

    Provided: That no person will receive a rate of pay that is less than a person that
    is under his or her supervision.

3. Any person hired, or promoted, after the July 1 implementation date will be paid
    at the Entry rate of the job, unless it would mean that he or she would make more
    than a person already employed who is at the Entry level but paid below the
    Entry rate (due to 4, below), in which case the newly hired or promoted person
    would be paid the same rate as the employee(s) already on the job, at the Entry
    level.

4. No employee shall receive more than $1,200.00 in base salary increases during
    the fiscal year beginning July 1. This applies to the initial implementation of the
    classification and pay plan and to any increase from the Entry to the Interim level,
    or from the Interim to the Job- rate level due to length of time in job. It does not
    apply to promotions. However, rule 3, above, would be the overriding consider-
    ation in the case of promotions, when applicable.

5. Beginning July 1 (of the year following implementation), all employees affected
    by the $1,200.00 ceiling in rule 4 will receive the actual rate of pay at the correct
    level according to their time completed in job. This may be adjusted according to
    revenue availability and the adopted pay schedule. Any salary schedule
    adjustments made by the mayor and council for that fiscal year would apply to
    these persons as well as to all other city employees.

- *Maximum pay in highest pay grade.* The council thought the salary of $23,884 was too high for the city to pay a department director. They set $21,392 as the maximum amount to be paid any department director and $16,800 as the lowest amount.
- *Implementation cost.* After a review of the total budget and in consideration of the $1,200 ceiling placed on the amount of increase to be granted to any one employee, the council decided that the city could implement the plan.
- *Pay to be received by specific employees.* Some of the council members felt that certain individual employees did not deserve the pay as proposed. This subject was discussed, and it was pointed out that the city had no valid and reliable way at that time to appraise employee performance. It was further pointed out that the recommended pay was not based on individual performance but on the responsibilities and duties of the job. The discussion emphasized that the Factor Evaluation System considers only the job, not the person who occupies it.
- *Forty-one employees receiving no increase.* The council discussed each of the forty-one employees in some detail. They outlined job responsibilities and pay for similar jobs in other jurisdictions. In some cases they reviewed the factors for the job in question. Prior to this review, a number of the council members felt that everyone should receive some pay increase. Upon completion of this discussion, however, only five jobs had their pay adjusted upward. The council decided that no employee would receive a cut in pay; rather, those outside of the pay range

Exhibit 10-2. Council Members and FES Rankings of Department Director Jobs

Department	Council Ranking	FES Ranking
Police	1	1
Fire	2	2
Administrative Services	3	3
Water	4	9
Public Works	5	4
Communications	6	10
Electrical	7	8
Sanitation	8	13
Buildings and Grounds	9	12
Garage	10	14
Personnel	11	7
Recreation	12	11
Inspection	13	5
Community Development	14	6

would be "red circled" and would continue to receive their present rate of pay until the pay scale caught up with their red-circled rates of pay.

IV. The council approves the classification and pay plan.

V. Mayor vetoes the classification and pay plan. In the two weeks between the veto and the next scheduled council meeting there were several favorable newspaper articles about the proposed plan. In addition, a memo was circulated by concerned citizens, and city employees (who remained anonymous) regarding their support of the plan. At the meeting in which the vetoed ordinance came before the council for reconsideration, the chamber was filled with employees and citizens who spoke in favor of passing the proposed plan. It should be noted that an upcoming council election, which involved four of the eight councilmembers, played an important role in this issue.

VI. Council modifies plan and adopts it, overriding the mayor's veto. Following the remarks and discussion from the audience, the mayor and council went into a closed executive session to reconsider the classification and pay plan. During the closed session, they advanced the following jobs one pay grade: the director of communications, the director of sanitation, the director of buildings and grounds, and the garage director. After these changes, the council voted to override the mayor's veto and adopt the plan. The final pay grade assignments for department director jobs are shown in Exhibit 10-3.

The most important tool in selling the proposal to top management is to provide enough information so that the system is understood. In Olympia every question or objection raised was answered as thoroughly and completely as possible. The Factor Evaluation System facilitated this because of the data it generated and the relative ease of compiling this information in a readable format. The evaluation system focused on the responsibilities and duties of the job, rather than on incumbent personalities. Even in a political climate it is possible to reduce "political" decisions.

Exhibit 10-3. Final Pay Grade Assignments for Department Directors

Department	Final Pay Grade Assigned
Police	A
Fire	A
Administrative Services	B
Public Works	B
Sanitation	B
Water	C
Communications	C
Electrical	C
Buildings and Grounds	C
Garage	C
Recreation	C
Inspection	C
Community Development	C
Personnel	D

Chapter 11

Providing Opportunities to Learn and Participate

A basic goal of the Olympia project was to design and implement a classification and pay system that would establish a trusting workplace environment. The project leaders began creating such an environment by providing as many employees as possible with an understanding of the entire process. Two major avenues for increased understanding were the use of project-related training programs and the involvement of employees in each step of the process.

All too often, managers and HR specialists act as if employees are not capable of understanding and do not wish to be involved in processes that are technical in nature or quantitatively oriented. In fact, just the opposite was found to be true. The following steps, however, are critical in obtaining employee participation:

1. Grant employees opportunities to participate in every stage of the process.
2. Explain the importance of each step in clear language, making sure the employees are familiar with all words and terms. Define words carefully and precisely to ensure understanding. These explanations should include discussions of how each phase leads into and influences phases to follow.

197

3. Present technical materials in a manner that makes them rational, practical, and intuitively appealing. For example, in discussing compensable factors, review how factors describe basic parts of any job. It is even possible to develop training sessions in which employees rank factors by importance, analyze different employee rankings, and discuss how, through the use of various statistical procedures incorporating the ranking by hundreds—even thousands—of experts, it is possible to develop a weighting for each factor.

4. Permit employee access to information regarding job content and evaluation results as soon as possible after completion of each phase of the process.

5. Open all information and procedures to employee review (and appeal, when possible).

Developing and implementing such a procedure requires considerable time at the initial design stage of the project. Project designers must make certain that each document— including the job evaluation standards, job analysis questionnaire, and job description—is presented in a format and in language that is logical, rational, and easily understood by rank-and-file-employees.

Checks and balances must be built into any open system where feedback is both provided and requested. There will always be some individuals who will devise methods for manipulating the system to their personal advantage. The better the check and balance procedures, the less the opportunity for devious manipulation. Documentation and justification of decisions are required at every stage of the process. Participation in programs such as the classification and pay of jobs is not possible without a rather substantial amount of paperwork. Many people abhor the very idea of additional paperwork in any phase of the operation of a business, but it must be recognized that improved understanding and common interpretation are only possible through well-designed, broadly promulgated communications. Such communications, in most cases, require documents for dissemination, review, and analysis purposes.

Broad-based ownership in the Olympia FES classification and pay plan was a major step in establishing a quality work-life environment for all employees. An open, documented, shared process included these major steps:

• Employees were informed at the beginning stage of the project what it was about, who was involved, how it was to be conducted, where various activities would take place, when different activities would happen, and why it was being done.

- All employees had an opportunity to complete a job analysis questionnaire and describe their jobs as they were now performing them.
- Approximately 50 percent of all incumbents were interviewed to ensure adequacy and accuracy of JAQ-provided information.
- Department directors reviewed all job descriptions for accuracy.
- Each employee was sent a completed job description and asked to make any revisions necessary to ensure its accuracy.
- Department directors and one employee of their choice took part in the evaluation of the jobs in their departments. (This process involved twenty-eight employees who received in-depth training on FES and the proper functioning of a job evaluation committee.)
- The mayor and city council were kept informed of each step of the project.
- The mayor and city council received complete financial data detailing costs involved in each compensation decision.
- The mayor and city council participated in the ranking of department director jobs.
- Employees were given the opportunity to appeal any classification decision. (Employees who appealed the classification of their jobs, as well as over eighty employees who were designated as possible members of a job classification appeals board, received in-depth instruction on FES and how to use it for evaluating jobs.)
- Final pay assignments considered the relative worth of each job, market demands, unusual job requirements, traditional considerations, and the financial capacity of the city.

Participation at Olympia was not passive acceptance. Rather, it was continuous involvement that had an impact on decisions reached at every stage. The right to challenge and criticize was up front; opportunities for subversion and subterfuge were minimized (but were always present). The training received by approximately one hundred Olympia employees on the whats, whys, and hows of FES and job evaluation was time-consuming. It did, however, facilitate an understanding and acceptance of the project. In order to create trust in the workplace, employees should be given access to training regarding the job evaluation and pay system used in their organization. No issue is surrounded with more employee suspicion than the pay system.

Appealing the Classification of Jobs

The final and possibly most critical phase of the Olympia classification and pay plan project was the design and implementation of the appeals process. Without this step, the pay plan would not have received the support it did from rank-and-file employees and, without that support, the mayor and council would not have adopted the plan.

This schedule was followed:
1. Mail final job descriptions to each employee with new established rate of pay for jobs and procedure for appealing classification.
2. Train Appeals Review Board participants.
3. Begin hearing appeals.

Determining the Appeals Procedure

One of the most important components of any job evaluation system is the appeals process. The right of an employee to appeal a classification decision adds to the credibility of the system in the eyes of the employee and strengthens the system by allowing for a check of the final product.

There are several ways to approach classification appeals. One rather common approach is to have appeals directed to the HR department for review and decision making. The benefits are (1) the work is performed by staff trained in classification procedures, (2) the work is a permanent assignment for staff specialists, and (3) HR staff are familiar with all jobs throughout the organization. The possibility, however, of lack of objectivity and the failure to gain credibility may outweigh these benefits. The natural tendency of the individual who made the original classification decision is to defend that position. This could result in viewing the job only as it was viewed originally, and some critical parts of the job may continue to be overlooked. Even if this is not the case, employees on the outside usually perceive it to be that way. If the appeals process is to be a viable one, it must be seen by employees as being fair and open.

Another method is to use a team composed of HR staff and employees from other departments of the organization. The primary benefit is the increased objectivity that the more diverse group brings to the process. One major drawback is the amount of time that must be spent in training the non-HR employees and the time those employees spend away from the job. If a few employees are selected to hear all appeals, the training time is minimized, but the time away from the job is greatly increased as those employees sit on appeal boards.

A variation to the team approach is to include the appellant on the appeals board and to let him or her select some of the team members. This maximizes openness and allows for greater participation in the system by affected employees. Again, the drawback is the time and cost of training and being away from the job.

In spite of these increased costs, this method has many advantages. In addition to greater employee input, more employees are a part of the system and thus are more likely to accept it; employees at all levels are encouraged to develop and use decision-making skills; the opportunity to participate in an obviously important function that could affect another employee's job and/or pay should be a morale booster; each person trained in the evaluation system can help to educate others in their work group; participation in the appeals process can identify employee qualities and skills that can be used in other areas of the organization where group dynamics is important.

Guidelines

For this project, the appellant was included as a member of the appeals board. Following are the guidelines used in Olympia for appealing job classifications:

1. Any incumbent employee filling a job that he or she believes is improperly classified may appeal the job classification.
2. The appeal and the reason for it shall be filed in writing (or the person appealing shall go to the HR department and make an oral appeal stating the reason, which will be transcribed) not later than fifteen days following receipt of the job description and approval of the classification plan by the city council. The appeal shall be filed with the HR department by an incumbent in the job that is being appealed.
3. The appeals procedure will consist of a reevaluation of the job by an appeals review board that will include the incumbent filing the appeal, the director, a supervisory and a nonsupervisory employee filling a job not in the same classification or pay grade as the job being appealed (these members must be mutually acceptable to the employee filing the appeal and the HR director), and an employee appointed by the city manager. If the appealing incumbent so desires, he or she may select a co-worker to sit with and speak for him or her on the review board. The FES will be used in the reevaluation.

4. The reevaluation procedure shall include, but not be limited to, a review of the job questionnaire originally completed, the job description as drafted from the questionnaire, information obtained from job audits, and the factors, including the supervisory accountability factor.

The first guideline limits an appeal to improper classification. Since the pay system is built on an ordering of jobs (using the FES) there is no basis for an appeal of pay alone. If an employee believes he or she is not being paid enough,the case must be proved through the FES, since it determines pay grade assignments.

Item 2 of the guidelines allows for an oral appeal. This is always necessary when there are employees in the work force who are illiterate or functionally illiterate. Care must be taken in a process where records and paperwork are essential not to neglect those who do not read or write. It is important to set a time limit in order to plan and organize the workload although the specific number of days is not significant.

The composition of the appeals review board is outlined in item 3 of the guidelines. Two members of the five-member board are the appellant and the HR director; the remaining three members are selected from a list initially assembled by the HR director. Supervisory and nonsupervisory employees who are interested in serving in this capacity are asked to apply. They are screened using the following criteria: ability to work in a group decision-making process, rationality, objectivity, fairness, and willingness to speak up and voice opinions. (A further check of the suitability of these people takes place in the training process.) The appeals process is explained to each person and a list of willing participants is compiled.

After making an appeal, the appellant is asked to review the list and strike the names of any individuals he or she does not want to serve on the board. From the appellant-approved list the HR director then appoints one supervisory employee and one nonsupervisory employee to serve on the board. The city manager also appoints a board member from the list that has been approved by the appellant. Interestingly, in the Olympia project most appellants eliminated very few names from the list. Some did strike all but three names, ensuring the composition of the board was their choice. This procedure for board selection worked very well and gave a great deal of credibility to the appeals process.

After the appeal is received, the person filing the appeal and the HR director review the information contained in the job analysis questionnaire (JAQ) and the job description. The reasons for the appeal are also clarified at this time.

Prior to the hearing, each of the items listed in number 4 of the guidelines is reviewed by the HR director. If the HR director determines the job description has been improperly written or contains elements that are not correct for the position being appealed, changes may be made. However this is only done after a full review with the appealing employee.

Appeals Review Board Hearing

Prior to the hearing, all appeals review board members are sent a copy of the job description so they can become familiar with the job. During the hearing, the appellant participates as an equal member of the team. The board does not have access to the original FES scores for the job in question. The board starts with a "clean slate." At the hearing, each board member completes a Position Evaluation Statement (see Exhibit 8-3, Chapter 8) and these are retained as part of the record. The results of the individual evaluations are discussed and consensus is reached. The result of the board evaluation constitutes the new FES points. When it is not possible to reach a consensus on a factor or factors, then each member states his or her final score and all individual scores are recorded. The HR director is responsible for maintaining the records and reviewing the final scores with the entire board before the hearing is adjourned.

Report to City Manager

The HR director reviews comparable salary data for the job in question, and the relationship of the new evaluation to the other jobs in the pay system. A file is sent to the city manager that includes:

1. The letter of appeal.
2. Notes from the meeting held between the appellant and the HR director to review records and clarify the appeal.
3. The job analysis questionnaire.
4. Any job audit information.
5. The original job description.
6. The final job description with any changes noted.
7. A list of persons serving on the appeals review board.
8. Position evaluation statements completed and signed by each member of the appeals review board.

Accompanying this file is a letter with the recommendation of the HR director to the city manager concerning the appeal. This letter includes the appellant's present pay grade and step; his or her annual salary; a statement describing the changes made in the job description; the board evaluation and corresponding pay grade; information concerning the board's understanding of the process and any special circumstances such as extreme emotions, etc.; pertinent market data, including source and salary information; and the final recommendation with its justification. The city manager also has a matrix showing the FES evaluation by departments and within occupational groupings across department lines.

The city manager makes the final decision and notifies each appellant in writing. In making final allocation decisions, it is important to have one person accountable for reconciling any differences in order to maintain the validity of the system.

Lessons Learned

After using the appeals review board initially in Olympia, it is recommended that an additional member be added to the board: the department director (or a designee) to serve as a nonparticipating member and a resource. This person could answer any questions regarding the relationship of the appellant's job to other jobs in the department. At the hearing some appellants expanded the scope of responsibility of their jobs. Although this was not part of the authorized job description and could not be given much credence, it did have an effect on the board members. This was not a widespread problem.

The greatest lesson learned was the verification that employees working together in this capacity make rational, thoughtful decisions. They gain an appreciation for the system and for the work of other employees. Perhaps the most significant comment was from the appellant who said "I don't like the decision, but I understand how it was made and I know it is fair." That's about all you can ask from a pay system!

Training for Appeals Review Board

Training for employees who participate on the Appeals Review Board is critical. The success of the appeals process depends on the actions of these people. The class size is limited, so there can be "hands on" experience and plenty of time for questions and discussion. Ten participants per class is ideal, fifteen is maximum. Eight hours are needed to cover the material and thoroughly prepare employees to serve as board members. In the initial Olympia project three and a half hours were allotted for training. The consistent feedback was that more time was needed. A notebook is provided for participants that can be used for review and as a resource during the hearing.

In the Olympia project eighty people were trained to serve on the boards. A large pool of potential appeals review board members has many benefits. It gives appellants a variety of people to choose from, ensures availability, allows representation of jobs categories, and reflects the diverse makeup of the work force.

The following topics are covered in training:

- An explanation of classification and a brief description of some classification/job evaluation systems different from the one selected.
- The Factor Evaluation System and the reasons for its selection.
- The allocation of jobs to pay grades. In addition to internal equity, as determined by the FES, other factors are part of the decision-making process. These include such things as: market salary data, labor availability, and the ability of the organization to fund.
- What is appealable? Although this is covered with the appellants, it is important for the appeals review board members to understand that employees may only appeal their classification, not their pay.
- A review of the complete classification process and the role of the employee in it, including completion of questionnaires, job audits, job descriptions, review of job descriptions by supervisors and employees, and the evaluation process.
- The procedure for appeal, including the role of the appeals review board members. A video is shown of a simulated hearing.
- A review and explanation of the standards used in the FES.

With this background, the participants are prepared to spend time using the standards to evaluate jobs. It is most effective to begin with factors 9 (work environment) and 8 (physical demands), and work backwards through the other seven factors. This builds understanding and allows participants to gain the confidence to deal with the more complex factors such as supervisory controls and knowledge required by the job. The final step in the training is to have the participants work through a mock appeal in teams of five. This is videotaped, then reviewed and critiqued. This is also an opportunity to ensure that each participant demonstrates the knowledge and ability to be a viable member of a board.

Employees are encouraged to participate as appeals review board members and training classes are scheduled on a regular basis. This makes it possible to increase the number of people involved and provides a refresher for those who continue to serve. Refresher training could be effectively done in three hours with the mock appeal and review of tapes.

A sample Appeals Review Board training outline is shown in Exhibit 11-1.

Exhibit 11-1. Appeals Review Board Hearing Training Session

Outline for Training Session for Appeals Review Board Hearing
8:00 - 5:00

N (indicates material included in participant notebook)

8:00	Welcome, introductions, ice-breaker
8:20	Review agenda (N) and expectations
8:30	Explain classification. Give a brief description of classification/job evaluation systems different from the one selected. -samples (N)
8:45	Factor Evaluation System, reasons for selection -factors (N) -video of factors in action, using a variety of jobs (filmed at own organization)
9:15	Explain allocation of jobs to pay grades -sample market data (N) -actual pay grades (N)
9:30	Break
9:45	Employees can appeal classification not pay -guidelines for appeal (N)
10:00	Review of classification process -sample job analysis questionnaire completed (N) -sample job audit notes (N) -sample job description (N) -video of process: employee on job, completing JAQ, talking with job analyst, analyst writing job description, review by supervisors and employee, team evaluation process, department committee evaluation
10:45	Appeal procedure, discussion of the role of board members -procedural guidelines (N) -video of simulated hearing
11:15	Review and explanation of the FES standards -standards (N) -FES position evaluation statement (N)
Noon	Lunch
1:00	Review, questions, concerns, comments
1:20	Practice using standards, from factors nine to one -one exercise at a time, discussing results after each -exercises for each factor (N)
2:30	Break
2:45	Divide into two teams of five and hear a simulated appeal -video tape each team separately -review and critique
4:45	Closing comments
5:00	Adjourn

Other Opportunities for Employee Training

Line Supervisor Training

Training for line supervisors prior to the distribution of the JAQ facilitates the entire process. It is useful to prepare a video of the entire classification process. Camcorders make this an inexpensive option, and everyone enjoys seeing folks they know on the big screen. It begins with an employee shown on the job, then moves to the employee completing the JAQ. Another segment has the employee talking with a job analyst. This is an excellent way to introduce the analysts to the work force. Next, the analyst is shown writing the job description, then a review by supervisors and the employee. Finally, the job evaluation process, with a department evaluation committee, is shown in action.

Also, ideas for motivating employees to complete the JAQ thoughtfully and accurately are discussed. Techniques are given for assisting those employees who are semiliterate. This involvement of supervisors not only increases their knowledge of the system but it allows them to be a more effective conduit between employees and the job analyst. This training can also be used as an ongoing part of supervisory development for those promoted in the organization.

Initial Employee Meetings

The initial meetings with employees provide an excellent opportunity to increase employee understanding and involvement. A helpful technique is to use the classification video. The video format shows employees the connection between what they do on the job and the classification process. It also keeps them "tuned in" to the presentation through the use of their own work sites. It allows the same message to be communicated to all employees. It is best when introduced by a HR representative and followed by opportunities for questions and comments. However, it can be shown independently to employees who are not able to attend group meetings.

The classification process video is also used for informing elected officials and interested citizen groups and in training appeals review board members.

Training Department Evaluation Committees

Training for those who serve on the department evaluation committees increases the likelihood of sound results. This training is similar to that provided the appeals review board and some of the same material can be used. The factors-in-action video is particularly useful in this setting. It helps the group to see the connection between the factors and the real job. It is critical to give the participants an opportunity to practice evaluating and then to discuss the results. This not only ensure better results, but it builds confidence in the system.

Employee Rights

The legitimate rights of Olympia employees to be included in as many of the decision-making processes as possible was acknowledged prior to the start of the project. The design of each phase of the project attempted, within limits set by time and money constraints, to recognize these rights.

Although not a commonly recognized fact, the project consultant operated on the premise that all organizations "rent" the resources of their employees and that ownership of the human resource is retained by the individual employee. As such, each employee has a legitimate interest in the development and use of his or her own resources.

Self-management of one's own human resources includes economically analogous behaviors (such as investment in education), ultimately leading to the application of those unique resources in a workplace environment that will theoretically maximize the worker's expected utility. This utility is derived directly from all kinds of rewards received from employment. Such self-management is typically practiced only in those instances where the roles of employee and employer are merged (as with self-employed professionals). However, the absence of self-management in instances where there is no merger of employee/employer roles does not mitigate the desirability of greater employee participation in this area.

For an organization to function as a coordinated unit, and in order to take advantage of labor specialization in human resources management, it is to the employee's advantage to relinquish a substantial amount of control over this function to the HR specialist. A concerted effort should be made, however, to include the employee as much as possible in the management of human resources. Employee participation not only acknowledges the first-hand information the employee is able to provide concerning job content but also the legitimacy of the employee's interest in maintaining a role in the management of his or her greatest asset.

Even though it may mean improvement in the work life of all members, change of almost any kind in an organization is frequently met with resistance. Certainly change brought about by any classification and pay study will frequently fall into this category. To increase the acceptance of change or of a classification and pay study, employees must have information regarding what is to be changed and how the changes will be made. Additionally, they must be taught how the contemplated changes will be of benefit. Employees must recognize that they truly have some influence on the change-related processes and, through their inputs, can exercise some control over the directions and end results of these processes.

Much effort was expended in the Olympia project to demonstrate to employees that they do have a meaningful impact on the pay system. Their input into how their jobs are identified, described, and evaluated directly influences the pay they receive for the work they do. A basic premise, of employee involvement in HR activities such as pay systems is that it can and should be done *with* employees not for or to them. Designing employee involvement into the process benefits everyone.

Chapter 12

LAYING THE FOUNDATION FOR PAY FOR PERFORMANCE AND TOTAL QUALITY MANAGEMENT

In all of the previous discussions in this book, there has been little attention paid to two very critical subjects of the 1990s—pay for performance and Total Quality Management (TQM). The original design of a three-step pay plan for Olympia was predicated on the development of a workable performance appraisal rating system. In fact, those involved in the Olympia project originally wanted to establish pay grades with minimum and maximum rates of pay for each pay grade, and then, through a merit pay plan, to award pay increases based upon employees' annual performance ratings. This proposal turned out to be an unfulfilled dream. The measurement and rating of employee performance was recognized as a difficult, if not an almost impossible, assignment given the measurement technology available at that time.

Because of the lack of credible performance appraisal programs, we strongly recommended the development and use of pay grades with steps. Employees were denied a step increase when they received a less than satisfactory performance rating substantiated by written documentation establishing the reasons for the rating. This recommendation does not mean, however, that performance cannot be measured and that reward systems cannot be designed to pay for performance.

Before discussing the relationship between the focus of this book on job analysis and job descriptions and the evolving issues related to pay for performance and TQM, it is necessary to have a complete understanding of what is included within the compensation package of an organizational reward system. Compensation includes the following components: *base pay* (the major topic of this book) and *base pay addons* that include elements such as overtime pay, base pay increases for seniority or tenure, shift and weekend differentials, or hazardous pay, and *incentive pay* that also can include a wide variety of components from individual performance-based rewards, such as bonuses and commissions, individual bonuses (one-time re-earnable), to add-ons to base pay (permanent additions to base pay) such as merit pay and performance appraisal-based individual awards. Incentive pay can be an organization-wide profit-sharing program or programs such as gainsharing or team-based recognition and reward incentives for special groups of employees. The majority of these incentive components may be classified as variable pay components. However, those that become merged into the base pay plan have a strong fixed element.

The final and primarily fixed component of a compensation system is the package of employee benefits. For the past ten years, benefits have cost an average of 35 to 40 percent of base pay for most employers. In recent years, as the health care components of the employee benefits package have increased dramatically, employers have shifted some of the increased costs to employees. Not all compensation systems include incentive components, but all compensation systems include a benefits component—at a minimum, those benefits required by government legislation.

Pay for Performance

A long-time dream of many managers in all kinds of organizations—public and private, goods and service providing—is to have a part of all employees' compensation relate to performance. Performance measures could be organization-wide and based on the work unit, team, or individual. In recent years, experts on pay system design have promoted the concept of variable pay versus fixed pay, with the variable pay concept having its roots in some kind of pay-for-performance scheme. In any pay-for-performance system or plan, a certain amount of the employee's annual earnings is tied to the achievement of some established and understood objective, goal, or performance standard. Frequently, when an organization establishes a pay-for-performance system, the fixed portion of the pay system, such as base pay, base pay supplements, or seniority-based increases, are held constant, if not reduced. The opportunity to increase total annual income occurs through achievement of previously mentioned objectives, goals, and performance standards. Pay-for-performance concepts predate the Industrial Revolution, and if records from early times were available, they would indicate that pay for performance probably developed hand-in-glove with civilization.

The barrier to implementing and maintaining an effective pay-for-performance system is in the setting of performance standards at a desired level—organization-wide, division/department, team, or individual. The setting of achievable performance standards that benefit both the organization and the employee require considerable knowledge of organization inputs and outputs and employee work requirements. To outsiders or individuals not familiar with the inner workings and hidden mechanisms of organization life, it would be natural to think that organization inputs and outputs and employee activities are clearly established and well understood. This is seldom the case, and the greater the mystery related to these inputs, outputs, and activities, the more difficult it is to establish pay-for-performance systems that are effective for any period of time.

Pay-for-Performance in a Knowledge-based World

The turn of the twentieth century witnessed the decline of agricultural-based jobs and dominance of a farm-based society. Jobs in the manufacturing world began replacing many agricultural jobs. By the early 1900s, the Industrial Revolution had had 150 years to spawn factories and mills that provided better paying jobs and more freedom for workers, who had been serfs in feudal agricultural societies. It is true that the work in these factories and mills was not always pleasant and that the workers were frequently taken advantage of by the owners and supervisors. However, the benefits available to the work force and society as a whole through manufacturing-based jobs were far greater than those available through agricultural-based jobs. The shift away from agriculture has not been smooth. Here, at the end of the twentieth century, agricultural lobbies in even the most industrialized nations continue to have significant influence over political processes and, through these processes, to obtain favorable subsidies and tax relief and to control national import-export policies.

Just as the first half of the twentieth century saw the shift of agricultural employment from in excess of 30 percent of the work force to less than 3 percent, the last half of the twentieth century is witnessing a decline in the manufacturing-goods producing work force from in excess of 30 percent to less than 15 percent. Today and into the future, the service sector of the work force will dominate. Most workers in the service sector, even those in relatively low-paying jobs, will be knowledge-oriented workers who will have to constantly acquire more knowledge and new skills in order to perform their jobs satisfactorily.

The acquisition of new knowledge and skills will be based on a foundation of previously acquired knowledge and skills. As often mentioned, learning and skill acquisition will be a lifetime journey. A most difficult and complex issue facing managers and compensation professionals is how to measure the performance of knowledge-based workers. F. W. Taylor and his fellow industrial engineers of a century ago recognized that they could identify rather precisely and completely the activities a factory-worker must perform to produce a specific output.[1] Even in this setting, however, the development of performance standards is not as easy or as clearly defined as it may appear to be. All kinds of operating conditions can influence employee outputs beyond the physical efforts of the worker, and those conditions cause much concern and negotiation over the setting of performance standards in a manufacturing environment.

If the setting of performance standards is a difficult and complex assignment for a manufacturing job, it is far more difficult and complex for a service-type, knowledge-based job. The difficulty and complexity begin with a major difference between manufacturing, goods-producing jobs and knowledge-based, service-providing jobs. Many goods-producing jobs require the worker to perform routine assignments that vary little during the workday. Moreover, the assignments are repeated each day. Even in these jobs, however, conditions may arise that require some kind of intellectual effort to respond in a manner that meets productivity standards. Here, workplace experience usually provides the opportunity to acquire the knowledge and skills to react to these changing conditions.

However, even in relatively low-level, knowledge-based, service-providing jobs, work efforts are not routine. Job routines constantly change. Employee work effort varies according to the last direction received. It may be a personally delivered oral request from a fellow worker, a telephone call from a manager or a client of the organization, or it could be some kind of written notice, letter, or form. The activities of these workers cannot be described through the use of eight or ten action verbs with precise definitions such as *moves, transports, places,* and so forth. The verbs used to describe knowledge-oriented work range into the hundreds, and the same verb may have a very different meaning from one occupational setting to another. The nonroutine, complex nature of knowledge-based job activities makes it very difficult to set performance standards for these jobs.

There is, however, one strong foundation available to organizations in all kinds of settings that can establish performance standards for knowledge-based jobs. The foundation is the complete and precise description of work activities using the methods and processes discussed in this book. To summarize, these methods and processes produce a job definition—a set of responsibilities and assigned duties that completely and precisely describe the work of each employee. This definitional process involves the work of all employees from the CEO to the lowest-rated entry-level clerk. It must be recognized that as jobs increase in complexity and responsibility, the verbs used to describe the work activities are more general and less specific. In lower-level jobs, the verb-object-modifying phrase combination has or may almost have how-to requirements. It tells not only what the employee does but how the employee does it. The activity statement becomes a procedure. As knowledge-based jobs increase in complexity, the "what" and the "how-to" of the job become separate. The how-to relates to individual differences in knowledge, skill, effort, temperament, and values.

It is almost impossible and unnecessary to develop procedures for many knowledge-based, service-providing jobs. The procedures vary by the individual assigned to the job and the specific conditions or situations facing the jobholder. This does not mean that standards of performance cannot be established for this job. It just means that standard-setting is more difficult and complex.

Performance standards for high-level, knowledge-based jobs can be closely linked to the overall objectives of the organization or possibly to the goals of particular work units. The management-by-objectives (MBO) performance standards-setting process works well for these kinds of jobs. MBO becomes a weaker performance-setting process when the outputs of a job are co-mingled with the outputs of many other jobs in producing a work unit or organization measured output.

For these jobs, it is necessary to return the foundation for performance standards to the work activities (the responsibilities and duties) of the employee. The establishment of performance standards must have a participative base similar to those discussed in this book for developing job definitions. The individual responsible for performance review and rating and the individual whose performance is being measured must be able to move from job definitions to performance standards. There must be a clearly understood, well-defined audit trail from assigned job activities to measurable performance standards. The employee and the rating supervisor must be able to discuss how-to processes and procedures, but as long as the processes and procedures are legal, ethical, and non-life threatening, the knowledge-based worker can proceed on job assignments in a manner acceptable and workable to the individual whose performance is being measured and rated. What is critical is the output of these knowledge-based jobs. In some kind of a participative, open-communication process, rater and ratee identify and establish performance standards. This process must also recognize a clear link between the responsibilities and duties of the job and the performance standards. This linkage underscores the importance of solid job definitions. If agreement cannot be reached on the job definition, and if the job definition is not in written form, the opportunity to develop recognized and useful performance standards becomes not only difficult, but extremely weak and open to all kinds of arguments and disagreement.

As mentioned at the beginning of this chapter, performance appraisal (measurement) is possibly the most difficult and threatening assignment facing any manager. (Supervisors are actually murdered because of actions taken in this area. Check U.S. Postal Service problems to underscore the seriousness of this problem.) As jobs become more complex, the rating of employee performance becomes increasingly difficult, but *never unimportant.*

Pay-for-Performance—Individual, Team, Major Organizational Entity, and Organization

Pay-for-performance programs can take many forms. One way of analyzing pay-for-performance programs is to separate pay-for-performance components by those (1) based on some kind of individual performance or contribution, (2) recognizing membership within a certain team, (3) based on membership within a major organizational entity, and (4) recognizing membership in the organization.

Individual Performance. Merit pay (although many would argue there is no merit in merit pay) provides employees with the opportunity to enlarge their base pay by demonstrating a certain level of performance. Some merit pay plans provide a uniform dollar or percentage of pay increase. The actual amount of the increase depends on the employee's existing rate of pay, possibly tenure on the job, and performance ratings. Individuals may also receive special cash awards or bonuses for some special or exceptional contribution or achieved result.

Individual As Team Member. Team incentive plans must be tied in some manner to the outputs or results achieved by the team. Two issues facing team-based incentives are (1) establishing some kind of performance standards, expected results, or goals for the team; and (2) determining how a team incentive award will be divided among team members— that is, should more senior, more skilled, possibly more productive team members receive a larger share of the award than less qualified team members? The performance measurement issue is similar to that facing the rewarding of individuals based on individual performance. The issue of reward distribution among team members is a special case, although an option may be similar to that used in determining an individual's award in a gainsharing program.

Membership Within a Major Organizational Entity. Where it is possible to establish some kind of a productivity or results-achieved measure of performance, various kinds of cost reduction or gainsharing plans provide an ideal vehicle for rewarding all members of the identified organizational entity. For example, an individual's share of the total reward pool may be based on total individual earnings as a percentage of total earnings for all members of the entity.

Organizational Membership. There are a number of programs that are useful in linking the performance of all members of the organization to organizational success. Probably the oldest of these is profit sharing. Private-sector organizations with a profit motive can make use of such plans. Possibly the biggest weaknesses with profit sharing are the various kinds of tax legislation or other government mandates that can influence what an organization recognizes and states as profit. Accounting and financial rules can limit the value of almost any profit-sharing plan. As mentioned in the previous section, gainsharing or some kind of cost-reduction or broad-based performance measurement plan can be used to reward all employees in an organization. Any of these organization-wide plans can link individual performance awards, team-based awards, and major organizational unit awards.

For pay-for-performance systems to operate successfully, organizations must expend considerable effort to understand and document what is occurring and the results achieved at all levels within the organization.

For large, profit-making organizations, recent interest in pay for performance has been spurred by worldwide competition and high labor costs in the heavily industrialized nations such as the United States, Germany, and Japan. Not only are labor/compensation costs high in those nations, but labor costs have steadily increased as a percentage of total product costs. In addition, lagging employee interest and effort in providing quality output has become a major issue faced by managers at all levels. In public sector, nonprofit organizations, there is a limit to the amount of taxes to be paid by all members of society. Many public sector organizations are reaching their taxation limits, even as they face greater demands for public services, such as education, food, health care, housing, and safety. One opportunity available to all kinds and sizes of organizations to improve delivery and quality and lower the cost of output is through increased employee interest, effort, concern, and understanding. Both pay for performance and TQM are two concepts that provide a promise for achieving the lofty and desired goal of increased employee commitment to the organization and its product.

Total Quality Management (TQM)

TQM is an approach to managing human resources that can lead to long-term success through organization-wide efforts toward continuous improvement. Two of the respected leaders and promoters of TQM are W. Edwards Deming and Joseph M. Juran, who performed most of their pioneering TQM efforts in Japan. TQM, like pay for performance, comes packaged under a variety of labels such as Quality Management, Total Quality Leadership, and Continuous Improvement. Whatever the title, TQM programs contain five key concepts:

- Customer driven quality
- Strong quality leadership
- Continuous improvement
- Actions based on facts, data, and analysis
- Employee participation

In the late 1940s, Douglas MacArthur, in his efforts to democratize Japan and to stimulate the recovery of the war-ravaged Japanese economy, introduced Japanese leaders to Deming, who promoted the importance of quality in a manufacturing-based society. Although it took almost three decades for Deming's concepts to reach and be accepted in the United States, he is now recognized as the father of quality management, and those developing and promoting TQM programs faithfully follow his concepts and doctrines. Deming and his followers center their approach to TQM around his "fourteen points" and "deadly diseases." Of particular interest to the discussions presented in this book is his eleventh point, "eliminate numerical quotas for the work force and numerical goals of management." This point has been amplified by Deming and his followers to mean that performance appraisal is unnecessary and, in fact, a productivity-limiting tool. When talking and writing about "deadly diseases" within management, Deming and his followers attack the value and use of job descriptions.[2]

As noted, the keystone of the process discussed in this book is job analysis, and a major output of job analysis is the job description. In turn, the job description becomes the core of any performance measurement program. In many ways, concern with Deming's proposals regarding performance appraisal and job descriptions is similar to the old adage, "Don't throw out the baby with the bath water." There is no argument that, in the past—and often even now—job descriptions are poorly developed, provide only a cursory description of the work performed by the involved employees, and, in fact, become barriers to improved performance. Because they are so general and fail to adequately define job activities, they are of little use to the complex assignment of performance appraisal.

As previously mentioned, performance measurement and rating is a most difficult assignment in the knowledge-oriented society of today, where conditions and interactions constantly change, and these changes must be recognized when appraising employee performance. Two key parts of any TQM program are analysis of activities and measurement of performance. It is difficult to see how, in some manner, TQM programs can succeed without intense effort in job analysis and performance appraisal, no matter how they are titled.

Workplace Performance Measurement and TQM

Although many of the behavioral science theories developed and implemented over the past forty years within U.S. organizations are fundamental to TQM, it is essential to recognize that TQM is not a "touchy-feely" process. TQM, if anything, is based on "soft authoritarianism"—a hard but fair approach. Key to TQM are planning, orderliness, and constant vigilance. Key to TQM-based planning, orderliness, and vigilance is employee empowerment. Employee empowerment means that employees at all levels in all kinds of jobs have the right to make decisions, to be heard, to participate in the design of methods and processes, and to establish procedures for the work they do. To ensure cohesive efforts throughout the organization, TQM also requires the organization to provide a vision and mission. From the organization-wide vision and mission, individual jobs are defined and redefined. From job definitions, individuals develop their own set of procedures for doing their work and, in some manner, participating in the establishment of performance standards.

The TQM planning process is both top-down and bottom-up. The organization must establish policy, develop a mission, and set objectives and goals. Individuals, as sole contributors or as members of teams and work units, must design their work efforts and set performance standards to support top-down planning efforts or the modification of these efforts through bottom-up communication.

In some form, job analysis, job descriptions, and performance appraisals become critical components of the TQM process. When done properly, they provide orderliness to TQM. They permit and promote self-vigilance, self-control, and self-direction. This is what employee empowerment is all about. It spawns employee innovation and promotes individual discipline. It allows individuals to integrate their efforts within a cohesive team and to be part of a cooperative work force where all members join the effort to improve organizational productivity and promote organizational success.

TQM and Total Performance Measurement

Most performance appraisal systems, including those discussed in this book, focus on job-related behaviors, contributions, and output. TQM provides the opportunity for total performance measurement. Since TQM is dedicated to providing a quality product (good or service) to the customer, (the customer can be another member of the organization who is a recipient of an employee output—which can be a behavior—a client of the organization, or a member of society), the TQM process can recognize and reward such critical employee qualities as dependability, cooperation, courtesy, and support. These qualities in many performance appraisal systems go unrecognized or are merged in some manner with easier to measure output. In a TQM program, these individual attributes become critical issues that are identified and recognized within TQM and permit measurement at some time during a performance period.

Fables That Can Block Pay-for-Performance and TQM Success

Three phrases often quoted by individuals to explain or defend a certain action that can limit if not destroy quality-related performance are:
- "That's not on my job description."
- "Other duties as assigned."
- "We must reduce the number of classifications."

These three statements belong in the same garbage can as the infamous "If it ain't broke, don't fix it."

That's Not on My Job Description

Along with the development of a strong union movement in the 1930s and 1940s came the need to minimize what many workers felt to be the abusive power of the first-line supervisor. From the start of the Industrial Revolution to the rise of the twentieth century union movement, supervisors usually had the right to make any assignment to any employee at any time to accomplish the goals of the particular work unit. It was not unusual for supervisors to have favorite subordinates. Those employees not on the "right side" of the supervisor felt (and frequently with great justification) that they received all of the dirty, difficult, dangerous assignments no matter what their job duties were supposed to be. With the rise of unionism and labor-management contracts came the careful and precise detailing of what work could be assigned to each employee. If a subordinate's job classification (description) did not identify particular kinds and levels of work activities, a supervisor could not assign the undefined, unauthorized activities to that subordinate. These restrictions significantly reduced the authority of the supervisor. They also significantly increased labor costs and efficiency for the organization.

By not permitting supervisors or organizations to move employees to an area of work where there was an unusual but critical demand, many organizations had to maintain an excessively large work force to take care of the unusual and critical situation that could arise at irregular and infrequent intervals. The statement, "That's not on my job description," became as productivity abusive as supervisor favoritism was employee abusive.

Today, as the need for an adversarial relationship between labor and management becomes completely unacceptable, the term, "That's not on my job description," becomes archaic, with no place for it in organizational life. The following section discusses this same issue from a slightly different perspective and tells organizations what they can do to reduce if not eliminate the dysfunctional concepts related to this slogan.

Other Duties As Assigned

Many organizations, especially nonunion organizations, require this phrase at the end of the job activities (responsibilities and duties) section of all of their job descriptions. In many ways, this phrase is placed formally in this location to overcome the potential for the productivity blocking, "That's not on my job description."

However, the "other duties as assigned" statement is far too important to be the last statement on a list of job activities. Rather than placing the phrase, "other duties as assigned," on all job descriptions, this concept should be incorporated into the human resources/organization policy statement. It should be part of an employer-employee contract negotiated and signed at the time the employee is first hired by the organization. A paragraph such as the following should be clearly stated in the employment contract:

> The organization and its members with assigned supervisory responsibilities have the right to assign any employee to any work activity at any time to assist in the favorable operation of the organization. However, no employee will be assigned to any work activity that is illegal, immoral, life-threatening, or where lack of knowledge and skill on the part of the employee could cause the employee to perform the activity in a less than satisfactory manner or could be a danger to other employees or work-related individuals.

Possibly an additional paragraph should state that when an employee is given a temporary assignment that lasts more than 30 days, this assignment should be recognized and included within the employee's job description, and all organizational functions related to an employee's job description should note the new and additional assignment.

The need for flexibility in work assignments and the need for employee cooperation is so critical to organizational success that there must be no opportunity for supervisors to abuse the privilege and no desire for employees to refuse compliance with a supervisor's request for work-related assistance.

We Must Reduce the Number of Job Classifications

This third statement that is now being frequently heard and voiced by organizations and their productivity improvement specialists relates to the need to reduce the number of classifications. Over the past fifty years, many organizations developed job classifications (listings of work activities that can be assigned to specific groups of employees) as a result of labor-management contracts or even in nonunion settings where management thought this was part of good and acceptable management techniques. Over the years, all kinds of organizations have found these classifications to be barriers to improving organizational productivity. What must be recognized as a major and critical difference between the job classifications and the job descriptions discussed in this book is that the job classification covers a variety of jobs. The classification states in very generic terms what employees in the classification can be assigned to do.

Because they are somewhat general, employees, especially those in a strong unionized organization, can use them in refusing to perform an assignment because they *do not* specifically identify or define the new or additional assignment made by the supervisor.

What is absolutely imperative to understand about the job descriptions discussed in this book is that in no way are they meant to be "straitjackets." They are not meant to restrict or prohibit employee performance. They are first and last a communication device that permits the organization and its supervisors to clearly identify the work the employee must do. They inform employees about the assignments for which they are being held accountable. They minimize surprises. They aim to eliminate another unacceptable employee defense for not performing in an adequate or acceptable manner—"I didn't know I was supposed to do that."

A major reason organizations have not used the approach to writing precise and complete job/position descriptions in the past is that they did not have the administrative support to keep their job descriptions current and accurate. The updating process was far too costly. Today, however, word processing, computer technology, and computer networking permit both inexpensive and rapid updating of job description data. Computer-based storage can date and store changes to job description data for various compensation purposes. Also, this data is readily available to both the jobholders and their supervisors. This kind of information flow is essential to the success of both pay-for-performance and TQM programs.

Endnotes

1. Frederick W. Taylor, "A Piece Rate System," Transactions of the American Society of Mechanical Engineers, vol. XVI(1895), 856-905; Frederick W. Taylor, *Principles of Scientific Management,* (New York: Harper, 1911), 36-37; G. B. Gilbreath, *Motion Study*, (Princeton, New Jersey: Van Nostrand, 1911).

2. W. Edwards, Deming, *Out of the Crisis*, (Cambridge, Mass.: MIT Institute for Advanced Engineering Study, 1986); Walton, Mary, *The Deming Management Method*, (New York: Putnam, 1991)

Appendix A

FES Primary Standards

The Primary Standard serves as a "standard-for-standards" for the Factor Evaluation System (FES). Factor-level descriptions for position classification standards are point-rated against the Primary Standard. Thus, it serves as a basic tool for maintaining alignment across occupations.

The Primary Standard has descriptions of each of the nine FES factors and the levels within each factor as well as the point values appropriate for each level. The nine factors are:

Factor 1, Knowledge Required by the Position
Factor 2, Supervisory Controls
Factor 3, Guidelines
Factor 4, Complexity
Factor 5, Scope and Effect
Factor 6, Personal Contacts
Factor 7, Purpose of Contacts
Factor 8, Physical Demands
Factor 9, Work Environment

Also included in the Primary Standard is a master grade conversion table showing the total point ranges (based on sets of complete factors) for grades GS-1 through GS-15.

Reprinted from *Instructions for the Factor Evaluation System,* TS-27, U.S. Civil Service Commission, Bureau of Policies and Standards (U.S. Government Printing Office, Washington D.C., May 1977), pp. 13-21.

Factor 1: Knowledge Required by the Position

Factor 1 measures the nature and extent of information or facts which the workers must understand to do acceptable work (e.g., steps, procedures, practices, rules, policies, theories, principles, and concepts) and the nature and extent of the skills needed to apply those knowledges. To be used as a basis for selecting a level under this factor, a knowledge must be required and applied.

Level 1-1   *50 points*

Knowledge of simple, routine, or repetitive tasks or operations which typically includes following step-by-step instructions and requires little or no previous training or experience;

OR

Skill to operate simple equipment or equipment which operates repetitively, requiring little or no previous training or experience;

OR

Equivalent knowledge and skill.

Level 1-2   *200 points*

Knowledge of basic or commonly-used rules, procedures, or operations which typically requires some previous training or experience;

OR

Basic skill to operate equipment requiring some previous training or experience, such as keyboard equipment;

OR

Equivalent knowledge and skill.

Level 1-3   *350 points*

Knowledge of a body of standardized rules, procedures or operations requiring considerable training and experience to perform the full range of standard clerical assignments and resolve recurring problems;

OR

Skill, acquired through considerable training and experience, to operate and adjust varied equipment for purposes such as performing numerous standardized tests or operations;

OR

Equivalent knowledge and skill.

Level 1-4   *550 points*

Knowledge of an extensive body of rules, procedures or operations requiring extended training and experience to perform a wide variety of interrelated or nonstandard procedural assignments and resolve a wide range of problems;

OR

Practical knowledge of standard procedures in a technical field, requiring extended training or experience, to perform such work as: adapting equipment when this requires considering the functioning characteristics of equipment; interpreting results of tests based on previous experience and observations (rather than directly reading instruments or other measures); or extracting information from various sources when this requires considering the applicability of information and the characteristics and quality of the sources;

OR

Equivalent knowledge and skill.

Level 1-5

750 points

Knowledge (such as would be acquired through a pertinent baccalaureate educational program or its equivalent in experience, training, or independent study) of basic principles, concepts, and methodology of a professional or administrative occupation, and skill in applying this knowledge in carrying out elementary assignments, operations, or procedures;

OR

In addition to the practical knowledge of standard procedures in Level 1-4, practical knowledge of technical methods to perform assignments such as carrying out limited projects which involves use of specialized, complicated techniques;

OR

Equivalent knowledge and skill.

Level 1-6

950 points

Knowledge of the principles, concepts, and methodology of a professional or administrative occupation as described at Level 1-5 which has been either: (a) supplemented by skill gained through job experience to permit independent performance of recurring assignments, or (b) supplemented by expanded professional or administrative knowledge gained through relevant graduate study or experience, which has provided skill in carrying out assignments, operations, and procedures in the occupation which are significantly more difficult and complex than those covered by Level 1-5;

OR

Practical knowledge of a wide range of technical methods, principles, and practices similar to a narrow area of a professional field, and skill in applying this knowledge to such assignments as the design and planning of difficult, but well-precedented projects;

OR

Equivalent knowledge and skill.

Level 1-7

1250 points

Knowledge of a wide range of concepts, principles, and practices in a professional or administrative occupation, such as would be gained through extended graduate study or experience, and skill in applying this knowledge to difficult and complex work assignments;

OR

A comprehensive, intensive, practical knowledge of a technical field and skill in applying this knowledge to the development of new methods, approaches, or procedures;

OR

Equivalent knowledge and skill.

Level 1-8

1550 points

Mastery of a professional or administrative field to:
—Apply experimental theories and new developments to problems not susceptible to treatment by accepted methods;

OR

—Make decisions or recommendations significantly changing, interpreting, or developing important public policies or programs;

OR

Equivalent skill and knowledge.

Level 1-9   *1850 points*

Mastery of a professional field to generate and develop new hypotheses and theories;

OR

Equivalent knowledge and skill.

Factor 2, Supervisory Controls

"Supervisory Controls" covers the nature and extent of direct or indirect controls exercised by the supervisor, the employee's responsibility, and the review of completed work. Controls are exercised by the supervisor in the way assignments are made, instructions are given to the employee, priorities and deadlines are set, and objectives and boundaries are defined. Responsibility of the employee depends upon the extent to which the employee is expected to develop the sequence and timing of various aspects of the work, to modify or recommend modification of instructions, and to participate in establishing priorities and defining objectives. The degree of review of completed work depends upon the nature and extent of the review, e.g., close and detailed review of each phase of the assignment; detailed review of the finished assignment; spot-check of finished work for accuracy; or review only for adherence to policy.

Level 2-1   *25 points*

For both one-of-a-kind and repetitive tasks the supervisor makes specific assignments that are accompanied by clear, detailed, and specific instructions. The employee works as instructed and consults with the supervisor as needed on all matters not specifically covered in the original instructions or guidelines.

For all positions the work is closely controlled. For some positions, the control is through the structured nature of the work itself, for others, it may be controlled by the circumstances in which it is performed. In some situations, the supervisor maintains control through review of the work which may include checking progress or reviewing completed work for accuracy, adequacy, and adherence to instructions and established procedures.

Level 2-2   *125 points*

The supervisor provides continuing or individual assignments by indicating generally what is to be done, limitations, quality and quantity expected, deadlines, and priority of assignments. The supervisor provides additional, specific instructions for new, difficult, or unusual assignments including suggested work methods or advice on source material available.

The employee uses initiative in carrying out recurring assignments independently without specific instruction, but refers deviations, problems, and unfamiliar situations not covered by instructions to the supervisor for decision or help.

The supervisor assures that finished work and methods used are technically accurate and in compliance with instructions or established procedures. Review of the work increases with more difficult assignments if the employee has not previously performed similar assignments.

Level 2-3 275 *points*

The supervisor makes assignments by defining objectives, priorities, and deadlines; and assists employee with unusual situations which do not have clear precedents.

The employee plans and carries out the successive steps and handles problems and deviations in the work assignment in accordance with instructions, policies, previous training, or accepted practices in the occupation.

Completed work is usually evaluated for technical soundness, appropriateness, and conformity to policy and requirements. The methods used in arriving at the end results are not usually reviewed in detail.

Level 2-4 450 *points*

The supervisor sets the overall objectives and resources available. The employee and supervisor, in consultation, develop the deadlines, projects, and work to be done.

At this level, the employee, having developed expertise in the line of work, is responsible for planning and carrying out the assignment; resolving most of the conflicts which arise; coordinating the work with others as necessary; and interpreting policy on own initiative in terms of established objectives. In some assignments, the employee also determines the approach to be taken and the methodology to be used. The employee keeps the supervisor informed of progress, potentially controversial matters, or far-reaching implications.

Completed work is reviewed only from an overall standpoint in terms of feasibility, compatibility with other work, or effectiveness in meeting requirements or expected results.

Level 2-5 650 *points*

The supervisor provides administrative direction with assignments in terms of broadly defined missions or functions.

The employee has responsibility for planning, designing, and carrying out programs, projects, studies, or other work independently.

Results of the work are considered as technically authoritative and are normally accepted without significant change. If the work should be reviewed, the review concerns such matters as fulfillment of program objectives, effect of advice and influence of the overall program, or the contribution to the advancement of technology. Recommendations for new projects and alteration of objectives are usually evaluated for such considerations as availability of funds and other resources, broad program goals or national priorities.

Factor 3, Guidelines

This factor covers the nature of guidelines and the judgment needed to apply them. Guides used in General Schedule occupations include, for example: desk manuals, established procedures and policies, traditional practices, and reference materials such as dictionaries, style manuals, engineering handbooks, the pharmacopoeia, and the Federal Personnel Manual.

Individual jobs in different occupations vary in the specificity, applicability and availability of the guidelines for performance of assignments. Consequently, the constraints and judgmental demands placed upon employees also vary. For example, the existence of specific instructions, procedures, and policies may limit the opportunity of the employee to make or recommend decisions or actions. However, in the absence of procedures or under broadly stated objectives, employees in some occupations may use considerable judgment in researching literature and developing new methods.

Guidelines should not be confused with the knowledges described under Factor 1, Knowledge Required by the Position. Guidelines either provide reference data or impose certain constraints on the use of knowledges. For example, in the field of medical technology, for a particular diagnosis there may be three or four standardized tests set forth in a technical manual. A medical technologist is expected to know these diagnostic tests. However, in a given laboratory the policy may be to use only one of the tests; or the policy may state specifically under what conditions one or the other of these tests may be used.

Level 3-1   *25 points*

Specific, detailed guidelines covering all important aspects of the assignment are provided to the employee.

The employee works in strict adherence to the guidelines; deviations must be authorized by the supervisor.

Level 3-2   *125 points*

Procedures for doing the work have been established and a number of specific guidelines are available.

The number and similarity of guidelines and work situations requires the employee to use judgment in locating and selecting the most appropriate guidelines, references, and procedures for application and in making minor deviations to adapt the guidelines in specific cases. At this level, the employee may also determine which of several established alternatives to use. Situations to which the existing guidelines cannot be applied or significant proposed deviations from the guidelines are referred to the supervisor.

Level 3-3   *275 points*

Guidelines are available, but are not completely applicable to the work or have gaps in specificity.

The employee uses judgment in interpreting and adapting guidelines such as agency policies, regulations, precedents, and work directions for application to specific cases or problems. The employee analyzes results and recommends changes.

Level 3-4   *450 points*

Administrative policies and precedents are applicable but are stated in general terms. Guidelines for performing the work are scarce or of limited use.

The employee uses initiative and resourcefulness in deviating from traditional methods or researching trends and patterns to develop new methods, criteria, or proposed new policies.

Level 3-5   *650 points*

Guidelines are broadly stated and nonspecific, e.g., broad policy statements and basic legislation which require extensive interpretation.

The employee must use judgment and ingenuity in interpreting the intent of the guides that do exist and in developing applications to specific areas of work. Frequently, the employee is recognized as a technical authority in the development and interpretation of guidelines.

Factor 4, Complexity

This factor covers the nature, number, variety, and intricacy of tasks, steps, processes, or methods in the work performed; the difficulty in identifying what needs to be done; and the difficulty and originality involved in performing the work.

Level 4-1   *25 points*

The work consists of tasks that are clear-cut and directly related.

There is little or no choice to be made in deciding what needs to be done.

Actions to be taken or responses to be made are readily discernible. The work is quickly mastered.

Level 4-2   *75 points*

The work consists of duties that involve related steps, processes, or methods.

The decision regarding what needs to be done involves various choices requiring the employee to recognize the existence of and differences among a few easily recognizable situations.

Actions to be taken or responses to be made differ in such things as the source of information, the kind of transactions or entries, or other differences of a factual nature.

Level 4-3   *150 points*

The work includes various duties involving different and unrelated processes and methods.

The decision regarding what needs to be done depends upon the analysis of the subject, phase, or issues involved in each assignment, and the chosen course of action may have to be selected from many alternatives.

The work involves conditions and elements that must be identified and analyzed to discern interrelationships.

Level 4-4   *225 points*

The work typically includes varied duties requiring many different and unrelated processes and methods such as those relating to well-established aspects of an administrative or professional field.

Decisions regarding what needs to be done include the assessment of unusual circumstances, variations in approach, and incomplete or conflicting data.

The work requires making many decisions concerning such things as the interpreting of considerable data, planning of the work, or refining the methods and techniques to be used.

Level 4-5   *325 points*

The work includes varied duties requiring many different and unrelated processes and methods applied to a broad range of activities or substantial depth of analysis, typically for an administrative or professional field.

Decisions regarding what needs to be done include major areas of uncertainty in approach, methodology, or interpretation and evaluation processes resulting from such elements as continuing changes in program, technological developments, unknown phenomena, or conflicting requirements.

The work requires originating new techniques, establishing criteria, or developing new information.

Level 4-6   *450 points*

The work consists of broad functions and processes of an administrative or professional field. Assignments are characterized by breadth and intensity of effort and involve several phases being pursued concurrently or sequentially with the support of others within or outside of the organization.

Decisions regarding what needs to be done include largely undefined issues and elements, requiring extensive probing and analysis to determine the nature and scope of the problems.

The work requires continuing efforts to establish concepts, theories, or programs, or to resolve unyielding problems.

Factor 5, Scope and Effect

Scope and Effect covers the relationship between the nature of the work, i.e., the purpose, breadth, and depth of the assignment, and the effect of work products or services both within and outside the organization.

In General Schedule occupations, effect measures such things as whether the work output facilitates the work of others, provides timely services of a personal nature, or impacts on the adequacy of research conclusions. The concept of effect alone does not provide sufficient information to properly understand and evaluate the impact of the position. The scope of the work completes the picture, allowing consistent evaluations. Only the effect of properly performed work is to be considered.

Level 5-1   *25 points*

The work involves the performance of specific, routine operations that include a few separate tasks or procedures.

The work product or service is required to facilitate the work of others; however, it has little impact beyond the immediate organizational unit or beyond the timely provision of limited services to others.

Level 5-2   *75 points*

The work involves the execution of specific rules, regulations, or procedures and typically comprises a complete segment of an assignment or project of broader scope.

The work product or service affects the accuracy, reliability, or acceptability of further processes or services.

Level 5-3   *150 points*

The work involves treating a variety of conventional problems, questions, or situations in conformance with established criteria.

The work product or service affects the design or operation of systems, programs, or equipment; the adequacy of such activities as field investigations, testing operations, or research conclusions; or the social, physical, and economic well being of persons.

Level 5-4   *225 points*

The work involves establishing criteria; formulating projects; assessing program effectiveness; or investigating or analyzing a variety of unusual conditions, problems, or questions.

The work product or service affects a wide range of agency activities, major activities of industrial concerns, or the operation of other agencies.

Level 5-5   *325 points*

The work involves isolating and defining unknown conditions, resolving critical problems, or developing new theories.

The work product or service affects the work of other experts, the development of major aspects of administrative or scientific programs or missions, or the well-being of substantial numbers of people.

Level 5-6   *450 points*

The work involves planning, developing, and carrying out vital administrative or scientific programs.

The programs are essential to the missions of the agency or affect large numbers of people on a long-term or continuing basis.

Factor 6, Personal Contacts

This factor includes face-to-face contacts and telephone and radio dialogue with persons not in the supervisory chain. (NOTE: Personal contacts with supervisors are covered under Factor 2, Supervisory Controls.) Levels described under this factor are based on what is required to make the initial contact, the difficulty of communicating with those contacted, and the setting in which the contact takes place (e.g., the degree to which the employee and those contacted recognize their relative roles and authorities). Above the lowest level, points should be credited under this factor only for contacts which are essential for successful performance of the work and which have a demonstrable impact on the difficulty and responsibility of the work performed.

The relationship of Factors 6 and 7 presumes that the same contacts will be evaluated for both factors. Therefore, use the personal contacts which serve as the basis for the level selected for Factor 7 as the basis for selecting a level for Factor 6.

Level 6-1   *10 points*

The personal contacts are with employees within the immediate organization, office, project, or work unit, and in related or support units;

AND/OR

The contacts are with members of the general public in very highly structured situations (e.g., the purpose of the contact and the question of with whom to deal are relatively clear). Typical of contacts at this level are purchases of admission tickets at a ticket window.

Level 6-2   *25 points*

The personal contacts are with employees in the same agency, but outside the immediate organization. People contacted generally are engaged in different functions, missions, and kinds of work, e.g., representatives from various levels within the agency such as headquarters, regional, district, or field offices or other operating offices in the immediate installations;

AND/OR

The contacts are with members of the general public, as individuals or groups, in a moderately structured setting (e.g., the contacts are generally established on a routine basis, usually at the employee's work place; the exact purpose of the contact may be unclear at first to one or more of the parties; and one or more of the parties may be uninformed concerning the role and authority of other participants). Typical of contacts at this level are those with persons seeking airline reservations or with job applicants at a job information center.

Level 6-3   *60 points*

The personal contacts are with individuals or groups from outside the employing agency in a moderately unstructured setting (e.g., the contacts are not established on a routine basis; the purpose and extent of each contact is different and the role and authority of each party is identified and developed during the course of the contact). Typical of contacts at this level are those with persons in their capacities as attorneys; contractors; or representatives of professional organizations, the news media, or public action groups.

Level 6-4   *11 0 points*

The personal contacts are with high-ranking officials from outside the employing agency at national or international levels in highly unstructured settings (e.g., contacts are characterized by problems such as: the officials may be relatively inaccessible; arrangements may have to be made for accompanying staff members; appointments may have to be made well in advance; each party may be very unclear as to the role and authority of the other; and each contact may be conducted under different ground rules). Typical of contacts at this level are those with members of Congress, leading representatives of foreign governments, presidents of large national or international firms, nationally recognized representatives of the news media, presidents of national unions, state governors, or mayors of large cities.

Factor 7, Purpose of Contacts

In General Schedule occupations, purpose of personal contacts ranges from factual exchanges of information to situations involving significant or controversial issues and differing viewpoints, goals, or objectives. The personal contacts which serve as the basis for the level selected for this factor must be the same as the contacts which are the basis for the level selected for Factor 6.

Level 7-1   *20 points*

The purpose is to obtain, clarify, or give facts or information regardless of the nature of those facts, i.e., the facts or information may range from easily understood to highly technical.

Level 7-2   *50 points*

The purpose is to plan, coordinate, or advise on work efforts or to resolve operating problems by influencing or motivating individuals or groups who are working toward mutual goals and who have basically cooperative attitudes.

Level 7-3   *120 points*

The purpose is to influence, motivate, interrogate, or control persons or groups. At this level the persons contacted may be fearful, skeptical, uncooperative, or dangerous. Therefore, the employee must be skillful in approaching the individual or group in order to obtain the desired effect, such as, gaining compliance with established policies and regulations by persuasion or negotiation, or gaining information by establishing rapport with a suspicious informant.

Level 7-4   *220 points*

The purpose is to justify, defend, negotiate, or settle matters involving significant or controversial issues. Work at this level usually involves active participation in conferences, meetings, hearings, or presentations involving problems or issues of considerable consequence or importance. The persons contacted typically have diverse viewpoints, goals, or objectives requiring the employee to achieve a common understanding of the problem and a satisfactory solution by convincing them, arriving at a compromise, or developing suitable alternatives.

Factor 8, Physical Demands

The "Physical Demands" factor covers the requirements and physical demands placed on the employee by the work assignment. This includes physical characteristics and abilities (e.g., specific agility and dexterity requirements) and the physical exertion involved in the work (e.g., climbing, lifting, pushing, balancing, stooping, kneeling, crouching, crawling, or reaching). To some extent the frequency or intensity of physical exertion must also be considered, e.g., a job requiring prolonged standing involves more physical exertion than a job requiring intermittent standing.

NOTE: Regulations governing pay for irregular or intermittent duty involving unusual physical hardship or hazard are in Chapter 550, Federal Personnel Manual.

Level 8-1   *5 points*

The work is sedentary. Typically, the employee may sit comfortably to do the work. However, there may be some walking; standing; bending; carrying of light items such as papers, books, small parts; driving an automobile, etc. No special physical demands are required to perform the work.

Level 8-2   *20 points*

The work requires some physical exertion such as long periods of standing; walking over rough, uneven, or rocky surfaces; recurring bending, crouching, stooping, stretching, reaching, or similar activities; recurring lifting of moderately heavy items such as typewriters and record boxes. The work may require specific, but common, physical characteristics and abilities such-as above-average agility and dexterity.

Level 8-3   *50 points*

The work requires considerable and strenuous physical exertion such as frequent climbing of tall ladders, lifting heavy objects over 50 pounds, crouching or crawling in restricted areas, and defending oneself or others against physical attack.

Factor 9, Work Environment

The "Work Environment" factor considers the risks and discomforts in the employee's physical surroundings or the nature of the work assigned and the safety regulations required. Although the use of safety precautions can practically eliminate a certain danger or discomfort, such situations typically place additional demands upon the employee in carrying out safety regulations and techniques.

NOTE: Regulations governing pay for irregular or intermittent duty involving unusual physical hardship or hazard are in Chapter 550, Federal Personnel Manual.

Level 9-1   *5 points*

The work environment involves everyday risks or discomforts which require normal safety precautions typical of such places as offices, meeting and training rooms, libraries, and residences or commercial vehicles, e.g., use of safe work practices with office equipment, avoidance of trips and falls, observance of fire regulations and traffic signals, etc. The work area is adequately lighted, heated, and ventilated.

Level 9-2   *20 points*

The work involves moderate risks or discomforts which require special safety precautions, e.g., working around moving parts, carts, or machines; with contagious diseases or irritant chemicals; etc. Employees may be required to use protective clothing or gear such as masks, gowns, coats, boots, goggles, gloves, or shields.

Level 9-3   *50 points*

The work environment involves high risks with exposure to potentially dangerous situations or unusual environmental stress which require a range of safety and other precautions, e.g., working at great heights under extreme outdoor weather conditions, subject to possible physical attack or mob conditions, or similar situations where conditions cannot be controlled.

Appendix B

Factor Level Descriptions, Occupational Standards

Factor Level Descriptions

This section defines the levels of the nine factors as they apply to the Secretary Series.

Factor 1: Knowledge Required by the Position

Factor 1 measures the nature and extent of information or facts which the secretary must understand to do acceptable work (e.g., steps, procedures, practices, rules, policies, principles, and concepts) and the nature and extent of the skills needed to apply those knowledges. To be used as a basis for selecting a level under this factor, a knowledge must be required and applied.

The same type of knowledge may be found at different point levels depending upon the extent of knowledge required. For this occupation the extent of knowledge required is related, in part, to the work situation in which the position is found.

Work situation refers to the complexity of the organization served (i.e., the immediate office in which the secretary works, and any subordinate offices) which affects the extent of office rules, procedures, operations, and priorities the secretary must apply to maintain a proper and smooth flow of work within the organization and between organizations.

Reprinted from *Position-Classification Stndard for Secretary Series GS-318,* TS-34, Office of Personnel Management, Occupational Standards Branch (U.S. Government Printing Office, Washington, D.C., January 1979), pp. 11-28.

This standard defines four basic types of knowledge required and three basic types of work situations.

Knowledge Type I—Assign Level 1-2 (200 points) regardless of work situation:

Knowledge of basic or commonly used rules, procedures, or operations which typically require some previous experience or training. For example, this level is appropriate for positions providing routine receptionist, typing, timekeeping, correspondence control, and filing services for an office. Some examples of knowledge commonly found at this level include:

— general knowledge of the office routine and procedures sufficient, for example, to receive and refer phone calls and visitors to staff members;

— knowledge of a range of common clerical practices and procedures sufficient, for example, to file material and obtain requested data from files;

— knowledge of grammar, spelling, punctuation, and required formats sufficient to recognize and correct such errors in correspondence and reports.

Knowledge Type II—Assign Level 1-3 (350 points) regardless of work situation:

In addition to Type I knowledges, positions at this level require knowledge of an extensive body of rules, procedures, or operations applied to clerical assignments, and knowledge of the organization and functions of the office in order to perform all of the procedural work of the office. This includes knowledge to carry out and coordinate, in a timely and effective manner, many different procedures, each of which might involve numerous steps, such as all of those needed to:

— obtain and monitor a full range of office support services such as printing, maintenance, and supply services. This requires knowledge of the procedures applicable to the control, authorization, securing, and justification of such services;

— request various types of personnel training actions or services;

— prepare a wide variety of recurring internal reports and documents from information obtained from the staff, files, and other sources.

This level may also include the knowledge required to advise clerks or secretaries in subordinate organizations of the appropriate procedures to use.

Knowledge Type III—Assign:

Level 1-3 (350 points) in combination with Work Situation A;
Level 1-4 (550 points) in combination with Work Situation B;
Level 1-5 (750 points) in combination with Work Situation C.

In addition to Type II knowledges, positions at this level require knowledge of the duties, priorities, commitments, policies, and program goals of the staff sufficient to perform non-routine assignments such as: independently noting and following-up on commitments made at meetings and conferences by staff members; shifting clerical staff in subordinate offices to take care of fluctuating workloads; or locating and summarizing information from files and documents when this requires recognizing which information is or is not relevant to the problem at hand.

At this level, the secretary is fully responsible for coordinating the work of the office with the work of other offices, and for recognizing the need for such coordination in various circumstances. This may include advising secretaries in subordinate organizations concerning such matters as the information to be provided by the subordinate organizations for use in conferences or reports.

Knowledge type IV—Assign:

Level 1-5 (750 points) in combination with Work Situation B;
Level 1-6 (950 points) in combination with Work Situation C.

(Note: Work Situation A does not permit application of Knowledge Type IV. Work Situation B rarely involves application of Knowledge Type IV.)

In addition to the knowledges and skills required at the lower levels, employees at this level must have as a continuing requirement:

— A basic foundation of administrative concepts, principles, and practices sufficient to perform independently such duties as eliminating conflict and duplication in extensive office procedures; determining when new procedures are needed; systematically studying and evaluating new office machines and recommending acceptance or rejection of their use; studying the clerical activities of the office and subordinate offices and recommending a specific restructuring of the way activities are carried out. The presence of these knowledges is shown by skills such as:

- skill in adapting policies or procedures to emergency situations and establishing practices or procedures to meet new situations; and
- skill in recognizing how and when certain policies, procedures, or guidelines will be confusing to others;

AND

— A comprehensive knowledge of the supervisor's policies and views on all significant matters affecting the organization that would enable the secretary to perform duties such as:
- developing material for supervisor's use in public speaking engagements. After ascertaining subject matter, develops background information and prepares outline for speech; submits outline to the supervisor or the supervisor's subordinate for final writing;
- briefing or advising staff members or persons outside the organization on supervisor's views on current issues facing the organization, e.g., supervisor feels that a proposed reorganization would increase the effectiveness of the program because it reduces some administrative burdens.

Work Situation A

These organizations are small and of limited complexity. Although the organization may include several subordinate sections or subgroups, the employee's supervisor directs the staff primarily through face-to-face meetings, and internal procedural and administrative controls are simple and informal. Within the supervisor's organization, there are few complicated problems of coordination requiring formal procedures and controls for adequate solution.

Work Situation B

The staff is organized into subordinate segments which may in turn be further divided. Direction of the staff is exercised through intermediate supervisors, and the subordinate groups differ from each other in such aspects as subject matter, functions, relationships with other organizations, and administrative requirements in ways that place demands upon the secretary that are significantly greater than those described Work Situation A. The presence of subordinate supervisors does not by itself mean that Work Situation B applies. (For example, a processing or records organization divided into several units, each performing identical work, would not meet the definition of Work Situation B.)

There is a system of formal internal procedures and administrative controls, and a formal production or progress reporting system. Coordination among subordinate units is sufficiently complex to require continuous attention.

Also at this level are organizations described as Work Situation A in terms of internal coordination when they have extensive responsibility for coordinating work outside of the organization. Such organizations may be placed in Work Situation B when the responsibility for coordination of work outside the organization requires procedures and administrative controls equivalent to those described above for this level.

Work Situation C

In addition to conditions described in Work Situation B, staffs of organizations in this situation are augmented by various staff specialists in such fields as personnel, management analysis, and administration. The organization is typically divided into three or more subordinate levels' with several organizations at each level. In addition, such organizations typically have one of the following (or equivalent) conditions which increase the knowledges required by the work:

1. The program is interlocked on a direct and continuing basis with the programs of other departments, agencies, or organizations, requiring constant attention to extensive formal clearances and procedural controls.
2. The program is directly affected by conditions outside the organization which vary widely in nature and intensity, and which frequently require organizational, procedural, or program adjustments in the supervisor's organization.
3. There is active and extensive public interest or participation in the program which results in the supervisor spending a substantial portion of the time in personal contacts such as those with citizens groups, professional societies, the media, educational groups, officials of State or local governments, or community leaders.

Factor 2: Supervisory Controls

This factor covers the nature and extent of direct or indirect controls exercised by the supervisor, the secretary's responsibility, and the review of completed work. Controls are exercised by the supervisor in the way assignments are made, instructions are given, priorities and deadlines are set, and objectives and boundaries are defined. The responsibility of the secretary depends upon the extent to which the supervisor expects the secretary to develop the sequence and timing of various aspects of the work, to modify or recommend modification of instructions, and to participate in establishing priorities and defining objectives. The degree of review of completed work depends upon the nature and extent of the review, e.g., close and detailed review of each phase of the assignment; detailed review of the finished assignment; spotcheck of finished work for accuracy; or review only for adherence to policy.

Supervisory controls over secretaries may be exercised by the head of the organization served and, in part, through direction provided by secretaries at higher echelons, or

---

The number of organizational echelons is not necessarily the controlling element in determining that the definition of Work Situation C is met. The presence of conditions such as augmenting staff specialists performing management analysis, administration, personnel management, and similar functions in the organizational structure, or the degree of managerial autonomy, may be more significant as criteria in certain situations.

occasionally by other staff members. For the sake of editorial simplicity, the term "supervisor" in the following factor level descriptions may refer to any one of these sources of supervision.

The level determination under this factor should be based on the same duties that served as the basis for the level determination under Factor 1.

Level 2-1   *25 points*

For both one-of-a-kind and routine tasks, the supervisor provides specific assignments that are accompanied by detailed and specific instructions.

The secretary works as instructed and consults with the supervisor as needed on all matters not specifically covered in the original instructions.

The work is closely controlled, either by the structured nature of the work itself or by the supervisor's review which may include checking progress or reviewing completed work for accuracy, adequacy, and adherence to instructions or procedures.

Level 2-2   *125 points*

The supervisor provides assignments, indicating generally what is to be done, quantity expected, deadlines, and priority of assignments. The supervisor provides additional, specific instructions for new, difficult, or unusual assignments including suggested work methods or advice on the availability of source materials.

The secretary uses initiative in carrying out the recurring work of the office independently, referring only problems and unfamiliar situations not covered by instructions to the supervisor for help. For example, the employee performs the following duties in accordance with established procedures:

— receives and refers phone calls; personally answers routine questions, such as those concerning standard office procedures;

— reviews outgoing correspondence for procedural, grammatical, and typographical accuracy;

— maintains control records on incoming correspondence and action documents; notifies staff member when due date is near to insure timely reply;

— searches for and obtains information in files on request.

The supervisor assures that finished work is accurate and in compliance with instructions and established procedures.

Level 2-3   *275 points*

The supervisor defines the overall objectives and priorities of the work in the office and assists the secretary with some special assignments. The secretary plans and carries out the work of the office and handles problems and deviations in accordance with established instructions, priorities, policies, commitments and program goals of the supervisor, and accepted practices in the occupation. For example, the secretary:

— receives telephone calls and visitors, screening those which can he handled without the supervisor's help. At this level, the secretary personally takes care of many matters and questions including answering substantive questions not requiring technical knowledge;

— keeps the supervisor's calendar, schedules appointments and conferences without prior approval, and sees that the supervisor is fully briefed on the matters to be considered before the scheduled meeting;

— receives requests for information concerning the organization's programs which can be assembled from the record based on a knowledge of the organization, advises when the material can he furnished, and prepares it personally or follows up to see that it is prepared by the staff within the specified time;

— based upon the information provided by the supervisor concerning the purpose of the conference and people to attend, makes necessary arrangements for conferences, including space, time, contacting people, and other matters; assembles background material for the supervisor; attends the meetings; and reports on the proceedings;

— receives and reads incoming correspondence and reports, screening those items which can be handled personally, forwarding the rest to the supervisor or the staff. Actions taken personally include:

- drafting replies to general inquiries not requiring a technical knowledge of the program; and
- relaying instructions to subordinate offices, collecting data, preparing reports for higher echelons, or otherwise acting on requests received concerning procedural or administrative requirements.

— Reads outgoing correspondence for procedural and grammatical accuracy, conformance with general policy, factual correctness, and adequacy of treatment; advises the writer of any deviations or inadequacies;

— Assists supervisor's subordinates in the procedural aspects of expediting the work of the office, including such matters as shifting clerical help in subordinate offices to take care of fluctuating workload; helping supervisor's subordinates to implement supervisor's instructions concerning procedures; explaining reporting requirements and arranging with subordinate officials for the collection and submission of data; and assembling data into general reports of the total work of the office;

— Signs routine correspondence of a nontechnical nature in the supervisor's name or in own name as secretary to the supervisor.

The methods used by the incumbent are almost never reviewed in detail. Completed work is evaluated for adequacy, appropriateness, and conformance to established policy. By its very nature, much of the work cannot be reviewed in detail.

Level 2-4   *450 points*

The supervisor sets the overall objectives of the work. The secretary and the supervisor, in consultation, develop the deadlines and the work to be done.

At this level, the secretary handles a wide variety of situations and conflicts requiring use of initiative to determine the approach to be taken or methods to use. This level is most likely to be found in organizations of such size and scope that many complex office problems arise which cannot be brought to the attention of the supervisor. For example:

— The secretary notes the commitments made by the supervisor during the meetings, informs the staff of those commitments, and arranges for the staff to implement them;

— When reviewing correspondence for the supervisor's signature, the secretary calls the writer's attention to any conflict reflected in the file or any departure from policies and attempts to resolve conflict before matter is presented to supervisor;

— In addition to arranging conferences as described at the lower level, the secretary at this level may decide to arrange for a subordinate of the supervisor to represent the organization at a conference. Such decisions would be based on a knowledge of the supervisor's views;

— The secretary drafts letters of acknowledgment, commendation, notification, etc., when the need arises; e.g., a secretary whose supervisor makes it a practice to acknowledge all commendatory remarks concerning the organization's program in periodicals, publications, or speeches, may review publications for such remarks and prepare appropriate letters for the supervisor's signature;

— The secretary insures that all official social obligations are met, arranges luncheons, issues invitations, insures proper seating arrangements, and insures that all details are covered, (e.g., that guest speakers are invited sufficiently in advance, and adequate provisions are made for protocol requirements). When necessary, the secretary settles accounts with the restaurant, club, or caterer;

— The secretary obtains information, the sources of which are not initially known and which may be available in only one or very few places. Subject matter is generally specialized and not a matter of widespread knowledge or is complicated because it is scattered in numerous documents or only in the memories of a few employees Frequently the information is obtained orally from a variety of sources. The employee organizes the material and draws attention to the most important parts;

— Using personal initiative, the employee observes need for administrative or procedural notices or instructions to the staff, prepares the necessary issuances, and presents them for signature or signs them personally. The employee devises and installs office procedures.

Completed work is reviewed only for overall effectiveness.

Factor 3: Guidelines

This factor covers the nature of guidelines and the judgment needed to apply them. Guides used in this occupation include, for example, reference materials such as dictionaries and style manuals, agency instructions concerning correspondence, and operating procedures of the organization served.

Individual jobs vary in the specificity, applicability, and availability of the guidelines for performance of assignments. Consequently, the constraints and judgmental demands placed upon secretaries also vary. For example, the existence of specific instructions, procedures, and policies may limit the opportunity of the secretary to make or recommend decisions or actions. However, secretaries may use considerable judgment in applying generally stated policies or objectives to individual cases.

Level 3-1   *25 points*

Specific, detailed guidelines cover the work, and the secretary works in strict adherence to them. Guidelines include dictionaries, style manuals, agency instructions governing time and leave, correspondence and handling of classified information, and operating procedures of the office. Assignments are made in a way that leaves no doubt as to which guide applies.

Level 3-2   *125 points*

Guidelines typically include dictionaries; style manuals; agency instructions concerning such matters as correspondence, or the handling of classified information; and operating policies of the supervisor or organization served.

The secretary locates and selects the appropriate guidelines, references, and procedures for application to specific cases, referring situations to which the existing guidelines cannot be applied or significant proposed deviations to the supervisor. The secretary may also determine which of established alternatives to use.

Level 3-3   *275 points*

Guidelines include a large body of unwritten policies, precedents, and practices which are not completely applicable to the work or are not specific and which deal with matters relating to judgment, efficiency, and relative priorities rather than with procedural concerns. For example, they may include decisions made by the supervisor in cases that are similar, but not completely analogous. The secretary applies and adapts guidelines, such as regulations or the supervisor's policies, to specific problems for which the guidelines are not clearly applicable .

Factor 4: Complexity

This factor covers the nature, number, variety, and intricacy of tasks, steps, processes, or methods in the work performed; the difficulty in identifying what needs to be done; and the difficulty and originality involved in performing the work.

Level 4-1   *25 points*

The work consists of a few clear-cut tasks. The secretary typically provides typing or stenographic services, maintains simple office files, sorts mail into a few categories, and refers phone calls and visitors to staff members.

There is little choice in deciding what needs to be done or when it should be done. Work is performed either as it arrives or in an order set by someone else.

Actions to be taken are readily discernible, e.g., phone calls are simply referred to the requested staff member; otherwise, the secretary requests assistance.

Level 4-2   *75 points*

The work consists of duties that involve various related steps, processes, or methods. In addition to duties as varied as those described at level 4-1, secretaries at this level perform a full range of procedural duties in support of the office, including such duties as requisitioning supplies, printing, or maintenance service; filling out various travel forms for staff members; arranging for meeting rooms; and preparing scheduled reports from information readily available in the tiles.

Decisions regarding what needs to be done involve various choices requiring the secretary to recognize the existence of and differences among clearly recognizable situations.

Actions to be taken or responses to be made differ in such things as the sources of information, the kind of transactions or entries, or other readily verifiable differences. Decisions at this level are based on a knowledge of the procedural requirements of the work coupled with an awareness of the specific functions and staff assignments of the office.

Level 4-3   *150 points*

The work includes various duties involving different and unrelated processes and methods. For example, in addition to duties described at levels 4-1 and 4-2, the secretary performs a number of duties comparable to the following:

— prepare one-of-a-kind reports from information in various documents when this requires reading correspondence and reports to identify relevant items, and when decisions are based on a familiarity with the issues involved and the relationships between the various types of information; and

— set up conferences requiring the planning and arranging of travel and hotel accommodations for conference participants when this is based on a knowledge of the schedules and commitments of the participants.

Decisions regarding what needs to be done, and how to accomplish them, are based on the secretary's knowledge of the duties, priorities, commitments, policies, and program goals of the supervisor and staff, and involve analysis of the subject, phase, or issues involved in each assignment. The chosen courses are selected from many alternatives.

Factor 5: Scope and Effect

Scope and Effect covers the relationship between the nature of the work, i.e., the purpose, breadth, and depth of the assignment, and the effect of work products or services both within and outside the organization.

In this occupation, effect measures such things as whether the work output facilitates the work of others, provides timely services of a personal nature, or affects the adequacy of systems of clerical and administrative support. Effect alone does not provide sufficient information to properly understand and evaluate the impact of the position. The scope of the work completes the picture, allowing consistent evaluations. Only the effect of properly performed work is to be considered.

Level 5-1   *25 points*

The purpose of the assignment is the performance of routine operations involving a few tasks or procedures. At this level, the secretary typically provides typing or stenography services, maintains time and leave records for the organization, maintains the office files, and refers phone calls and visitors to staff members. The work has little impact beyond the immediate organization.

Level 5-2   *75 points*

At this level, the purpose of the work is to carry out specific procedures. The work affects the accuracy and reliability of further processes.

Duties frequently appearing at this level include:
— serving as liaison between the supervisor and subordinate units;
— consolidating reports submitted by subordinate units;
— arranging meetings involving staff from outside the immediate office.

Level 5-3   *150 points*

Positions at this level serve offices that clearly and directly affect a wide range of agency activities, operations in other agencies, or a large segment of the public or business community. The secretary at this level modifies and devises methods and procedures that significantly and consistently affect the accomplishment of the mission of the office. The secretary identifies and resolves various problems and situations that affect the orderly and efficient flow of work in transactions with parties outside the organization.

Factor 6: Personal Contacts

This factor includes face-to-face telephone contacts with persons not in the supervisory chain. (NOTE: Personal contacts with supervisors are covered under Factor 2, Supervisory Controls.) Levels described under this factor are based on what is required to make the initial contact, the difficulty of communicating with those contacted, and the setting in which the contact takes place (e.g., the degree to which the employee and those contacted recognize their relative roles and authorities).

Above the lowest level, points should be credited under this factor only for contacts which are essential for successful performance of the work and which have a demonstrable impact on the difficulty and responsibility of the work performed.

The relationship between Factors 6 and 7 presumes that the same contacts will be evaluated for both factors. Therefore, use the personal contacts which serve as the basis for the level selected for Factor 7, as the basis for selecting a level for Factor 6.

Level 6-1   *10 points*

The personal contacts are with employees within the immediate organizations office, project or work unit, or in related units involved in functions similar to that of unit served; in support units, for example, a messenger service; or employees in other offices with whom contacts are so frequent and close that they are comparable to contacts made in the same office, e.g., the contacts a division office secretary might have with employees in the bureau office immediately over the division.

AND/OR

The contacts are with members of the general public in very highly structured situations (e.g., the purpose of the contact and the question of with whom to deal are relatively clear). A typical contact might include receiving visitors to the office who have appointments with other staff members.

Level 6-2   *25 points*

The personal contacts are with employees in the same agency, but outside the immediate organization. People contacted generally are engaged in different functions, missions, and kinds of work, e.g., representatives from various levels within the agency such as headquarters, regional, district, or field offices, or other operating offices in the immediate installation;

AND/OR

The contacts are with members of the general public, as individuals or groups, in a moderately structured setting (e.g., the contacts are generally established on a routine basis, usually at the employee's work place; the exact purpose of the contact is frequently unclear at first to one or more of the parties; and one or more of the parties may be uninformed concerning the role and authority of the other participants).

Contacts at this level are typically found in offices where visitors and callers contact the office, or are contacted by the office for several different purposes, to find several different kinds of information, or to receive one of several different services. Regardless of the purpose of the contact as described under Factor 7 (i.e., to exchange information or coordinate work), this requires the secretary to clarify first why the caller or visitor is in contact with the office.

Level 6-3   *60 points*

The personal contacts are with individuals or groups from outside the employing agency in a moderately unstructured setting, for example, the contacts are not established on a routine basis, requiring the secretary to identify and locate the appropriate person to contact or to apply significant skill and knowledge in determining to whom a telephone call or visitor should be directed; the purpose and extent of each contact is different, and the role and authority of each party is identified and developed during the course of the contact. Typical contacts at this level might include people in their capacities as attorneys, contractors, or representatives of professional organizations, the news media, or public action groups when the office deals with them on a variety of issues.

Level 6-4   *110 points*

The personal contacts are with high-ranking officials from outside the employing agency at national or international levels in highly unstructured settings (e.g., contacts are characterized by problems such as: the officials may be relatively inaccessible; arrangements may have to be made for accompanying staff members; appointments may have to be made well in advance; each party may be very unclear as to the role and authority of the other; and each contact may be conducted under different ground rules).

Typical contacts at this level might include Members of Congress. Leading representatives of foreign governments, presidents of large, national or international firms, nationally recognized representatives of the news media, presidents of national unions, State governors, or mayors of large cities.

Factor 7: Purpose of Contacts

In this occupation, purpose of personal contacts may range from factual exchanges of information to resolving problems affecting the efficient operation of the office. The personal contacts which serve as the basis for the level selected for this factor must be the same as the contacts which are the basis for the level selected for Factor 6.

Level 7-1   *20 points*

The purpose is to obtain, clarify, or give facts or information directly related to the work, for example, exchanging information when providing telephone and receptionist service and informing staff members of their leave balances.

Level 7-2   *50 points*

The purpose of the secretary's work is to plan, coordinate, or advise on work efforts or to resolve operating problems. Typical duties normally evaluated at this level include; insuring that reports and responses to correspondence are submitted by the staff on time and in the proper format, making travel arrangements, and scheduling conferences.

Factor 8: Physical Demands

This factor covers the requirements and physical demands placed on the employee by the work assignment. This includes physical characteristics and abilities (e.g., specific agility and dexterity requirements) and the physical exertion involved in the work (e.g., climbing, lifting, pushing, balancing, stooping, kneeling, crouching crawling, or reaching). To some extent the frequency or intensity of physical exertion must also be considered, e.g., a job requiring prolonged standing involves more physical exertion than a job requiring intermittent standing.

(Note: regulations governing pay for irregular or intermittent duty involving unusual physical hardship or hazard are in chapter 550, Federal Personnel Manual.)

Level 8-1   *5 points*

The work is sedentary. Typically, the employee may sit comfortably to do the work. However, there may be some walking; standing; bending; carrying of light items such as papers, books, small parts; driving an automobile, etc. No special physical demands are required to perform the work.

Factor 9, Work Environment

This factor considers the risks and discomforts in the employee's physical surroundings or the nature of the work assigned and the safety regulations required. Although the use of safety precautions can practically eliminate a certain danger or discomfort, such situations, typically place additional demands upon the employee in carrying out safety regulations and techniques.

NOTE: regulations governing pay for irregular or intermittent duty involving unusual physical hardship or hazard are in chapter 550, Federal Personnel manual.

Level 9-1   *5 points*

The work environment involves everyday risks or discomforts which require normal safety precautions typical of such places as offices, meeting and training rooms, libraries, and residences or commercial vehicles, e.g., use of safe work practices with office equipment, avoidance of trips and falls, observance of fire regulations and traffic signals, etc. The work area is adequately lighted, heated, and ventilated.

Secretary (Typing)

Duties

The incumbent serves as the principal clerical assistant in an office, performing various clerical tasks in accordance with established procedures.

— Maintains established office files and records. Obtains data requested by other employees in the unit.
— Receives and refers visitors and telephone calls. Distributes mail and messages, recording the receipt, suspense, and completion dates as appropriate.
— Types narrative and tabular material from rough draft or revised typed draft. Types memoranda, reports, viewgraphs, and similar material in accordance with established guidelines for review by originators. Corrects grammatical and spelling errors in drafts.

Factor 1. Knowledge required by the position

Level 1-2   *200 points*

Knowledge Type I

— Knowledge of the unit's organization and function sufficient to refer visitors, telephone calls, and mail by specific name request or request by a specific functional area.
— Knowledge of clerical procedures and forms used in the organization.
— Knowledge of spelling, punctuation, and syntax sufficient identify and correct grammatical errors and type materials in final form.
— Skill in operating typewriter. A qualified typist is required.

Appendix C

Occupational Standards for City of Olympia

CLERICAL SERIES

Series Coverage

This series covers a wide range of positions involving the performance and supervision of secretarial, clerical (e.g., including filing, record keeping, and answering the telephone and routing calls), typing, or similar activities. General office work not requiring specialized experience or training is always included in this series.

Occupational Information

This series covers a group of closely related occupations; consequently, there are a variety of different activities which are performed by the positions included. Areas of work which are found in these positions involve work related to

- secretarial support (e.g., serving as a personal assistant, performing a variety of clerical and administrative duties which are auxiliary to the work of the supervisor and which do not require a technical or professional knowledge of a specialized subject-matter area);
- general clerical and typing support;
- fiscal activities (e.g., bookkeeping or customer service);
- information gathering or processing (e.g., operating a keypunch and verifier to encode information concerning customer accounts; or reading water or electricity meters to record usage information); or
- store keeping (e.g., inventory control).

Factor-Level Descriptions

Factor-level descriptions are used to describe the characteristics of each job content factor used in the Factor Evaluation System of job classification. The factor-level descriptions used in the Primary Standard serve as a reference guide and are not written in terms of a specific occupation. Therefore, classification standards include factor-level descriptions which are more specific to an occupation (NOTE: Classification standards may be written for a narrowly defined occupation or for a group of related occupations). Classification standards do not change the essential meaning of Primary Standard factor-level descriptions; they merely redefine them in terms more descriptive of the occupation, allowing easier evaluation of the various job content factors.

Only those factor-levels that are applicable to positions in the occupation are described in the classification standard. For example, the highest levels of "Knowledge Required," as defined in the Primary Standard, would not exist in clerical work and, therefore, would not be described in the factor-levels for that occupation. If a position is encountered which does not fit well in any of the occupations for which classification standards exist, or if a position in an occupation appears to fall outside the established range of levels for a particular job content factor, then use of the Primary Standard is indicated and will permit evaluation.

Factor 1: Knowledge Required by the Job

This factor measures the nature and extent of information or facts which the worker must understand to do acceptable work (e.g., steps, procedures, practices, rules, policies, theories, principles, and concepts) and the nature and extent of the skills needed to apply those knowledges. To be used as a basis for selecting a level under this factor, a knowledge must be required and applied.

Level 1-2   *200 points*

Positions at this level typically require a basic knowledge of the departments for, or through which, services are being provided; this includes knowledge of departmental

- functions and activities;
- budgetary process (to compile relevant information);
- operating procedures, rules, and policies; and filing and record keeping systems.

In addition, some positions require knowledge specific to the department or to the position such as a basic knowledge of

- routes and procedures followed in reading water and electricity meters;
- accounts payable procedures to post items to accounts;
- terminology (e.g., police, fire);
- facilities maintained or operated (e.g., water plant);
- equipment or materials utilized by the department (e.g., heavy equipment used in construction to identify type of equipment in communicating with others; or parts used in electrical work); or
- City or State codes or ordinances applicable to departmental functions or activities (e.g., State regulations concerning vehicle registration; or City ordinances concerning garbage collection) to either comply with these laws or to communicate their requirements to others.

Many positions at this level also require a working knowledge of City Personnel Rules and Regulations to advise others and to aid departmental compliance.

These knowledges enable the worker to provide a number of services such as maintaining and updating files, records, and accounts; routing information or problems to proper personnel or departments; acting as a communication link between persons within the immediate organizational unit, other employees of the City, and the general public or those consuming services provided by the department; or explaining interpretations concerning departmental policy or procedures.

The worker typically demonstrates skill (varying in degree and number according to importance in the individual position) in

- operating typewriters, Dictaphones, adding machines, or copiers to type memoranda and reports and to perform related clerical duties;
- operating two-way radios to communicate with work crews;
- operating a switchboard to answer and route incoming telephone calls;
- operating a keypunch and verifier;
- using simple hand tools to expose and clean water meter faces so they can be read; or
- communicating with others, both in person and on the telephone, primarily to exchange information.

Level 1-3   *350 points*

In addition to the knowledges found at the next lowest level, positions at this level typically require

- greater knowledge of City organization, functions, and activities to coordinate work with other departments on a frequent basis and to refer nonstandard problems to proper personnel or departments; and/or
- greater knowledge of departmental record keeping and filing systems to develop new systems and to maintain and update records and files which are greater in number and/or are more complex than those maintained in positions at the next lowest level (e.g., court docket; City personnel files; or fire run reports).

Some positions require knowledge specific to the department or to the position such as

- knowledge of municipal bookkeeping, accounting, and bond accounting practices and City, State, and Federal laws and ordinances concerning municipal financial activities to maintain City financial accounts and to provide other bookkeeping services; or
- knowledge of City Code as it regulates electrical, heating, building, and plumbing construction, zoning, and the issuance of Business Licenses to provide information or explain interpretations of these Codes.

In addition to the skills found at the next lowest level, positions at this level typically require skill, achieved through considerable training and experience, in performing one or more of the following activities including

- composing correspondence for department head which may be sent out without review;
- operating a duplicating machine to provide mimeograph services for all departments;
- taking shorthand dictation of correspondence or notes of meetings;
- making appointments and maintaining appointment calendar for department head or other personnel; or
- directing the work of less skilled personnel, primarily clerk-typists.

Level 1-4   *550 points*

Positions at this level typically require
- a basic knowledge of administrative concepts, principles, and practices sufficient to enable the worker to recognize the relationships between a specific
  problem or requirement and similar existing or potential problems or requirements; and
- a thorough knowledge of the supervisor's policies and views sufficient to enable the worker to decide how the supervisor would want a problem handled
  when a decision must be made by the worker without assistance or specific
  guidelines provided by the supervisor.

The worker demonstrates a high degree of skill in communicating with others to
function as spokesman for the supervisor or for the organizational unit (e.g., preparing
news releases for media publication).

These knowledges usually require extended training or experience to perform both
standard and nonstandard assignments and to resolve a wide range of problems.

Factor 2: Supervisory Controls

- This factor covers the nature and extent of direct or indirect controls exercised by the supervisor, the worker's responsibility, and the review of completed work.
- Controls are exercised by the supervisor in the way assignments are made,
  instructions are given to the worker, priorities and deadlines are set, and objectives and boundaries are defined.
- The worker's responsibility depends on the extent to which the worker is expected to develop the sequence and timing of various aspects of the work, to
  modify or recommend modification of instructions and to participate in establishing priorities and defining objectives.
- The review of completed work depends upon the nature and extent of the
  review, e.g., close and detailed review of each phase of the assignment; detailed review of the finished assignment; spot-check of finished work for accuracy; or review only for adherence to policy.

Level 2-1   *25 points*

Routine assignments are typically highly structured (e.g., answering and routing incoming telephone calls; or issuing parts from inventory upon receipt of requisition); the
supervisor provides detailed and specific instructions covering all important requirements of the assignment.

The employee works as instructed, referring to the supervisor all problems not specifically covered by the instructions. The supervisor is readily available to advise on
any problems encountered in the work assignment.

The work is closely reviewed. This review typically includes spot-checking work in
progress as well as reviewing completed work. Indirect review may occur through comments received by those for whom services are provided. The work is reviewed for
accuracy and compliance with instructions and established procedures.

Level 2-2   *125 points*

The supervisor gives general instructions on the priority and deadline of the assignment, often suggesting work methods, source materials, or persons to contact (e.g.,
format for a report; or files in which desired information can be found). Work activity

may also be initiated in response to requests from other employees or the general public (e.g., reservations of City facilities by citizens; complaints about utility services by consumers; or requests for typing services by departmental personnel).These requests, however, are usually covered by standing instructions provided by the supervisor.

The employee typically works independently and uses initiative in carrying out recurring assignments. The supervisor provides additional instructions concerning work in progress only when the work assignment is unusual and presents unfamiliar situations or calls for the employee to make significant deviations from instructions or established procedures.

Work is normally reviewed upon completion for accuracy and compliance with established procedures or instructions (e.g., accuracy in adding a column of figures; compliance with established procedures for processing records or dealing with the general public; or correct format to be used in a report). The work may also be spot-checked on an infrequent basis.

Level 2-3   *275 points*

The supervisor provides assignments by indicating objectives, priorities, and deadlines and assists the employee with unusual assignments.

The employee plans and carries out the successive steps in the assignment and handles most of the problems and deviations according to instructions, established procedures, or previous experience. Secretarial positions at this level may involve making physical arrangements (e.g., reservations) for conferences; drafting replies to general inquiries; and signing routine correspondence in the supervisor's name or in own name as secretary to the supervisor.

The work is reviewed infrequently; in some positions, review is conducted only on an annual basis. The work is reviewed for quality of results achieved, accuracy, propriety, and compliance with City policies.

Factor 3: Guidelines

This factor covers the nature of guidelines and the judgment needed to apply them. Guides used include, for example, desk manuals, established procedures and policies, traditional practices, City Personnel Rules and Regulations, applicable City ordinances, and reference materials such as dictionaries.

Individual jobs in different occupations vary in the specificity, applicability, and availability of the guidelines for performance of assignments. Consequently, the constraints and judgmental demands placed upon employees also vary. For example, the existence of specific instructions, procedures, and policies may limit the opportunity of the employee to make or recommend decisions or actions. However, in the absence of procedures or under broadly stated objectives, employees in some occupations may use considerable judgment in researching literature or developing new methods.

Guidelines should not be confused with the knowledges described under Factor 1, Knowledge Required by the Position. Guidelines either provide reference data or impose certain constraints on the use of knowledges.

Level 3-1   *25 points*

Specific and detailed guidelines are well established, readily available, and require little judgment to use. Many of these guidelines are oral (e.g., customer service procedures; departmental practices; or standing instructions) but also include written customer billing instructions; meter route books; or parts requisitions and invoices.

Level 3-2 *125 points*

Guidelines may include dictionaries, or style manuals; City Personnel Rules and Regulations; instructions concerning the handling of confidential information; municipal court procedures; procedures for format, preparation, and arrangement of correspondence; or departmental or City policies or Codes as they relate to departmental activities. The employee uses judgment in locating, selecting, and applying the appropriate guideline, procedure, or reference. The employee typically is required to select which of established alternatives to use. Situations involving significant proposed deviations from established guidelines or the absence of adequate guidelines are referred to the supervisor.

Level 3-3 *275 points*

Guidelines are available but are not completely applicable to the work. At this level, the employee uses judgment in adapting or making minor modifications in guidelines for application to specific situations. For example, the employee may modify bill collecting procedures for individual customers when extenuating circumstances exist. The employee may recommend changes in guidelines as a result of analyzing their use.

Factor 4: Complexity

This factor covers the nature, number, variety, and intricacy of tasks, steps, processes, methods, or activities in the work performed; and the degree to which the employee must vary the work, discern interrelationships and deviations, or develop new techniques, criteria, or information.

Level 4-1 *25 points*

The work consists of relatively few tasks which are clear-cut, largely repetitive, and directly related. These tasks include following a prescribed route, reading meters, and recording readings; answering and routing incoming telephone calls; or filling parts requisition orders. Actions to be taken or responses to be made are readily discernible.

Level 4-2 *75 points*

The work consists of duties involving several related sequential steps, processes, and methods (e.g., compiling information and formatting and preparing reports; receiving a number of financial account forms, verifying completeness or accuracy of information, and posting information to accounts; or preparing correspondence, maintaining departmental files, and answering incoming telephone calls). These duties require consideration of factors and conditions that are usually apparent, applicable, and readily verified. Actions to be taken or responses to be made vary in such things as sources of information, kinds of transactions or entries, or other differences of a factual nature.

Level 4-3 *150 points*

The work consists of various duties involving different processes or methods such as maintaining accounting ledgers, preparing City tax returns, and maintaining a variety of City bank accounts; or coordinating the work in more than one unrelated work area. Factors to be considered differ with the subject, phase, or issues involved in each assignment. The work involves conditions or elements which must be identified to discern interrelationships and deviations (e.g., how one account relates to another; or sources of error in account balances).

Factor 5: Scope and Effect

This factor measures the relationship between the nature of the work, i.e., the purpose, breadth, and depth of the assignments, and the effect of work products or services both within and outside the organization.

Effect measures such things as whether the work output facilitates the work of others, provides timely services of a limited nature, or impacts on major City programs. The concept of effect alone does not provide sufficient information to properly understand and evaluate the impact of the position. The scope of the work completes the picture, allowing consistent evaluations. Only the effect of properly performed work is to be considered.

Level 5-1   *25 points*

At this level, the purpose of the work is to perform specific, routine operations that include relatively few tasks or procedures (e.g., typing interdepartmental memoranda; maintaining relatively few and simple files and records; or issuing parts and materials from inventory).

The work product or service is required to facilitate the work of others; however, it has little impact beyond the immediate organizational unit or beyond the timely provision of limited services such as providing work materials.

Level 5-2   *75 points*

At this level, the purpose of the work is to carry out a number of specific procedures which typically comprise a complete segment of an assignment or project of broader scope. Examples of duties frequently appearing at this level include
- transcribing or composing and typing all correspondence and reports for a department and all interdepartmental forms;
- compiling departmental budget information to assist in budget report preparation;
- developing and maintaining a number of department function record and file systems (e.g., personnel files; or fire run records); or
- scheduling appointments and maintaining appointment calendar for department head.

The work product or service affects the reliability or acceptability of further processes or services (e.g., further processing of job applicants; acceptability of budget report; or the efficient retrieval of information from files).

Level 5-3   *150 points*

At this level, the purpose of the work is to handle a variety of conventional problems, questions, or situations in conformance with established criteria such as would be involved in maintaining City financial records and bank account balances in accordance with specific bookkeeping practices and laws regulating municipal financial activities; or coordinating and supervising the activities of more than one unrelated work unit.

The work product or service typically affects the operation of systems (e.g., City financial accounting system or meter reading operations) or programs and may impact on the costs associated with these systems or programs.

Factor 6: Personal Contacts

This factor includes the face-to-face contacts and telephone and radio dialogue with persons not in the supervisory chain. (NOTE: Personal contacts with supervisors are covered under Factor 2, Supervisory Controls; personal contacts with subordinates are covered under Factor 10, Supervisory Accountability*). Levels described under this factor are based on what is required to make the initial contact, the difficulty of communicating with those contacted, and the setting in which the contact takes place (e.g., the degree to which the employee and those contacted recognize their relative roles and authority).

Above the lowest level, points should be credited under this factor only for contacts which are essential for the successful performance of the work and which have a demonstrable impact on the difficulty and responsibility of the work performed.

The relationship of Factors 6 and 7 presumes that the same contacts will be evaluated for both factors. Therefore, use the personal contacts which serve as the basis for the level selected for Factor 7 as the basis for selecting a level for Factor 6.

Level 6-1   *10 points*

Personal contacts are primarily with co-workers or other employees within the immediate organizational unit. Some contact is made with employees of the City in other (usually related) departments. Any personal contact made outside the scope of City government is in a highly structured situation (e.g., the purpose of the contact and the question of with whom to deal are relatively clear).

Level 6-2   *25 points*

Personal contacts are typically with employees within the City, but outside the immediate organizational unit. These employees are often involved in different kinds of work (e.g., elected City officials). Contacts may be with employees of organizations outside City government involved in unrelated work (e.g., suppliers of equipment, parts, or materials used by the department). Contacts may also be with the general public or persons consuming services which are provided by the City such as electricity, water, or sewage disposal; these contacts typically take place in moderately structured situations (e.g., the contacts are generally established on a routine basis, usually at the employee's work place; the exact purpose of the contact may be unclear at first to one or more of the parties; and one or more of the parties may be uninformed concerning the role and authority of other participants).

The extent that these three basic types of personal contacts occur will vary according to the nature and function of the individual position.

Factor 7: Purpose of Contacts

Purposes of personal contacts range from factual exchanges of information to situations involving significant or controversial issues and differing viewpoints, goals, or objectives. The personal contacts which serve as the basis for the level selected for this factor must be the same as the contacts which are the basis for the level selected for Factor 6.

Level 7-1   *20 points*

Contacts are primarily for the purpose of providing services or obtaining, clarifying, or giving facts or information directly related to the work. Duties normally evaluated at this level include providing telephone and receptionist services, advising departmental employees of personnel or departmental rules and regulations, and clarifying correspondence to be typed.

Level 7-2   *50 points*

Contacts are primarily for the purpose of planning, coordinating, or advising on work

---

* Factor 10, Supervisory Accountability, was added by the authors to the nine FES Factors for the Olympia project. See Chapter 8 for a discussion of this Factor.

efforts; or to resolve operating problems. Duties normally evaluated at this level include ensuring that reports and responses to correspondence are submitted by other personnel on time and in the proper format, making travel arrangements, and scheduling conferences.

Factor 8: Physical Demands

This factor covers the requirements and physical demands placed on the employee by the work assignment. This includes physical characteristics and abilities (e.g., specific agility and dexterity requirements) and the physical exertion involved in the work (e.g., climbing, lifting, pushing, balancing, stooping, kneeling, crouching, crawling, or reaching). To some extent, the frequency or intensity of physical exertion must also be considered, e.g., a job requiring prolonged standing involves more physical exertion than a job requiring intermittent standing.

Level 8-1   *5 points*

The work is primarily sedentary (e.g., typing); the employee typically sits to do the work. However, there may be some walking, bending, or carrying of light objects.

Level 8-2   *20 points*

The work requires some physical exertion such as prolonged walking or standing (e.g., walking a route to read water meters), bending, crouching, or stooping. The employee frequently lifts light objects weighing under 25 pounds and occasionally lifts objects weighing up to 50 pounds (e.g., lifting and carrying automotive parts).

Factor 9: Work Environment

This factor considers the risks and discomforts in the employee's physical surroundings or the nature of the work assigned and the safety regulations required. Although the use of safety precautions can practically eliminate a certain danger or discomfort, such situations typically place additional demands upon the employee in carrying out safety regulations and techniques.

Level 9-1   *5 points*

The work is normally performed in an office or similar setting (e.g., stockroom) which is adequately lighted, heated, and ventilated.

Level 9-2   *20 points*

The work involves regular and recurring exposure to moderate discomforts and risks such as machinery and its moving parts, noise, or toxic fumes. The work may be performed outdoors, sometimes in inclement weather.

INSPECTION SERIES

Series Coverage

This series covers positions involving the supervision and performance of inspection activities. While these inspections are primarily of buildings or other structures, positions involving the general inspection of premises for safety conditions and of business activity for possession of proper permits and licenses are also classified in this series.

When positions involve duties not related to the general field of inspection (e.g., arson investigation), the predominance of inspection activities will allow evaluation under this series; however, care must be taken to consider all activities performed by the employee in order to correctly evaluate the position.

Occupational Information

Positions included in this series primarily involve activities designed to ensure compliance with certain laws established by the City Code of Ordinances (either through direct inclusion in the Code or adopted by reference). Inspection activities typically fall into one of the following three broad categories:

- safety requirements (e.g., building design, construction, and maintenance including all plumbing, electrical and heating and air-conditioning systems; fire prevention; or containment or elimination of hazardous materials or conditions);
- zoning restrictions (e.g., use of property; special requirements of zoning classification); or
- business activity restrictions (e.g., specific proscriptions or limitations; license or permit requirements; or excise tax requirements).

These duties are typically carried out through on-site inspections; these inspections may be programmed (e.g., periodic inspections of industrial and commercial sites), part of a larger project (e.g., neighborhood housing rehabilitation), or may result from specific complaints. In addition, permit or license requirements are frequently used to aid identification of work to be done (e.g., inspection of building plans prior to issuance of building permit) or as a check on previous and/or continuing compliance with established ordinances (e.g., business license requirements).

Depending on the nature and complexity of the subject area, some positions may require specialized knowledges and skills (e.g., knowledge of plumbing to determine the adequacy of proposed or existing facilities). While there may be substantial differences in the duties performed, the commonalty of the inspection function allows evaluation of these specialized positions under this series.

Factor-Level Descriptions

Factor-level descriptions are used to describe the characteristics of each job content factor used in the Factor Evaluation System of job classification. The factor-level descriptions used in the Primary Standard serve as a reference guide and are not written in terms of a specific occupation. Therefore, classification standards include factor-level descriptions which are more specific to an occupation (NOTE: Classification standards may be written for a narrowly defined occupation or for a group of related occupations). Classification standards do not change the essential meaning of Primary Standard factor-level descriptions; they merely redefine them in terms more descriptive of the occupation, allowing easier evaluation of the various job content factors.

Only those factor-levels that are applicable to positions in the occupation are described in the classification standard. For example, the highest levels of "Knowledge Required," as defined in the Primary Standard, would not exist in clerical work and, therefore, would not be described in the factor-levels for that occupation. If a position is encountered which does not fit well in any of the occupations for which classification standards exist, or if a position in an occupation appears to fall outside the established range of levels for a particular job content factor, then use of the Primary Standard is indicated and will permit evaluation.

Factor 1: Knowledge Required by the Position

This factor measures the nature and extent of information or acts which the worker must understand to do acceptable work (e.g., steps, procedures, practices, rules, policies, theories, principles, and concepts) and the nature and extent of the skills needed to apply those knowledges. This factor includes the knowledges and skills required to perform supervisory functions (e.g., training and performance appraisal); this differs from the responsibility placed on the employee for the activities of subordinates (covered in Factor 10, Supervisory Accountability). To be used as a basis for selecting a level under this factor, a knowledge must be required and applied.

Level 1-3   *50 points*

Positions at this level typically require a thorough knowledge of related inspection practices, procedures, and techniques and local, state, or federal laws, codes, ordinances, or programs regulating such areas as

- building (e.g., residential dwellings) rehabilitation to enforce minimum Housing Code through on-site inspection; or
- business license, permit, or excise tax requirements to ensure compliance by the City business community and to ensure prompt and accurate payment of all related fees.

The employee is required to have a thorough knowledge of the procedures to be followed in dealing with violators which may include preparing cases for prosecution in court.

The employee demonstrates skill in communicating and interacting with others (e.g., residential or commercial property owners) to influence or motivate them to comply with established regulations. The employee may also demonstrate skill in determining actions or improvements necessary for compliance with regulations (e.g., housing repairs such as rewiring) and the estimated cost of these improvements or actions.

These knowledges and skills typically require a considerable amount of training and experience to perform the full range of standard assignments in the field of work.

Level 1-4   *50 points*

Positions at this level typically require an extensive knowledge of building inspection procedures, practices, techniques, or operations used in, and the relevant laws, ordinances, or codes concerning the inspection of residential, commercial, and industrial installations, both old and under construction, to

- ensure compliance with adopted City Code regulating structural, plumbing, electrical, and heating and air-conditioning specifications;
- locate fire hazards and assist property owners in eliminating or minimizing these hazards and to ensure compliance with City Code concerning fire hazards; or
- coordinate housing rehabilitation inspection programs of limited scope, provide technical assistance and training to subordinate inspectors, and participate in enforcing Minimum housing Code requirements.

In some positions, the employee is also required to have a thorough knowledge of a building trade (e.g., electrical, plumbing, or carpentry) or other extensive body of information in order to

- prepare and administer professional examinations in skilled trades (e.g., Master electrician or Master Plumber examinations); or
- inspect structures after fire or other damage to determine what repair or

other action is necessary to meet code requirements (e.g., City Building Code; or Fire Prevention Code) or to determine the cause of fires of nonsuspicious origin.

The employee typically demonstrates a high degree of skill in

- applying inspection related knowledges to detect deficiencies, locate defects or fire hazards, or determine the cause of fires;
- using tools and equipment such as measuring and calibration devices, heat and flow gauges, and velocity meters to perform various inspection activities (e.g., checking the load capacity of an electrical circuit);
- communicating with others to motivate and influence persons to comply with regulatory requirements or to perform supervisory functions such as training, performance appraisal, or quality control; or
- interpreting code requirements in specific situations.

These knowledges and skills typically require extended training and experience to perform both standard and nonstandard assignments and to solve a wide range of problems.

Level 1-5   *750 points*

Positions at this level typically require a practical knowledge of the concepts and methodology in the inspections field such as knowledge of the aims and objectives of establishing building, housing, zoning, or fire safety standards or ordinances and methods by which compliance with such standards and ordinances can be achieved. The employee typically demonstrates a high degree of skill in

- performing nonstandard inspections, those which are unusually complex in nature, or require the use of complicated, specialized techniques;
- coordinating full-scale inspections programs typically comprising a specialty area; or
- communicating with others to motivate and influence persons who may be hostile and uncooperative to comply with regulatory requirements, to interrogate witnesses or suspects in fire inspection, or to perform supervisory functions such as training, performance appraisal, or quality control.

Factor 2: Supervisory Controls

- This factor covers the nature and extent of direct or indirect controls exercised by the supervisor, the worker's responsibility, and the review of completed work.
- Controls are exercised by the supervisor in the way assignments are made, instructions are given to the worker, priorities and deadlines are set, and objectives and boundaries are defined.
- The worker's responsibility depends on the extent to which the worker is expected to develop the sequence and timing of various aspects of the work, to modify or recommend modification of instructions, and to participate in establishing priorities and defining objectives.
- The review of completed work depends upon the nature and extent of the review, e.g., close and detailed review of each phase of the assignment; detailed review of the finished assignment; spot-check of finished work for accuracy; or review only for adherence to policy.

Level 2-2   *125 Points*

The supervisor typically provides continuing or individual assignments by indicating generally what is to be done (e.g., list of buildings or a fire scene to be inspected).

The supervisor may also suggest work methods or persons to contact in specific situations.

The employee uses initiative in carrying out recurring assignments independently according to established procedures and previous experience and may develop the sequencing of tasks within narrow guidelines (e.g., determining order in which to inspect a number of buildings or check various items in one inspection). Deviations, problems and unfamiliar situations not covered by instructions or precedent (e.g., unusually hostile persons or borderline violations) are referred to the supervisor for assistance.

The work is typically spot-checked to ensure proper inspections procedures or specific instructions are followed.

Level 2-3   *275 Points*

The supervisor provides assignments by indicating objectives, priorities, and deadlines (e.g., time requirements to inspect a particular building or group of buildings). The employee may also develop assignments on own initiative (e.g., checking various areas of the City for unlicensed business activity).

The employee plans and carries out the successive steps in the assignment and handles most of the problems and deviations encountered according to instructions, established procedures, or previous experience. At this level the employee seldom has to consult with the supervisor after the assignment is made except for technical assistance.

Completed work is reviewed infrequently. At this level, review is for the purpose of evaluating technical soundness, appropriateness of action taken, and conformity to established departmental or City policies.

Level 2-4   *450 points*

The supervisor sets the overall objectives and resources available (e.g., defining inspection program objectives and setting number of subordinates or amount of time available). The employee and supervisor, in consultation, develop the deadlines, priorities, projects, and work to be done.

At this level the employee, having developed expertise in the specialty inspections area, is responsible for planning and carrying out the assignment; resolving most of the conflicts which arise (e.g., persons not willing to comply with regulations); coordinating the work of or with others as necessary; and interpreting relevant City Codes or departmental policies in terms of established objectives. The employee may determine the approach to be taken or methodology to be used (e.g., area of inspection given greater attention; depth, intensity, or frequency of inspection). The employee keeps the supervisor informed of progress, potentially controversial matters, or significant deviations made from established procedures or regulations (e.g., determining that electrical wiring, while not up to Code specification, is safe and will not require rework).

Completed work is reviewed only from an overall standpoint in terms of effectiveness in meeting requirements or expected results or in terms of organizational objectives (e.g., standards of safety) or compatibility with other work (e.g., inspections of various facilities owned, operated, or controlled by the same person).

Factor 3: Guidelines

This factor covers the nature of guidelines and the judgment needed to apply them. Guides used include, for example, desk manuals; City Code regulating building, plumbing, heating, air-conditioning, and wiring specifications and standards; Minimum Housing Code; trade manuals; technical bulletins; National Fire Prevention Code; traditional practices; and established procedures and policies.

Individual jobs in different occupations vary in the specificity, applicability, and availability of the guidelines for performance of assignments.

Consequently, the constraints and judgmental demands placed upon employees also vary. For example, the existence of specific instruction, procedures, and policies may limit the opportunity of the employee to make or recommend decisions or actions. However, in the absence of procedures or under broadly stated objectives, employees in some occupations may use considerable judgment in researching literature or developing new methods.

Guidelines should not be confused with the knowledges described under Factor 1, Knowledge Required by the Position. Guidelines either provide reference data or impose certain constraints on the use of knowledges.

Level 3-2   *125 points*

The employee is provided a number of written and oral guidelines, most of which are directly applicable. Guidelines which may be used by the employee include City Code establishing building, plumbing, electrical wiring, heating, and air-conditioning standards and construction permit requirements; Minimum Housing Code; departmental procedures and policies; commonly used inspection practices; and previous experience. Judgment is used in locating and selecting the most appropriate guidelines and alternative courses of action. The employee may make minor deviations to adapt guidelines to specific situations; however, significant proposed deviations are referred to the supervisor.

Level 3-3   *275 points*

Guidelines provided the employee, in addition to those at Level 3-2, may include City and State Codes establishing business license and permit requirements; HUD Rehabilitation Financing Handbook; National Fire Prevention Association Code; various fire prevention manuals; and national or regional Codes regulating building standards. At this level, guidelines may not be completely applicable to the problems encountered or may have gaps in specificity. The employee is often required to interpret and adapt these guidelines with reference to the specific situation or assignment (e.g., allowing wiring which does not meet code requirements to remain when the employee determines that the work product is, nonetheless, safe; or allowing building materials just introduced into the market and not formally approved for use to be used in construction when the employee determines their use to be safe). In some positions, the employee may recommend specific changes in departmental procedures, policies, or City Code (e.g., modifying National Electrical Code for use in City Code, taking into account conditions such as climate which are specific to the City).

Factor 4: Complexity

This factor covers the nature, number, variety, and intricacy of tasks, steps, processes, methods, or activities in the work performed; and the degree to which the employee must vary the work, discern interrelationships and deviations, or develop new techniques, criteria, or information

Level 4-2   *75 points*

Positions at this level require performance of several related duties involving consideration of choices of appropriate procedures or actions to be taken in a variety of situations (e.g., issuing business licenses and permits, maintaining records of their issuance, and inspecting business premises or investigating complaints of unlicensed business activity to ensure compliance with City Code regulating business activity). Assignments usually have many similar elements limiting the need to use judgment in deciding what needs to be done. Problem analysis may be required (e.g., determining the best way to influence uncooperative persons to comply with regulatory requirements, using prosecution under the law as a last resort).

Level 4-3   *50 points*

Positions at this level require performance of several duties involving different and unrelated processes or methods (e.g., conducting fire prevention inspections, public awareness programs, and investigating the cause of both routine and suspicious-origin fires). There is a substantial amount of problem analysis involved which requires consideration of existing conditions and problem elements to discern interrelationships (e.g., analysis of building construction blueprints to determine acceptability of wiring, plumbing, heating and air-conditioning, or other system specifications). The employee is often required to improvise in order to meet deadlines or other constraints.

Factor 5: Scope and Effect

This factor measures the relationship between the nature of the work, i.e., the purpose, breadth, and depth of the assignments, and the effect of work products or services both within and outside the organization.

Effect measures such things as whether the work output facilitates the work of others, provides timely services of a limited nature, or impacts on major City programs. The concept of effect alone does not provide sufficient information to properly understand and evaluate the impact of the position. The scope of the work completes the picture, allowing consistent evaluations. Only the effect of properly performed work is to be considered.

Level 5-3   *150 points*

At this level, the purpose of the work is to handle a variety of conventional problems, questions, or situations in conformance with established criteria. examples include inspecting construction projects for compliance with City Code regulating electrical wiring, plumbing, and other standards of safety or investigating the cause of fires.

The work product or service typically affects the operation of inspection programs, the achievement of program objectives, and the physical and economic well-being of persons (e.g., offsetting the safety of a construction project against the cost of requiring rework).

Level 5-4   *225 points*

The work involves establishing criteria, formulating inspection projects, assessing inspection program effectiveness, or investigating or analyzing a variety of unusual conditions, problems, or questions. At this level, the employee is often required to provide technical assistance to other inspectors encountering problems of unusual difficulty.

The work product or service affects a wide range of departmental activities, the safety of major construction projects, or the operation of other departments. The work also has a major impact on the cost of various building projects through the formulation of safety standard enforcement policy.

Factor 6: Personal Contacts

This factor includes the face-to-face contacts and telephone and radio dialogue with persons not in the supervisory chain. (NOTE: Personal contacts with supervisors are covered under Factor 2, Supervisory Controls; personal contacts with subordinates are covered under Factor 10, Supervisory Accountability). Levels described under this factor are based on what is required to make the initial contact, the difficulty of communicating with those contacted, and the setting in which the contact takes place (e.g., the degree to which the employee and those contacted recognize their relative roles and authority).

Above the lowest level, points should be credited under this factor only for contacts which are essential for successful performance of the work and which have a demonstrable impact on the difficulty and responsibility of the work performed.

The relationship of Factors 6 and 7 presumes that the same contacts will be evaluated for both factors. Therefore, use the personal contacts which serve as the basis for the level selected for Factor 7 as the basis for selecting a level for Factor 6.

Level 6-2   *25 points*

Personal contacts are with co-workers and employees of the City, but outside the immediate organizational unit. Extensive contacts are made with residential, commercial, and industrial property owners, builders, and contractors in making on-site inspections and investigations. Contacts with the general public are made in a moderately structured setting (e.g., the contacts are generally established on a routine basis, normally in the field; the exact purpose of the contact may be unclear at first to one or more of the parties; and one or more of the parties may be uninformed concerning the role and authority of other participants).

Level 6-3   *60 points*

Personal contacts are with individuals or groups outside the immediate organizational unit or outside City government in a moderately unstructured setting (e.g., the contacts are not established on a routine basis; the purpose and extent of each contact is different and the role and authority of each party is identified and developed during the course of the contact). Typical of contacts at this level are directors of other departments, engineers, contractors, attorneys, surveyors, land planners, or representatives from real estate organizations and the State Environmental Department.

Factor 7: Purpose of Contacts

Purposes of personal contacts range from factual exchanges of information to situations involving significant or controversial issues and differing viewpoints, goals, or objectives. The personal contacts which serve as the basis for the level selected for this factor must be the same as the contacts which are the basis for the level selected for Factor 6.

Level 7-2   *50 points*

Contacts are primarily for the purpose of resolving problems (e.g., investigating unlicensed business activity) by influencing or motivating individuals or groups. These persons are usually cooperative and not working towards conflicting goals.

Level 7-3   *120 points*

The purpose of personal contacts at this level is to influence, motivate, or control persons or groups. Persons contacted may be skeptical, uncooperative, or dangerous. The employee must be skillful in approaching the individual or group in order to obtain the desired effect, such as gaining compliance with established regulatory requirements by persuasion or negotiation with contractors, engineers, or property owners.

Factor 8: Physical Demands

This factor covers the requirements and physical demands placed on the employee by the work assignment. This includes physical characteristics and abilities (e.g., specific agility and dexterity requirements) and the physical exertion involved in the work (e.g., climbing, lifting, pushing, balancing, stooping, kneeling, crouching, crawling, or reaching). To some extent, the frequency or intensity of physical exertion must also be considered, e.g., a job requiring prolonged standing involves more physical exertion than a job requiring intermittent standing.

Level 8-1   *5 points*

The work is primarily sedentary (e.g., filling out inspection report forms). However, there may be some standing, stooping, bending, or crouching when conducting field inspections. The employee may be required to lift objects weighing under 25 pounds.

Level 8-2   *20 points*

The work requires some physical exertion such as prolonged walking or standing, bending, crouching, or stooping when making field inspections. The employee frequently lifts objects weighing under 25 pounds and, occasionally, objects weighing 25 to 50 pounds. The employee may be required to climb ladders or use tools or equipment requiring above-average dexterity.

Factor 9: Work Environment

This factor considers the risks and discomforts in the employee's physical surroundings or the nature of the work assigned and the safety regulations required. Although the use of safety precautions can practically eliminate a certain danger or discomfort, such situations typically place additional demands upon the employee in carrying out safety regulations and techniques.

Level 9-1   *5 points*

The work is usually performed in an office and, occasionally, outdoors under pleasant conditions. The employee is infrequently required to use special safety precautions (e.g., the use of hard hats at construction sites) when conducting field inspections.

Level 9-2   *20 points*

The work is typically performed in the field (e.g., construction sites; existing residential, commercial, or industrial facilities; or fire scenes), seldom in inclement weather. The employee is exposed to regular and recurring risks and discomforts such as machinery and its moving parts, high voltage electrical equipment, noise, or fire-damaged structures which reassure the employee to use a number of standard safety precautions.

<u>LABOR AND TRADES SERIES</u>

Series Coverage

This series covers positions involving the supervision and performance of
- maintenance and/or construction of public works facilities (e.g., dirt and paved roads; storm drainage and sewage disposal systems and facilities; rock walls used as erosion barriers; and sidewalks) and public utilities facilities (e.g., water and electrical power distribution systems and facilities);
- custodial operations and maintenance of City buildings and grounds (e.g., jani-

torial and painting activities and repair of heating and air-conditioning systems);

- operation of vehicles or equipment (ranging from small garbage pushers to heavy equipment such as bulldozers or back hoes);
- maintenance and repair of City vehicles and equipment;
- collection and disposal of refuse; or
- performance of related work when such duties primarily require the application of the knowledge and skills established in this series.

As the series title indicates, positions covered in this series are usually categorized within either the labor or trades occupations. This intraseries categorization is not necessary for the purposes of classification and factor-level evaluation; distinctions will not be made between the two in the factor-level descriptions.

Positions which are primarily involved with the management or administration of labor-related programs are excluded from this series and are classified under the Staff/Administrative Series.

Occupational Information

Positions included in the Labor and Trades Series encompass a wide range of activities; these positions are distinguished by the manual performance of these activities or supervision of employees whose jobs are primarily manual in nature.

There are four major functional areas in which these positions operate including

- construction (e.g., water mains and service lines; sewer lines; storm drains; sidewalks; road signs; and electrical power lines and transformer banks);
- maintenance (e.g., water and sewer lines; automotive and heavy equipment; power line ; lawns; street surfaces and rights-of-way; swimming pools; building structures; and street lighting, fire alarm and traffic signal systems);
- equipment operation (e.g., bulldozers; bucket trucks; back hoes; and tractor-trailer rigs); and
- refuse collection and disposal (e.g., garbage; trash; litter; and dead animals).

Positions often involve performance of activities in more than one functional area (e.g., construction and maintenance of water or sewer lines). There are also positions which perform the activities of one functional area within another (e.g., operating back hoes to dig ditches as part of a construction or maintenance project; or operating refuse trucks to collect and dispose of trash and garbage).

Supervisory Positions

In all functional areas there exist positions which have varying degrees of supervisory responsibility, ranging from a general foreman responsible for the activities of four construction and maintenance crews to a crew leader responsible for the activities of two manual laborers in the absence of a formal supervisor. These positions should be distinguished from those whose primary function is to design, plan, manage, or administer labor-related work projects. To be classified in this series, the supervisor should be skilled in the types of work activities subordinates are performing in order to train subordinates in requisite knowledges and skills, coordinate and direct work activities, provide technical assistance, and to ensure quality control of subordinates' work products or services.

Factor-Level Descriptions

Factor-level descriptions are used to describe the characteristics of each job content factor used in the Factor. Evaluation System of job classification. The factor-level descriptions used in the Primary Standard serve as a reference guide and are not written in terms of a specific occupation. Therefore, classification standards include factor-level descriptions which are more specific to an occupation (NOTE: Classification standards may be written for a narrowly defined occupation or for a group of related occupations). Classification standards do not change the essential meaning of Primary Standard factor-level descriptions; they merely redefine them in terms more descriptive of the occupation, allowing easier evaluation of the various job content factors.

Only those factor-levels that are applicable to positions in the occupation are described in the classification standard. For example, the highest levels of "knowledge required," as defined in the Primary Standard, would not exist in clerical work and, therefore, would not be described in the factor-levels for that occupation. If a position is encountered which does not fit well in any of the occupations for which classification standards exist, or if a position in an occupation appears to fall outside the established range of levels for a particular job content factor, then use of the Primary Standard is indicated and will permit evaluation .

Factor 1: Knowledge Required by the Position

This factor measures the nature and extent of information or facts which the worker must understand to do acceptable work (e.g., steps, procedures, practices, rules, policies, theories, principles, and concepts) and the nature and extent of the skills needed to apply those knowledges. This factor includes the knowledges and skills required to perform supervisory functions (e.g., training and performance appraisal); this differs from the responsibility placed on the employee for the activities of subordinates (covered in Factor 10, Supervisory Accountability). To be used as a basis for selecting a level under this factor, a knowledge must be required and applied.

Level 1-1   *50 points*

Positions at this level require a knowledge of simple, routinized or repetitive tasks, requiring little or no previous experience or training, to perform such tasks as
  * cleaning bathrooms, buildings, or other facilities;
  * cutting grass or pruning trees and hedges using lawn mowers and pruning shears; or
  * lifting and carrying heavy objects.

Knowledge of commonly used safety precautions is also required, especially when working with tools, equipment, or materials which are potentially hazardous .

At this level, the worker demonstrates skill in operating simple tools or equipment such as hand tools, mops, shovels, lawn mowers, gas pumps, or axes to perform their related activities.

Level 1-2   *200 points*

Positions at this level typically require a knowledge of the basic practices, techniques, or operations used in one of a variety of activities including
  * public works or water distribution facility construction and maintenance (e.g., checks grade of sewer ditches against established markers, handles pipe, and cements pipe joints to lay sewer and storm drain lines; or places and fits sec-

tions of water line pipe together, inserts rubber gaskets, iron joint rings and valves, and tightens nuts and bolts with a pipe wrench to seal pipe joints and lay water lines);

- building and grounds maintenance (e.g., uses chain saws to fell and cut up trees; removes existing surface finishes and old putty and caulking, repairs surface using plaster or other filler, and applies paints, varnishes, stains and shellacs using brushes, rollers, and spray guns; or mows fields, lawns, and rights-of-way using tractor with a mower attachment);
- vehicle or equipment operation (e.g., operates refuse trucks to follow prescribed routes and transport solid waste to transfer station or landfill; operates street sweeper to maintain street and parking lot surfaces; uses water line tapping machine to connect service lines to water main under pressure; or drives utility or pickup trucks to transport tools, equipment, materials or personnel); or
- vehicle equipment maintenance or servicing (e.g., operates gas pumps; changes, repairs, and balances tires; changes oil and all filters; and greases and lubricates vehicles or equipment).

Knowledge of commonly used safety precautions is also required, especially when working with tools, equipment, or materials which are potentially hazardous; the worker uses this knowledge to ensure his own safety as well as that of others.

In using the knowledges described above, the worker typically demonstrates skill in operating a variety of tools or equipment. The identification of the tools or equipment used by the worker does not determine factor-level evaluation; to correctly evaluate the position, it is necessary to consider the extent of the knowledge required of operations performed using the equipment or the level of skill required to perform specific operations.

Positions at this level typically require some previous training or experience.

Level 1-3   *350 points*

Positions at this level typically require a thorough knowledge of a body of standardized procedures, practices, or operations used in activities such as

- operating heavy equipment requiring a high degree of skill (e.g., digging ditches using a large back hoe in close proximity to water, sewer, natural gas, and electrical power lines; transporting heavy equipment such as bulldozers using a tractor and low-boy trailer rig where wind resistance varies and loads may not be completely secured or centered; or moving earth or other materials to composition or level specifications);
- performing a full range of standard vehicle or equipment maintenance or repair operations (e.g., performing automobile engine tune-ups; or repairing, replacing, and painting damaged automobile and truck body parts; or
- coordinating, directing, and supervising a work crew involved in laying or repairing water or sewer mains or service lines (e.g., including resolution of standard or recurring problems; and provision of supervisory functions such as training, quality control, and performance appraisal).

Positions at this level typically require a considerable amount of training and experience to perform the full range of standard assignments.

Level 1-4   *550 points*

Positions at this level typically require knowledge of an extensive body of rules, procedures, or operations to perform a wide variety of interrelated or nonstandard assignments and resolve a wide range of problems. Duties typically evaluated at this level include

- inspecting, dismantling, adjusting, and repairing a variety of motorized equipment including heavy-duty water pumps, hydraulic motors, transmitters, telemeters, motor starters, and chemical feeders at a number of water plant facilities;
- diagnosing failures in one-ton or heavier trucks and heavy-duty equipment (e.g., bulldozers, back hoes, and fire trucks), dismantling and repairing fuel, ignition, electrical, brake, and drive train parts and systems;
- constructing and repairing high and low voltage power lines, transformer banks, voltage regulators and other related electrical distribution equipment (including troubleshooting equipment failure and determining necessary repairs);
- coordinating, supervising, and assisting the activities of several skilled mechanics and unskilled laborers involved in the servicing and repair of a wide range of automotive and heavy equipment; or
- coordinating and directing (typically through other work crew supervisors) construction and maintenance projects in public works such as sewer and storm drain systems or streets and sidewalks (e.g., including providing technical assistance, analyzing the work to be done or problem to be solved, and allocating limited resources such as personnel or heavy equipment to work crews to ensure most effective utilization).

The employee demonstrates a high degree of skill in analyzing the work assignment or problem to determine the necessary course of action in both recurring and unusual or nonstandard situations.

Positions at this level typically require extended training and experience.

Factor 2: Supervisory Controls

- This factor covers the nature and extent of direct or indirect controls exercised by the supervisor, the worker's responsibility, and the review of completed work.
- Controls are exercised by the supervisor in the way assignments are made, instructions are given to the worker, priorities and deadlines are set, and objectives and boundaries are defined.
- The worker's responsibility depends on the extent to which the worker is expected to develop the sequence and timing of various aspects of the work, to modify or recommend modification of instructions, and to participate in establishing priorities and defining objectives.
- The review of completed work depends upon the nature and extent of the review, e.g., close and detailed review of each phase of the assignment; detailed review of the finished assignment; spot check of finished work for accuracy; or review only for adherence to policy.

Level 2-1   *25 points*

Routine assignments are usually highly structured; the supervisor indicates specific results to be achieved, e.g., a field to be mowed; work materials to be assembled; a ditch to be dug; or a sign post to be installed. New and nonrecurring assignments are made through specific and detailed instructions.

The employee works as instructed utilizing past experience and instructions given in similar situations and consults with the supervisor as needed on all matters not specifically covered in the original instructions or guidelines.

The work is closely reviewed. This review typically includes checking progress as well as reviewing completed work for accuracy, adequacy, and adherence to instructions and established procedures.

Level 2-2   *125 points*

The supervisor typically provides continuing or individual assignments by indicating generally what is to be done. At this level, the employee may also receive written work orders and may, on a limited basis, develop assignments on own initiative (e.g., observing a water line maintenance problem outside the scope of the work order and determining the impact of handling the problem on established priorities). The supervisor provides additional, specific instructions for new, difficult, or unusual assignments.

The employee typically uses initiative in carrying out recurring assignments independently, according to established procedures and previous experience, and may develop the sequencing of tasks within narrow guidelines. Deviations, problems, and unfamiliar situations not covered by instructions or precedent are referred to the supervisor for assistance.

The work is reviewed directly at various stages of completion or may only be spot-checked; this review is undertaken to ensure accuracy and compliance with instructions or established procedures. The work may also be reviewed indirectly through complaints received or a recurrence of a problem supposedly solved.

Level 2-3   *275 points*

The supervisor makes assignments through both written and oral work orders and standing instructions which provide objectives, priorities, and deadlines concerning the assignment. The employee may also develop assignments on own initiative

The employee independently plans and executes the successive steps in the assignment and handles most deviations encountered according to past experience, instructions, or guidelines.

Completed work is reviewed to ensure propriety of results and compliance with established policies and procedures. Work may also be reviewed while in progress.

Factor 3: Guidelines

This factor covers the nature of guidelines and the judgment needed to apply them. Guides used include, for example, desk manuals, established procedures and policies, traditional practices, and reference materials such as manufacturers' product manuals, blueprints, and City Personnel Rules and Regulations.

Individual jobs in different occupations vary in the specificity, applicability, and availability of the guidelines for performance of assignments. Consequently, the constraints and judgmental demands placed upon employees also vary. For example, the existence of specific instruction, procedures, and policies may limit the opportunity of the employee to make or recommend decisions or actions. However, in the absence of procedures or under broadly stated objectives, employees in some occupations may use considerable judgment in researching literature or developing new methods.

Guidelines should not be confused with the knowledges described under Factor 1, Knowledge Required by the Position. Guidelines either provide reference data or impose certain constraints on the use of knowledges.

Level 3-1   *25 points*

Specific and detailed guidelines, primarily oral, are provided which are directly applicable and cover all important aspects of the work assignment. Any deviations from these guidelines must be authorized by the supervisor.

Level 3-2   *125 points*

The employee is provided a number of written and oral guidelines, most of which are directly applicable. Guidelines which may be used by the employee includes State and City laws, ordinances, and codes which are applicable to specific activities (e.g., building or electrical codes, traffic laws, and laws concerning the transportation and use of dynamite and working in City rights-of-way); departmental procedures and policies; City Personnel Rules and Regulations; schematic drawings and blueprints; repair manuals and manufacturers' catalogs and specifications; and commonly used practices and previous experience. Judgment is used in locating and selecting the most appropriate guidelines and alternative courses of action. The employee may make deviations to adapt guidelines to specific situations; however, significant proposed deviations are referred to the supervisor.

Level 3-3   *275 points*

Guidelines provided the employee are substantially the same as in the previous level; however, for problems dealt with at this level, these guidelines often are not completely applicable to the work or have gaps in specificity. The employee is often required to interpret and adapt these guidelines with reference to the specific situation or assignment and may recommend changes in departmental procedures or policies (e.g., modifying standard procedures for working in deep ditches to ensure a high degree of safety).

Factor 4: Complexity

This factor covers the nature, number, variety, and intricacy of tasks, steps, processes, methods, or activities in the work performed; and the degree to which the employee must vary the work, discern interrelationships and deviations, or develop new techniques, criteria, or information.

Level 4-1   *25 points*

Positions at this level require performance of clear-cut, largely repetitive tasks such as digging ditches; operating jack hammers to cut street pavement; checking fluid levels in automobiles; mowing lawns; or similar tasks in which the actions and steps to be taken are easily discernible.

Level 4-2   *75 points*

Positions at this level require performance of several related duties involving consideration of choices of appropriate procedures or actions to be taken in a variety of situations. Assignments usually have many similar elements limiting the need to use judgment in deciding what needs to be done. Problem analysis may be required (e.g., troubleshooting damaged water or sewer lines; or accomplishing assignments with understaffed work crews)and the employee may improvise in reaching problem solutions.

Level 4-3   *150 points*

Positions at this level require performance of several duties involving different and unrelated processes or methods. There is a substantial amount of problem analysis involved which requires consideration of existing conditions and problem elements to discern interrelationships (e.g., coordinating the work of two or more crews, taking into account their limitations and other variables such as weather conditions, available resources, task difficulty, and established priorities and deadlines). The employee is often required to improvise in order to meet deadlines or other constraints.

Factor 5: Scope and Effect

This factor measures the relationship between the nature of work, i.e., the purpose, breadth, and depth of the assignment, and the effect of work products or services both within and outside the organization.

Effect measures such things as whether the work output facilitates the work of others, provides timely services of a limited nature, or impacts on the quality of construction projects. The concept of effect alone does not provide sufficient information to properly understand and evaluate the impact of the position. The scope of the work completes the picture, allowing consistent evaluations. Only the effect of properly performed work is to be considered. This factor is not intended to account for the consequences of error or hazards associated with the job.

Level 5-1   *25 points*

Positions at this level primarily involve the performance of specific, routine operations that include relatively few separate tasks or procedures (e.g., routine automobile servicing; basic janitorial tasks; assembling work materials for other workers; or driving trucks along well-defined routes).

The work product or service is required to facilitate the work of others; however, it has little impact beyond the immediate organizational unit or beyond the timely provision of limited services to others.

Level 5-2   *75 points*

Positions at this level primarily involve the performance of specific procedures or execution of specific rules and typically comprise a complete segment of an assignment or project of broader scope. Examples include operating a street sweeper or other heavy equipment; supervising and directing a work crew; or providing a full range of semi-skilled labor services.

The work product or service affects the accuracy, reliability, or acceptability of further processes or services, and may affect the performance and morale of other employees. The work product often impacts on the cost of projects such as construction of water distribution facilities and the need for re-work.

Level 5-3   *150 points*

Positions at this level involve treating a variety of conventional problems, questions, or situations in conformance with established criteria. Examples include analyzing machinery and equipment to determine the nature and cause of malfunction and to effect repairs; or coordinating work crews and providing technical assistance to construct public works facilities.

The work product or service typically affects the construction or operation of systems, facilities, or equipment, with regard to their economy, efficiency, and safety.

Factor 6: Personal Contacts

This factor includes the face-to-face contacts and telephone and radio dialogue with persons not in the supervisory chain. (NOTE: Personal contacts with supervisors are covered under Factor 2, Supervisory Controls; personal contacts with subordinates are covered under Factor 10, Supervisory Accountability). Levels described under this factor are based on what is required to make the initial contact, the difficulty of communicating with those contacted, and the setting in which the contact takes place (e.g., the degree to which the employee and those contacted recognize their relative roles and authority).

Above the lowest level, points should be credited under this factor only for contacts which are essential for successful performance of the work and which have a demonstrable impact on the difficulty and responsibility of the work performed.

The relationship of Factors 6 and 7 presumes that the same contacts will be evaluated for both factors. Therefore, use the personal contacts which serve as the basis for the level selected for Factor 7 as the basis for selecting a level for Factor 6.

Level 6-1   *10 points*

Personal contacts are primarily with employees in the immediate work unit, and also in related work units or departments.

Level 6-2   *25 points*

Personal contacts are with co-workers and employees of the City but outside the immediate organizational unit such as work crew foremen in other departments. There may also be contact with the general public in a moderately structured setting (e.g., sewage disposal or water service consumers having problems with leakage or line breaks).

Factor 7: Purpose of Contacts

Purposes of personal contacts range from factual exchanges of information to situations involving significant or controversial issues and differing viewpoints, goals, or objectives. The personal contacts which serve as the basis for the level selected for this factor must be the same as the contacts which are the basis for the level selected for Factor 6.

Level 7-1   *20 points*

Contacts are primarily for the purpose of providing services or exchanging information.

Level 7-2   *50 points*

Contacts are for the purpose of resolving operating problems; planning, coordinating, or advising on work efforts; or exchanging information. Resolution of problems may involve influencing or motivating individuals who are basically cooperative (e.g., persuading the foreman of a work crew to temporarily transfer a laborer in order to accomplish an assignment; or influencing a work crew foreman in another department to expedite part of a joint project).

Factor 8: Physical Demands

This factor covers the requirements and physical demands placed on the employee by the work assignment. This includes physical characteristics and abilities (e.g., specific agility and dexterity requirements) and the physical exertion involved in the work (e.g., climbing, lifting, pushing, balancing, stooping, kneeling, crouching, crawling, or reaching). To some extent, the frequency or intensity of physical exertion must also be considered, e.g., a job requiring prolonged standing involves more physical exertion than a job requiring intermittent standing.

Level 8-1   *5 points*

The work is primarily sedentary, although there may be some walking, bending, or carrying of light objects.

Level 8-2   *20 points*

The work requires some physical exertion such as prolonged standing, bending, crouching, occasional lifting of objects weighing up to 50 pounds, or similar activities. The employee may work with tools or equipment requiring a high degree of dexterity.

Level 8-3   *50 points*

The work requires considerable and strenuous physical exertion such as frequent climbing of utility poles, lifting objects weighing over 50 pounds, crouching or crawling in restricted areas, or prolonged use of equipment requiring considerable physical strength and stamina (e.g., jack hammers, picks, or shovels).

Factor 9: Work Environment

This factor considers the risks and discomforts in the employee's physical surroundings or the nature of the work assigned and the safety regulations required. Although the use of safety precautions can practically eliminate a certain danger or discomfort, such situations typically place additional demands upon the employee in carrying out safety regulations and techniques.

Level 9-1   *5 points*

The work is normally performed in an office or shop which is adequately lighted, heated, and ventilated. Some work may be performed outdoors under pleasant conditions.

Level 9-2   *20 points*

The work involves regular and recurring exposure to moderate discomforts and risks such as working with heavy equipment (e.g., bulldozers, back hoes, or tractors), sharp tools, or power equipment (e.g., chain saws, power mowers or jack hammers). The work also involves exposure to noise, machinery and its moving parts, or toxic fumes. The employee is often required to use protective equipment or clothing such as masks, gloves, or goggles. Work is often performed outdoors, sometimes in inclement weather.

Level 9-3   *50 points*

The work involves regular and recurring exposure to a high degree of discomfort or risk requiring a wide range of safety precautions. The employee is frequently exposed to conditions such as working with live high voltage power lines; in ditches where dirt walls may not be stable; in mud, water, or occasionally raw sewage; where levels of noise, heat, or cold are considered excessive; or around the unpleasant odor of garbage. Work is normally performed outdoors, often in inclement weather.

PUBLIC SAFETY SERIES

Series Coverage

This series covers positions in the field of public safety whose broad mission is to protect lives and property and preserve order within the community. Public safety positions are typically found in the Fire or Police Departments.

Positions which are primarily involved with the management or administration of public safety programs or the performance of staff functions (e.g., training) are excluded from this series and are classified under the Staff/Administrative Series. Positions which are primarily involved with the provision of technical support (e.g., fingerprinting and photographing) are excluded from this series and are classified under the Technician Series.

Occupational Information

Positions covered in the Public Safety Series involve a wide range of activities all of which are related to the recognition by government that the provision of services to protect lives and property and preserve civil order and stability is an obligation of paramount importance. Activity areas in which public safety positions operate include
- fire suppression and investigation;
- fire prevention and safety education;
- emergency rescue operations;
- traffic control and accident investigation;
- crime prevention and deterrence;
- crime investigation;
- police intelligence operations; and
- detention and incarceration of persons who have violated established laws.

Many public safety positions are characterized by wide fluctuations in the demands placed upon an employee's knowledges and skills or other job content factors; in some situations, the employee may only be standing by, ready to provide services as needed. Consequently, emphasis must be placed on what is expected of the employee for purposes of evaluation. In addition, care must be taken to avoid reference to actions which are beyond those normally expected of the employee.

A ranking system, as part of the paramilitary nature of most public safety agencies, does not play a role in job evaluation. Rank is used only as a means of establishing a formal chain-of-command and provides, at best, only a rough indication of job content. Furthermore, the set of duties and responsibilities ascribed to a particular rank in one jurisdiction may vary considerably from those in another. Therefore, one should take care to avoid giving any consideration in the evaluation process to the rank held by the individual whose job is being evaluated.

Factor-Level Descriptions

Factor-level descriptions are used to describe the characteristics of each job content factor used in the Factor Evaluation System of job classification. The factor-level descriptions used in the Primary Standard serve as a reference guide and are not written in terms of a specific occupation. Therefore, classification standards include factor-level descriptions which are more specific to an occupation (NOTE: Classification standards may be written for a narrowly defined occupation or for a group of related occupations). Classification standards do not change the essential meaning of Primary Standard factor-level descriptions; they merely redefine them in terms more descriptive of the occupation, allowing easier evaluation of the various job content factors.

Only those factor-levels that are applicable to positions in the occupation are described in the classification standard. For example, the highest levels of "Knowledge Required," as defined in the Primary Standard, would not exist in clerical work and, therefore, would not be described in the factor-levels for that occupation. If a position is encountered which does not fit well in any of the occupations for which classification standards exist, or if a position in an occupation appears to fall outside the established range of levels for a particular job content factor, then use of the Primary Standard is indicated and will permit evaluation.

Factor 1: Knowledge Required by the Position

This factor measures the nature and extent of information or facts which the worker must understand to do acceptable work (e.g., steps, procedures, practices, rules, policies, theories, principles, and concepts) and the nature and extent of the skills needed to apply those knowledges. This factor includes the knowledges and skills required to perform supervisory functions (e.g., training and performance appraisal); this differs from the responsibility placed on the employee for the activities of subordinates (covered in Factor 10, Supervisory Accountability). To be used as a basis for selecting a level under this factor, a knowledge must be required and applied.

Level 1-2   *200 points*

Positions at this level typically require a basic knowledge of commonly used public safety rules and procedures, usually acquired through some training and experience, to perform such duties as

- maintaining order and supervising the inmates (typically numbering 10-20) of the City jail (e.g., including providing transportation; assigning and supervising work activities; ensuring provision of medical treatment, visitation rights, and telephone privileges; and planning and supervising the preparation and distribution of meals); or

- dealing with persons who fail to appear in court (e.g., including typing and mailing form letters of notification; locating offenders, serving bench warrants, and transporting offenders to police station for further processing; and completing necessary reports).

Level 1-3   *350 points*

Positions at this level typically require knowledge of a large body of standardized public safety rules and procedures (including relevant Federal, State, and City laws, ordinances, and court decisions), usually acquired through considerable training and experience, to perform the full range of standard assignments in a public safety field. Typical of duties evaluated at this level are

- performing basic fire suppression activities (e.g., including laying, connecting, and directing fire hoses; removing persons from danger and administering first aid; ventilating burning structures; and performing salvage operations such as placing salvage covers, sweeping water, and removing debris; or

- providing basic law enforcement services (e.g., including patrolling assigned area or staking-out target area; detecting or responding to crimes in progress, conducting initial field investigations, and taking necessary action such as issuing citations, arresting suspects, or searching persons and property to locate and preserve evidence; completing detailed incident reports and arrest records; and testifying in court).

The employee typically demonstrates skill in using a wide variety of equipment which may include

- operating police vehicles, often at a high rate of speed;
- operating fire equipment such as fire hoses, chemical extinguishers, air masks, pry bars, hooks, and lines;

- operating weapons such as handguns, rifles, or shotguns; or
- installing and operating surveillance equipment.

Level 1-4   *550 points*

Positions at this level typically require knowledge of an extensive body of rules (including relevant Federal, State and City laws, ordinances, and court decisions), procedures, and/or operations, acquired through extended training and experience, to perform a wide variety of interrelated or nonstandard public safety assignments. Typical of duties evaluated at this level are

- handling (or assisting less skilled public safety personnel in handling) unusually difficult or dangerous assignments (e.g., riot control; hostage negotiations; or the apprehension of armed, extremely dangerous suspects);
- conducting or coordinating investigations (typically subsequent to initial investigation) ranging from routine follow-ups to cases of unusual difficulty or complexity;
- preparing special reports, studies, or surveys in a public safety field requiring extensive knowledge of the subject matter (e.g., crime incidence analysis; or fire safety analysis);
- performing the full range of both routine and nonstandard assignments in a specialized field of public safety such as juvenile crime or intelligence operations (e.g., organized crime or narcotics investigations) requiring the use of specialized knowledges and skills (e.g., knowledge of undercover techniques or organized crime operations; or skill in dealing with juvenile offenders and their families); or
- coordinating fire suppression activities (e.g., including evaluating the extent of involvement to determine manpower and apparatus requirements; establishing priority of actions to be taken; coordinating personnel and apparatus to best utilize limited resources; and providing technical assistance such as techniques to use in unusual situations).

In a few positions, a high degree of skill in operating heavy equipment or apparatus will allow evaluation at this level. These positions are characterized by expertise in this operation such as would be demonstrated by adapting heavy fire apparatus for use at fire scenes where nonstandard situational elements (e.g., inadequacy of equipment or water supply) require considering the functional nature of the equipment.

Level 1-5   *750 points*

Positions at this level typically require knowledge of the basic principles, concepts, and methodology of a public safety field (e.g., police or fire science) and skill in applying this knowledge in carrying out such assignments as serving as watch commander for an entire public safety department (or one or more large divisions), performing activities including

- identifying and communicating goals and objectives;
- making assignments and coordinating and supervising all activities through subordinate supervisors;
- interpreting departmental policy, laws, or ordinances in ambiguous situations or providing other technical or procedural assistance;
- keeping abreast of current developments and advancements in the field and communicating this information to subordinates; and
- participating in line activities of significant importance (e.g., investigations of crimes of serious or potentially controversial nature; or suppression activities at major fires).

Factor 2: Supervisory Controls

- This factor covers the nature and extent of direct or indirect controls exercised by the supervisor, the worker's responsibility, and the review of completed work.
- Controls are exercised by the supervisor in the way assignments are made, instructions are given to the worker, priorities and deadlines are set, and objectives and boundaries are defined.
- The worker's responsibility depends on the extent to which the worker is expected to develop the sequence and timing of various aspects of the work, to modify or recommend modification of instructions, and to participate in establishing priorities and defining objectives.
- The review of completed work depends upon the nature and extent of the review, e.g., close and detailed review of each phase of the assignment; detailed review of the finished assignment; spot check of finished work for accuracy; or review only for adherence to policy.

Level 2-2   *125 points*

The supervisor provides continuing assignments by indicating generally what is to be done (e.g., geographic area to be patrolled; warrants to be served). Specific instructions may be given for new or nonrepetitive tasks. The supervisor may suggest work methods or provide other technical assistance for difficult or unusual assignments (e.g., serve as back-up officer on dangerous calls; advise on best method of ventilating a burning structure).

The employee uses initiative and judgment in carrying out recurring assignments and handling problems independently according to standard operating procedures. The supervisor is usually available to help with deviations or unfamiliar situations; infrequently, situations necessitate adopting unusual work methods or deviating from normal operating procedures on own initiative but within established priorities.

The supervisor typically reviews finished work and the methods used through written and oral reports to ensure accuracy and compliance with instructions or established procedures. Review typically increases with the difficulty of the assignment (e.g., nature of crime being investigated; size or involvement of fire) if the employee has not previously performed similar assignments or encountered similar situations or as part of standard operating procedures.

Level 2-3   *275 points*

The supervisor provides assignments by defining objectives, priorities, and deadlines. Once the assignment is made, the supervisor provides assistance only when the assignment is unusually difficult or has no clear precedent.

The employee plans and carries out the successive steps in the assignment and handles problems and deviations in accordance with policies, previous experience, or accepted practices in the public safety field.

Completed work is reviewed for technical soundness, appropriateness, and conformity to policy. The methods used by the employee are usually not reviewed in detail.

Level 2-4   *450 points*

The supervisor sets the overall objectives and resources available (e.g., personnel available; general objectives in the field of public safety). The supervisor and employee, in consultation, develop the deadlines, projects, and operating procedures to be used.

The employee is responsible for planning and carrying out assignments; resolving most of the conflicts or problems which arise; coordinating the work with other personnel, both within and outside the department ; and interpreting policy on own initiative in terms of established objectives. The employee determines the methodology or approach to be used, contacting the supervisor only to advise on progress or potentially controversial matters.

Completed work is reviewed only in terms of effectiveness in meeting requirements or expected results.

Factor 3: Guidelines

This factor covers the nature of guidelines and the judgment needed to apply them. Guides used include, for example, all criminal and related laws and court decisions; standard operating procedures; and departmental policies.

Individual jobs in different occupations vary in the specificity, applicability, and availability of the guidelines for performance of assignments Consequently, the constraints and judgmental demands placed upon employees also vary. For example, the existence of specific instruction, procedures, and policies may limit the opportunity of the employee to make or recommend decisions or actions. However, in the absence of procedures or under broadly stated objectives, employees in some occupations may use considerable judgment in researching literature or developing new methods.

Guidelines should not be confused with the knowledges described under Factor 1, Knowledge Required by the Position. Guidelines either provide reference data or impose certain constraints on the use of knowledges.

Level 3-2   *125 points*

The employee is provided a number of written guidelines, both regulatory (e.g., Federal, State, and City laws and ordinances) and procedural (e.g., building ventilation, forcible entry, or search and seizure procedures). Other guidelines provided include-departmental rules and regulations; accepted practices in the public safety field; and previous training and experience. The number and similarity of guidelines and variety of work situations require the employee to use judgment in locating and selecting the most appropriate guideline to use and in making minor deviations to adapt guidelines to specific situations. The employee typically determines which of several established courses of action to take. Significant proposed deviations from the guidelines are referred to the supervisor.

Level 3-3   *275 points*

Guidelines used are substantially the same as in Level 3-2; however, these guidelines may not be completely applicable to the types of problems or work assignments handled at this level or may have gaps in specificity (e.g., when performing undercover operations; or when sizing up nature and extent of fires). At this level, standard operating procedures are frequently not applicable to the decisions which have to be made and more reliance is placed on previous experience in similar situations. The employee uses judgment in interpreting and adapting guidelines such as departmental policies for use in specific cases and may recommend changes or modification in standard operating procedures or departmental regulations.

Factor 4: Complexity

This factor covers the nature, number, variety, and intricacy of tasks, steps, processes, methods, or activities in the work performed; and the degree to which the employee must vary the work, discern interrelationships and deviations, or develop new techniques, criteria, or information.

Level 4-2   *75 points*

Positions at this level require performance of duties involving a limited number of related processes or operations in a public safety field (e.g., maintaining order and supervising the activities of approximately 10-20 inmates at the city jail). Assignments usually have many similar elements, thus limiting the need to use judgment in deciding what needs to be done (e.g., serving and processing warrants for failure to appear in municipal court). Situations are usually well-defined, leaving the employee to choose from a few easily recognizable alternative courses of action.

Level 4-3   *125 points*

Positions at this level require performance of several duties involving different and unrelated processes or methods used to provide the full range of services in a public safety field. There is a substantial amount of problem analysis involved in determining what needs to be done or how best to approach a problem. The employee is required to identify and analyze conditions and situational elements to discern interrelationships (e.g., analyzing conditions and elements present at a fire scene to determine actions necessary to suppress the fire). The chosen course of action may have to be selected from many alternatives.

Level 4-4   *225 points*

Positions at this level typically require the performance of many different and unrelated operations or methods in a public safety field (e.g., planning and supervising the work of several unrelated police divisions; supervising and participating in all criminal investigations of a serious nature; and securing and recording all confiscated property). Decisions regarding what needs to be done include the assessment of unusual circumstances, variations in approach, and incomplete or conflicting data. The work requires making many decisions concerning such things as the interpreting of considerable data, planning of the work, or refining the methods and techniques to be used.

Factor 5: Scope and Effect

This factor measures the relationship between the nature of the work, i.e., the purpose, breadth, and depth of the assignments, and the effect of work products or services both within and outside the organization.

Effect measures such things as whether the work output facilitates the work of others, provides timely services of a limited nature, or impacts on major City programs. The concept of effect alone does not provide sufficient information to properly understand and evaluate the impact of the position. The scope of the work completes the picture, allowing consistent evaluations. Only the effect of properly performed work is to be considered.

Level 5-2   *75 points*

At this level, the purpose of the work is to perform specific procedures or execute rules, which typically comprise a complete segment of an assignment or project of broader scope (e.g., supervising City jail operations including maintaining order and supervising the activities of approximately 10-20 inmates).

The work product or service typically affects the accuracy, reliability, or acceptability of further processes or services (e.g., acceptability of prisoner treatment; or serving and processing of warrants for failure to appear in municipal court).

Level 5-3   *150 points*

At this level, the purpose of the work is to handle a variety of problems, questions, or situations in conformance with established criteria. Positions at this level typically involve providing a full range of public safety services at any of several levels within the department's organizational structure. Some positions may operate within a specialized area (e.g., drug investigation).

The work product or service typically affects the operation of public safety service programs (e.g., fire suppression and prevention; or law enforcement and other peace-keeping activities) and/or the adequacy of field investigations (e.g., cause of a fire; commission of a crime). In addition, the work typically affects the social, physical, and economic well-being of the community.

Level 5-4   *20 points*

At this level, the purpose of the work is to establish criteria used in public safety operations; formulate special projects; assess the effectiveness of various public safety programs; and/or investigate or analyze a variety of unusual conditions, problems, or questions.

The work product or service affects a wide range of departmental activities and has a major impact on programs of community concern (e.g., effectiveness of law enforcement programs in meeting established objectives).

Factor 6: Personal Contacts

This factor includes the face-to-face contacts and telephone and radio dialogue with persons not in the supervisory chain. (NOTE: Personal contacts with supervisors are covered under Factor 2, Supervisory Controls; personal contacts with subordinates are covered under Factor 10, Supervisory Accountability). Levels described under this factor are based on what is required to make the initial contact, the difficulty of communicating with those contacted, and the setting in which the contact takes place (e.g., the degree to which the employee and those contacted recognize their relative roles and authority).

Above the lowest level, points should be credited under this factor only for contacts which are essential for successful performance of the work and which have a demonstrable impact on the difficulty and responsibility of the work performed.

The relationship of Factors 6 and 7 presumes that the same contacts will be evaluated for both factors. Therefore, use the personal contacts which serve as the basis for the level selected for Factor 7 as the basis for selecting a level for Factor 6.

Level 6-1   *10 points*

Personal contacts are primarily with co-workers and employees of related departments. Contacts with members of the general public are made in a highly structured setting (e.g., the purpose of the contact and the question of with whom to deal are clear). Typical of contacts at this level are City jail inmates, victims of fire or other emergency situations, and persons on tours of departmental facilities.

Level 6-2   *25 points*

Personal contacts are with co-workers, court officials, employees of other public safety organizations, and employees of other departments with the City. These persons are usually engaged in different functions or kinds of work. In a number of public safety positions at this level, personal contacts are with members of the general public in a moderately structured setting (e.g., the purpose of the contact may be unclear at first to one or more of the parties; and one or more of the parties may be uninformed concerning the role and authority of other participants). Typical of these contacts are crime suspects, witnesses to a crime, informants, and persons lodging complaints and/or requesting police services. Contacts at this level (other than those with crime suspects or offenders) are usually characterized by the employee responding to requests or emergency situations requiring public safety services.

Level 6-3   *60 points*

Personal contacts are with persons outside the department in a moderately unstructured setting (e.g., the contacts are not established on a routine basis, the purpose and extent of each contact is different, and the role and authority of each party is identified and developed during the course of the contact). Many contacts are characterized by the employee's initiative in making the initial contact (e.g., following up leads in a criminal investigation). Typical of contacts at this level are those with attorneys, the news media, persons having information about a crime or suspect, and family members of criminals. Contacts with criminals made during undercover operations are also evaluated at this level.

Factor 7: Purpose of Contacts

Purposes of personal contacts range from factual exchanges of information to situations involving significant or controversial issues and differing viewpoints, goals, or objectives. The personal contacts which serve as the basis for the level selected for this factor must be the same as the contacts which are the basis for the level selected for Factor 6.

Level 7-1   *20 points*

Contacts are primarily for obtaining, clarifying, or giving information or providing services. Positions at this level typically have limited public safety duties which do not require many involved contacts.

Level 7-2   *50 points*

Contacts are made primarily to plan, coordinate, or advise on work efforts with co-workers; conduct demonstrations or presentations with business, school, or civic groups; or resolve a variety of operating problems. The employee is required to influence or motivate those contacted to stimulate performance, ensure compliance with requirements, or resolve conflicts. Persons contacted at this level are usually working toward a common goal and have basically cooperative attitudes.

Level 7-3   *120 points*

Contacts are made primarily to influence, motivate, interrogate, or control persons or groups. Contacts may be for the purpose of arresting or detaining suspicious, hostile, or dangerous persons. The employee must demonstrate skill in dealing with these persons to obtain the desired effect, such as compliance with the law, cooperative behavior, or information about the criminal activities of others.

Factor 8: Physical Demands

This factor covers the requirements and physical demands placed on the employee by the work assignment. This includes physical characteristics and abilities (e.g., specific agility and dexterity requirements) and the physical exertion involved in the work (e.g., climbing, lifting, pushing, balancing, stooping, kneeling, crouching, crawling, or reaching). To some extent, the frequency or intensity of physical exertion must also be considered, e.g., a job requiring prolonged standing involves more physical exertion than a job requiring intermittent standing.

Level 8-1   *5 points*

The work requires little physical exertion (e.g., sitting at a desk, filling out police reports). There may be some field work requiring intermittent standing, walking, or carrying of light objects.

Level 8-2   *20 points*

Positions at this level require some physical exertion. The position may require regular performance of moderately strenuous activities (e.g., prolonged standing or walking or frequent lifting of objects weighing 25-50 pounds) or infrequent performance of heavily strenuous activities (e.g., extended periods of running; lifting heavy objects weighing over 50 pounds; or defending oneself or others against physical attack).

Level 8-3   *50 points*

Positions at this level require regular performance of heavily strenuous activities such as frequent lifting of objects weighing over 50 pounds; climbing and working from tall ladders; handling large diameter fire hoses under pressure; extended periods of running; or defending oneself or others against physical attack. The employee typically participates in a physical fitness program to ensure proper physical condition.

Factor 9: Work Environment

This factor considers the risks and discomforts in the employee's physical surroundings or the nature of the work assigned and the safety regulations required. Although the use of safety precautions can practically eliminate a certain danger or discomfort, such situations typically place additional demands upon the employee in carrying out safety regulations and techniques.

Level 9-1   *5 points*

The work is typically performed in an office setting. There may be infrequent exposure to moderate risk and discomfort (e.g., interrogating criminal suspects in a controlled environment).

Level 9-2   *20 points*

The work involves a moderate level of risk and discomfort. The position may require regular exposure to moderate risks and discomforts (e.g., supervising the activities of inmates at the City jail) or, in unusual situations, exposure to potentially dangerous situations (e.g., arresting an armed suspect or engaging in a vehicle pursuit at high speeds).

Level 9-3   *50 points*

The work involves regular and recurring exposure to potentially dangerous situations (e.g., subject to physical attack or mob conditions; working inside or near burning structures or near potentially explosive materials). These situations are characterized by conditions over which the employee has little control. Persons in positions encountering these types of situations typically receive specialized training to enable the employee to work as effectively as possible under the unusual environmental stress.

RECREATION SERIES

Series Coverage

This series covers positions which are primarily involved in providing recreation activities and programs to meet the needs of the community. Part-time positions are not included in this series for classification purposes but may appear in factor-level descriptions as examples, typically of lower-level jobs. Positions primarily involved with the maintenance of recreational facilities are excluded from this series and are classified under the Labor and Trades Series. Positions primarily involved with the administration or management of comprehensive recreation programs are excluded from this series and are classified under the Staff/Administrative Series.

Occupational Information

Positions covered in this series involve the full range of recreation program formulation, supervision, and implementation activities. Some of these activities include

- providing instructions and direction to recreation participants in organized or individual sports;
- supervising the activities at a recreation center (e.g., providing instruction in the use of facilities and equipment); or
- formulating recreation programs (e.g., including program subject; objectives; resource requirements and methods of implementation).

Some positions are involved primarily with providing support services (e.g., basketroom attendants at a City swimming pool). While these positions may not be included in a classification plan due to part-time status, they serve as effective examples of lower-level recreation positions.

Recreation programs offered by the City include intramural sports (youth and adult); free time, tennis, basketball, swimming, bicycling, etc.; and arts and crafts. In addition, the City periodically hosts tournaments (e.g., bicycle racing at the City velodrome) for regional and, occasionally, interstate competition. The positions included in this series are responsible for implementing these programs and special events.

Factor-Level Description

Factor-level descriptions are used to describe the characteristics of each job content factor used in the Factor Evaluation System of job classification. The factor-level descriptions used in the Primary Standard serve as a reference guide and are not written in terms of a specific occupation. Therefore, classification standards include factor-level descriptions which are more specific to an occupation (NOTE: Classification standards may be written for a narrowly defined occupation or for a group of related occupations). Classification standards do not change the essential meaning of Primary Standard factor-level descriptions; they merely redefine them in terms more descriptive of the occupation, allowing easier evaluation of the various job content factors.

Only those factor-levels that are applicable to positions in the occupation are described in the classification standard. For example, the highest levels of "Knowledge Required," as defined in the Primary Standard, would not exist in clerical work and, therefore, would not be described in the factor-levels for that occupation. If a position is encountered which does not fit well in any of the occupations for which classification standards exist, or if a position in an occupation appears to fall outside the established range of levels for a particular job content factor, then use of the Primary Standard is indicated and will permit evaluation.

Factor 1: Knowledge Required by the Position

This factor measures the nature and extent of information or facts which the worker must understand to do acceptable work (e.g., steps, procedures, practices, rules, policies, theories, principles, and concepts) and the nature and extent of the skills needed to apply those knowledges. This factor includes the knowledges and skills required to perform supervisory functions (e.g., training and performance appraisal); this differs from the responsibility placed on the employee for the activities of subordinates (covered in Factor 10, Supervisory Accountability). To be used as a basis for selecting a level under this factor, a knowledge must be required and applied.

Level 1-1   *50 points*

Positions at this level require knowledge of simple, routine, or repetitive tasks requiring little or no training or previous experience (e.g., keeping baskets of personal possessions for swimmers at a City pool).

Level 1-2   *200 points*

Positions at this level require knowledge of basic or commonly-used rules, procedures, or operations typically requiring some previous training or experience. Examples of duties evaluated at this level include

- acting as swimming pool lifeguard (e.g., including keeping a close watch on activities both in and around the pool area to prevent unsafe conditions or acts; providing first aid, water rescue, or other protective services; and enforcing all rules established for use at the pool);
- instructing persons in the fundamentals of individual sports such as swimming or tennis; or
- serving as a referee, umpire, or similar official for an organized sport such as basketball or softball (e.g., including enforcing all established rules of the game; ensuring that play is conducted under the safest conditions possible; and encouraging the use of principles of good sportsmanship).

Level 1-3   *350 points*

Positions at this level require knowledge of a body of standardized procedures or operations requiring considerable training and experience to perform the full range of standard assignments in one or more areas of recreation. Examples of duties normally evaluated at this level include

- organizing and directing the activities of an organized sport league (e.g., including making arrangements for necessary facilities, equipment, and game officials; publicizing league activities to generate interest and participation; scheduling games; purchasing and presenting awards; and preparing and/or administering budget for league expenditures);
- coordinating all activities performed and events held at a recreation center (e.g., including administering budget for center supplies and equipment; ensuring that facilities are properly maintained and used according to established rules; and supervising and assisting in the implementation of all programs and events held at the center); or

- coaching an organized sport team (e.g., including scheduling and holding practice sessions; instructing participants in the fundamental skills, strategies, and rules of the game and the principles of good sportsmanship; and attending scheduled games to serve as team leader).

In most positions at this level, the employee is required to have a working knowledge of an organized sport (e.g., softball, basketball, or football) as well as skill in instructing persons in the fundamental skills required to play the sport. The employee is also required to demonstrate skill in dealing with young persons, parents, and volunteer workers.

Level 1-4   *550 points*

Positions at this level require knowledge of an extensive body of rules, procedures, or operations requiring extended training and experience to perform a wide variety of interrelated or nonstandard assignments in the recreation field and to resolve a wide range of problems. Duties normally evaluated at this level include

- planning and directing the implementation of recreation programs to provide the community with varied, well-balanced recreation services (e.g., including evaluating effectiveness of past programs; assessing recreation needs of the community; developing program objectives and policies; providing assignments to subordinate personnel to implement programs; and monitoring progress and degree of success of programs with reference to established objectives);
- serving as tournament director for special competitive events (e.g., including contacting outside organization or agency to solicit funding; developing plan of tournament activities; scheduling necessary facilities and personnel; and supervising tournament operations); or
- attending workshops and seminars as departmental representative to gain ideas and information concerning recreation activities in other jurisdictions so that the employee can disseminate this information (e.g., suggestions for new program subjects) to others in the department.

Factor 2: Supervisory Controls

- This factor covers the nature and extent of direct or indirect controls exercised by the supervisor, the worker's responsibility, and the review of completed work.
- Controls are exercised by the supervisor in the way assignments are made, instructions are given to the worker, priorities and deadlines are set, and objectives and boundaries are defined.
- The worker's responsibility depends on the extent to which the worker is expected to develop the sequence and timing of various aspects of the work, to modify or recommend modification of instructions, and to participate in establishing priorities and defining objectives.
- The review of completed work depends upon the nature and extent of the review, e.g., close and detailed review of each phase of the assignment; detailed review of the finished assignment; spot check of finished work for accuracy; or review only for adherence to policy.

Level 2-1   *25 points*

The supervisor typically provides specific and detailed instructions for both outline and nonrecurring assignments. These instructions cover all important aspects of the assignment. The work at this level is usually highly structured (e.g., keeping personal possessions of those using City swimming pool).

The employee works as instructed; tasks are structured so that little or no initiative is required on the part of the employee (e.g., accepting admission receipts at an athletic event). Any deviations from instructions are referred to the supervisor.

The work is closely controlled, both through direct review by the supervisor (e.g., for accuracy and compliance with instructions) and indirect review (e.g., complaints received).

Level 2-2 125 points

At this level, the supervisor provides continuing assignments by indicating generally what is to be done (e.g., basketball team to organize and coach) and by qualifying these instructions (e.g., giving deadlines, limitations, and priority of assignment over other work). The supervisor may provide additional information (e.g., reference material on game strategies) for new or difficult assignments.

The employee uses initiative in carrying out recurring assignments independently without specific instruction (e.g., providing instructions in the fundamentals of the game to participants in an organized sport). Deviations or problems not covered by instructions are usually referred to the supervisor for decision or help.

The work is typically reviewed upon completion and occasionally while in progress to ensure compliance with established procedures and departmental policies. The supervisor may review the work more frequently or in greater detail if the employee has not previously performed assignments of similar difficulty (e.g., coaching a new sport or working with an unusually difficult age group for the first time).

Level 2-3 275 points

At this level, the supervisor provides assignments by defining recreation program objectives, priorities, and deadlines. The supervisor may assist the employee with unusual situations which do not have clear precedents.

The employee plans and carries out the successive steps in the assignment (e.g., contacting outside agencies and organizations to solicit funding for special recreation events; planning the event; and supervising its implementation). At this level, the employee typically handles most of the problems and deviations which occur according to departmental policies, previous experience, or accepted practices in the recreation field.

Completed work is usually evaluated for appropriateness, degree of success in achieving established objectives of the program, and conformity to departmental policies. The methods used in achieving program objectives are usually not reviewed in detail.

Level 2-4 450 points

The supervisor sets the overall objectives (e.g., objectives which all recreation programs have in common or broad objectives of the department) and resources available. The supervisor and employee, in consultation, develop the individual recreation programs or other projects to be undertaken and the accompanying deadlines and priorities.

The employee has full responsibility for planning and carrying out the assignment. Having established an expertise in the recreation field, the employee is expected to coordinate the work, as needed, with other individuals or groups, both within and outside City government; resolve most of the conflicts which arise; and interpret departmental and City policy on own initiative in terms of established objectives. The employee keeps the supervisor informed of progress of potentially controversial matters.

Completed work is reviewed only from an overall standpoint in terms of feasibility, compatibility with other programs or projects, or effectiveness in meeting expected results.

Factor 3: Guidelines

This factor covers the nature of guidelines and the judgment needed to apply them. Guides used include, for example, Georgia Recreation and Parks Society manual and 4th District supplement; rule books for a variety of organized sports; and departmental policies.

Individual jobs in different occupations vary in the specificity, applicability, and availability of the guidelines for performance of assignments. Consequently, the constraints and judgmental demands placed upon employees also vary. For example, the existence of specific instruction, procedures, and policies may limit the opportunity of the employee to make or recommend decisions or actions. However, in the absence of procedures or under broadly stated objectives, employees in some occupations may use considerable judgment in researching literature or developing new methods.

Guidelines should not be confused with the knowledges described under Factor 1, Knowledge Required by the Position. Guidelines either provide reference data or impose certain constraints on the use of knowledges.

Level 3-1   *25 points*

The employee is provided with specific, detailed guidelines covering all important aspects of the work. At this level, guidelines may include oral instructions or specific rules of play for an organized sport. The employee works in strict adherence to the guidelines. Any deviation or exception must be authorized by the supervisor.

Level 3-2   *125 points*

Departmental procedures have been established which cover many activities (e.g., the organization of a team; scheduling and use of facilities; and discipline of misbehaving persons). In addition, a number of specific guidelines exist which aid the employee in deciding what course of action to take. Examples include Georgia Recreation and Parks Society manual and 4th District supplement; technical aids such as recreation periodicals; and the bylaws of affiliated organizations (e.g., East Point Youth Sports, Inc.). The number and similarity of guidelines and work situations requires the employee to use judgment in locating and selecting the most appropriate guideline or procedure to follow and in making minor deviations to adapt guidelines to specific situations. Significant proposed deviations are referred to the supervisor. The employee may be required to select from several established alternative courses of action.

Factor 4: Complexity

This factor covers the nature, number, variety, and intricacy of tasks, steps, processes, methods, or activities in the work performed; and the degree to which the employee must vary the work, discern interrelationships and deviations, or develop new techniques, criteria, or information.

Level 4-1   *25 points*

At this level, the work consists of tasks which are clear-cut, directly related, and largely repetitive. There is little or no choice to be made in deciding what needs to be done (e.g., operating a basketroom at a City swimming pool, safeguarding personal possessions of those using the pool). Actions to be taken are readily discernible; the work is quickly mastered.

Level 4-2   *75 points*

At this level, the work consists of duties involving related steps, procedures, or methods (e.g., coaches organized sport teams; instructs individuals in fundamental recreation skills; and promotes participation in departmental programs). In deciding what needs to be done, the employee is required to recognize the existence of and differences among a few easily recognizable situations (e.g., availability of athletic facilities; ability of an individual to perform specific physical activities).

Level 4-3   *150 points*

At this level, the work includes performing various duties involving different processes and methods (e.g., developing program objectives and policies; attending recreation workshops and seminars as departmental representative; and coordinating facility and personnel schedules). Identifying what needs to be done involves analysis of interrelated elements (e.g., community needs; budget limitations; and capabilities of personnel and facilities); the chosen course of action may have to be selected from many alternatives.

Factor 5: Scope and Effect

This factor measures the relationship between the nature of the work, i.e., the purpose, breadth, and depth of the assignments, and the effect of work products or services both within and outside the organization.

Effect measures such things as whether the work output facilitates the work of others, provides timely services of a limited nature, or impacts on major City programs. The concept of effect alone does not provide sufficient information to properly understand and evaluate the impact of the position. The scope of the work completes the picture, allowing consistent evaluations. Only the effect of properly performed work is to be considered.

Level 5-1   *25 points*

The work involves the performance of specific, routine operations that include a few separate, largely repetitive tasks or procedures (e.g., accepting admission receipts and controlling access to City swimming pool).

The work has little impact beyond providing limited services to others or facilitating the work of others within the department.

Level 5-2   *75 points*

The work involves the execution of specific rules, regulations, or procedures and typically comprises a complete segment of an assignment (e.g., serving as a swimming pool lifeguard, providing first aid services and maintaining discipline).

The work product or service affects the reliability or acceptability of recreation services and may impact on the quality of the work of others.

Level 5-3   *150 points*

The work involves treating a variety of conventional problems or situations in conformance with established criteria (e.g., supervising the activities of a recreation center to provide persons with recreation facilities and instruction in their use; or organizing, planning, and promoting departmental programs to meet the recreational needs of a broad range of people).

The work product or service affects the design or operation of recreation programs and facilities and the social and physical well-being of community members.

Factor 6: Personal Contacts

This factor includes the face-to-face contacts and telephone and radio dialogue with persons not in the supervisory chain. (NOTE: Personal contacts with supervisors are covered under Factor 2, Supervisory Controls; personal contacts with subordinates are covered under Factor 10, Supervisory Accountability). Levels described under this factor are based on what is required to make the initial contact, the difficulty of communicating with those contacted, and the setting in which the contact takes place (e.g., the degree to which the employee and those contacted recognize their relative roles and authority).

Above the lowest level, points should be credited under this factor only for contacts which are essential for successful performance of the work and which have a demonstrable impact on the difficulty and responsibility of the work performed.

The relationship of Factors 6 and 7 presumes that the same contacts will be evaluated for both factors. Therefore, use the personal contacts which serve as the basis for the level selected for Factor 7 as the basis for selecting a level for Factor 6.

Level 6-1   *10 points*

Personal contacts are primarily with the general public (those that use department facilities or participate in recreation programs). Contacts are made in a very highly structured setting (e.g., with persons checking their personal possessions at a City swimming pool basketroom).

Level 6-2   *25 points*

Personal contacts are with co-workers, recreation personnel in other jurisdictions, and with the general public as described above. Contacts may also be made with members of the business community or other agencies and organizations, typically in a moderately structured setting (e.g., the contacts are generally established on a routine basis; the exact purpose of the contact may be unclear at first to one or more of the parties; and one or more of the parties may be uninformed concerning the role and authority of other participants).

Factor 7: Purpose of Contacts

Purposes of personal contacts range from factual exchanges of information to situations involving significant or controversial issues and differing viewpoints, goals, or objectives. The personal contacts which serve as the basis for the level selected for this factor must be the same as the contacts which are the basis for the level selected for Factor 6.

Level 7-1   *20 points*

Contacts are made primarily to exchange information or to provide services.

Level 7-2   *50 points*

Contacts are made primarily to plan and coordinate recreation activities or programs, instruct persons in fundamental recreation skills, coach organized sport teams, advise on work efforts, or resolve operating problems. These contacts involve influencing and motivating individuals or groups who have basically cooperative attitudes.

Factor 8: Physical Demands

This factor covers the requirements and physical demands placed on the employee by the work assignment. This includes physical characteristics and abilities (e.g., specific agility and dexterity requirements) and the physical exertion involved in the work (e.g., climbing, lifting, pushing, balancing, stooping, kneeling, crouching, crawling, or reaching). To some extent, the frequency or intensity of physical exertion must also be considered, e.g., a job requiring prolonged standing involves more physical exertion than a job requiring intermittent standing.

Level 8-1   *5 points*

The work primarily involves working at a desk, sitting comfortably. There may be some intermittent walking, standing, or driving automobiles. No special physical demands are required to do the work.

Level 8-2   *20 points*

The work involves some physical exertion such as prolonged walking, running, standing, or occasional lifting of weights in excess of 50 pounds. The work requires a full range of physical actions to demonstrate athletics.

Factor 9: Work Environment

This factor considers the risks and discomforts in the employee's physical surroundings or the nature of the work assigned and the safety regulations required. Although the use of safety precautions can practically eliminate a certain danger or discomfort, such situations typically place additional demands upon the employee in carrying out safety regulations and techniques.

Level 9-1   *5 points*

The work is performed primarily in an office setting; however, work is occasionally performed in recreation facilities (e.g., gymnasiums) or outdoors, seldom in inclement weather.

Level 9-2   *20 points*

The work involves moderate risks and discomforts such as demonstrating physical activities which expose the employee to a substantial risk of injury (e.g., sprained ankle) or performing activities outdoors under adverse weather conditions such as rain or excessive heat or cold.

STAFF/ADMINISTRATIVE SERIES

Series Coverage

This series covers positions involving the supervision and/or performance of activities in one of the following two broad areas:
- general administrative or managerial activities (e.g., managing a broad City program; planning and coordinating the activities of a department or large work unit; or developing long-range plans, capital improvement programs, and major projects); or
- specialized administrative activities or those requiring specialized training, typically comprising a segment of a broader project or program (e.g., serving as training officer for a large public safety department; or directing all phases of the City's purchasing activity).

Positions requiring specialized training to perform activities which are primarily technical in nature are excluded from this series and are classified under the Technician Series.

Occupational Information

Positions included in this series cover a variety of activities related through one of the two broad areas listed in the Series Coverage, staff and administrative functions.

Administrative positions typically involve planning, coordinating and implementing programs, projects or City services. These positions usually entail supervision of subordinate employees; the relative importance of providing supervisory functions (e.g., direction, training, and performance appraisals, and the extent of supervisory responsibilities) will vary according to the nature of the work being performed, the size of the work unit, and the specific function served by the position. Lower-level administrative positions may only involve duties designed to develop these administrative skills.

Staff positions typically involve specialized administrative functions or procedures requiring more specialized knowledges and skills. These positions may involve providing supervision as in administrative positions; however, the scope of supervision is typically limited and confined to subordinates involved in similar types of work.

Factor-Level Descriptions

Factor-level descriptions are used to describe the characteristics of each job content factor used in the Factor Evaluation System of job classification. The factor-level descriptions used in the Primary Standard serve as a reference guide and are not written in terms of a specific occupation. Therefore, classification standards include factor-level descriptions which are more specific to an occupation (NOTE: Classification standards may be written for a narrowly defined occupation or for a group of related occupations). Classification standards do not change the essential meaning of Primary Standard factor-level descriptions; they merely redefine them in terms more descriptive of the occupation, allowing easier evaluation of the various job content factors.

Only those factor-levels that are applicable to positions in the occupation are described in the classification standard. For example, the highest levels of "Knowledge Required," as defined in the Primary Standard, would not exist in clerical work and, therefore, would not be described in the factor-levels for that occupation. If a position is encountered which does not fit well in any of the occupations for which classification standards exist, or if a position in an occupation appears to fall outside the established range of levels for a particular job content factor, then use of the Primary Standard is indicated and will permit evaluation.

Factor 1: Knowledge Required by the Position

This factor measures the nature and extent of information or facts which the worker must understand to do acceptable work (e.g., steps, procedures, practices, rules, policies, theories, principles, and concepts) and the nature and extent of the skills needed to apply those knowledges. This factor includes the knowledges and skills required to perform supervisory functions (e.g., training and performance appraisal); this differs from the responsibility placed on the employee for the activities of subordinates (covered in Factor 10, Supervisory Accountability). To be used as a basis for selecting a level under this factor, a knowledge must be required and applied.

Level 1-3   *350 points*

Positions at this level typically require a working knowledge, gained through considerable training and experience, of the procedures, practices, techniques, or operations used in a limited-function staff or administrative area to perform a number of related standard assignments (e.g., knowledge of the procedures used to collect, record, and perform simple analysis of a large body of data or information and to prepare reports of the resulting analysis; or knowledge of the function and operation of a wide variety of weapons such as handguns, rifles, and tear gas and the laws regulating their use to train police personnel in the use of weapons and to teach them weapons related laws).

In addition to the skills needed to apply the knowledge referenced above, the employee typically demonstrates skill in coordinating a limited range of work activities (e.g., the activities of two or three assistants involved in the same type of work; or the activities of a training class). The employee may also demonstrate skill in providing supervisory functions (e.g., making assignments, appraising performance, and providing training) for a limited number of subordinates.

Level 1-4   *550 Points*

Administrative positions at this level typically require knowledge of an extensive body of rules, procedures, or operations achieved through extended training and experience to enable the employee to resolve a wide range of problems and to perform a wide variety of interrelated or nonstandard administrative assignments which may include the administration of a complete organizational unit or department of limited complexity. Typical of duties performed at this level are

- developing and maintaining major City services or programs (e.g., the collection and disposal of all trash and garbage within the City; or the maintenance and repair of all City vehicles and equipment);
- preparing and submitting an annual budget for the immediate organizational unit and monitoring expenditures to ensure compliance with budget constraints; and/or
- planning and coordinating the activities of a department or large work unit.

Staff positions at this level typically require a thorough knowledge of the standard procedures used in a specialized administrative function or departmental program to perform such work as

- developing, coordinating, and supervising all training programs and activities for a public safety department (e.g., Fire);
- directing all phases of the City's purchasing activity (e.g., development of item specifications; solicitation, review, and recommendation of bids; negotiation of contracts and agreements; and quality control analysis);
- performing duties related to grant application and administration (e.g., grant research activities; data collection and analysis; writing grant proposals; and monitoring, evaluating, and providing required financial information on funded projects).

As in administrative positions at this level, the knowledge required is typically gained through extended training and experience.

Level 1-5   *750 points*

Administrative positions at this level typically require knowledge of the basic principles, concepts, and methodology of public administration and skill in applying this knowledge in carrying out a broad range of assignments. In addition, the employee is normally required to have an extensive knowledge of the activities performed, services provided, or functions served by the department or organizational unit. Typical of duties performed at this level is the administration and direction of a large, complex organizational unit such as the Water or Electrical Department including such duties as

- establishing policies, procedures, and methods for the operation and maintenance of a large, complex system (e.g., supply, treatment, and distribution of water);
- conducting studies and evaluations of departmental operations and providing reports as required by the supervisor or agencies outside City government; and
- developing long-range plans, capital improvement programs, and major projects.

At this level, the employee typically utilizes the services of a consulting engineer or other professionals in the design of projects.

Staff positions at this level typically require, in addition to the knowledge required in Level 1-4, knowledge of the basic concepts, principles, and methodology of the specialized function or field to perform such duties as

- planning and administering the personnel function for the City (e.g., recruitment; pay and classification plan; development and training programs; employee records); or
- directing and coordinating the activities of the Communications Department (e.g., establishing operating procedures; developing dispatcher training programs; determining equipment requirements; and developing long-range plans for communication systems and programs.

Level 1-6   *950 points*

Staff and administrative positions at this level require knowledge of the principles, concepts, and methodology of public administration and the activities performed, services provided, or functions served by the department, or knowledge of a specialized program or administrative function as described at Level 1-5 which has been either (a) supplemented by skill gained through job experience to permit independent performance of assignments, or (b) supplemented by expanded administrative knowledge gained through relevant study or experience, which has provided skill in carrying out assignments, operations, and procedures in the field of work which are significantly more difficult and complex than those covered by Level 1-5. Examples of duties performed at this level include

- directing the construction, operation, and maintenance of public works facilities and systems (e.g., streets; sewage disposal systems; and storm drainage systems), including planning and development of projects and programs and designing facilities (requiring a bachelor's degree in civil engineering) and systems to be constructed; or
- formulating the policies, procedures, and methods and directing the operation of a complex law enforcement or fire protection agency or department.

Positions at this level normally do not need the services of consulting engineers or other professionals, having established a high degree of expertise in the field.

Factor 2: Supervisory Controls

- This factor covers the nature and extent of direct or indirect controls exercised by the supervisor, the worker's responsibility, and the review of completed work.
- Controls are exercised by the supervisor in the way assignments are made, instructions are given to the worker, priorities and deadlines are set, and objectives and boundaries are defined.

- The worker's responsibility depends on the extent to which the worker is expected to develop the sequence and timing of various aspects of the work, to modify or recommend modification of instructions, and to participate in establishing priorities and defining objectives.
- The review of completed work depends upon the nature and extent of the review, e.g., close and detailed review of each phase of the assignment; detailed review of the finished assignment; spot-check of finished work for accuracy; or review only for adherence to policy.

Level 2-2   *125 points*

The supervisor typically provides continuing or individual assignments by indicating generally what is to be done, often suggesting work methods (e.g., for data collection, work flow, or supervision of subordinates), source materials, or persons to contact. The supervisor provides additional, specific instructions for new, difficult, or unusual assignments.

The employee typically works independently and uses initiative in carrying out recurring assignments. Deviations, problems, and unfamiliar situations not covered by instructions or precedent are referred to the supervisor for assistance.

The work is reviewed upon completion for accuracy and compliance with established procedures or instructions. The work may also be spot-checked at various stages of completion.

Level 2-3   *275 points*

The supervisor makes assignments by defining objectives, priorities, and deadlines and assists the employee with unusual assignments.

The employee independently plans and executes the successive steps in the assignment and handles most deviations encountered according to past experience, guidelines, or instructions given in similar assignments.

The employee independently plans and executes the successive steps in the assignment and handles most deviations encountered according to past experience, guidelines, or instructions given in similar assignments.

The work is typically reviewed upon completion to ensure technical soundness, appropriateness, and conformity to policy (departmental and City) and requirements (e.g., guidelines for federal grant applications).

Level 2-4   *450 points*

The supervisor sets the overall objectives (e.g., departmental or program objectives) and resources available (e.g., departmental budget; personnel assigned). The employee and supervisor, in consultation, develop the deadlines, projects, and work to be done.

At this level, the employee, having developed expertise in the line of work, is responsible for planning and carrying out the assignment (e.g., coordinating, directing, and supervising the activities of an organizational unit or program); resolving most of the conflicts which arise; coordinating the work with others as necessary; and interpreting City policy on own initiative in terms of established objectives. In most assignments the employee also determines the approach to be taken and the methodology to be used. The employee keeps the supervisor informed of progress, potentially controversial matters, or far-reaching implications.

The work is reviewed only from an overall standpoint in terms of feasibility, compatibility with other work, or effectiveness in meeting requirements or expected results (e.g., provision of water services to meet the needs of consumers).

Level 2-5   *650 points*

The supervisor provides administrative direction with assignments in terms of broadly defined missions or functions. At this level, there may be professional organizations or associations which assist in or influence the formulation of goals and objectives (e.g., National Fire Protection Association).

The employee has full responsibility for planning, designing, and carryout programs, projects, studies, or other work independently. The employee may seek assistance from (or provide assistance to) others in similar positions in other jurisdictions.

Results of the work are considered as technically authoritative and are normally accepted without significant change. If the work should be reviewed, the review concerns such matters as fulfillment of program objectives, effect of advice and influence of the overall program, or the contribution to the advancement of technology in the field of work. Recommendations for new projects and alteration of objectives are usually evaluated for such considerations as availability of funds and other resources, broad program goals, or City priorities.

Factor 3: Guidelines

This factor covers the nature of guidelines and the judgment needed to apply them. Guides used may include, for example, technical manuals; established procedures and policies; City, State, or Federal laws or ordinances applicable to the field of work; and City Personnel Rules and Regulations.

Individual jobs in different occupations vary in the specificity, applicability of the guidelines for performance of assignments. Consequently, the constraints and judgmental demands placed upon employees also vary. For example, the existence of specific instruction, procedures, and policies may limit the opportunity of the employee to make or recommend decisions or actions. However, in the absence of procedures or under broadly stated objectives, employees in some occupations may use considerable judgment in researching literature or developing new methods.

Guidelines should not be confused with the knowledges described under Factor 1, Knowledge Required by the Position. Guidelines either provide reference data or impose certain constraints on the use of knowledges.

Level 3-1   *25 points*

Specific, detailed guidelines covering all important aspects of the assignment are provided to the employee (e.g., easily memorized equipment operating procedures). The employee works in strict adherence to the guidelines; any deviations must be authorized by the supervisor.

Level 3-2   *125 points*

The employee is provided with a number of guidelines, both written and oral, most of which are directly applicable. Examples of guidelines which may be used include City ordinances regulating solid waste disposal or City purchasing practices and procedures; City Personnel Rules and Regulations; commonly used procedures and techniques in the field of work; or previous experience. Judgment is used in locating and selecting the most appropriate guidelines and alternative courses of action. The employee may make minor deviations to adopt guidelines to specific situations; however, significant proposed deviations are referred to the supervisor.

Level 3-3 275 points

Guidelines are available, but many are not completely applicable to the work or have gaps in specificity. Guidelines which may be used include

- City, State, and Federal ordinances, laws, and court decisions such as those concerning law enforcement agencies, building and fire safety standards, employment practices and programs (e.g., Equal Pay Act and Title VII of the Civil Rights Act), the operation of municipal water treatment plants, or City financial activities;
- electrical distribution systems manuals;
- generally accepted principles and concepts in the field of work; or
- precedents and previous experience.

The employee uses judgment in interpreting, modifying, and adapting guidelines for application in specific situations to meet the requirements of the assignment. The employee analyzes the results of the use of guidelines and recommends changes (e.g., recommending modification in National Electrical Code for adaptation into the City Code of Ordinances).

Factor 4: Complexity

This factor covers the nature, number, variety, and intricacy of tasks, steps, processes, methods, or activities in the work performed; and the degree to which the employee must vary the work, discern interrelationships and deviations, or develop new techniques, criteria, or information.

Level 4-2 75 points

Positions at this level require performance of several related duties involving consideration of choices of appropriate procedures or actions to be taken in a variety of situations. Assignments usually have many similar elements, thus limiting the need to use judgment in deciding what needs to be done. Problems typically are readily solved by application of well-established practices or procedures. Work may consist of, for example, preparing reports of well-documented departmental activities; following well-defined procedures in conducting the purchasing activity for the City; or compiling and performing simple analyzes on a large body of data. The employee is required to discern differences of a factual nature when considering sources of information or analyzing a problem to be solved or work to be done.

Level 4-3 50 points

Positions at this level require performance of several duties involving different or unrelated processes or methods. There is often a substantial amount of problem analysis involved, requiring consideration of many alternative courses of action and the identification of conditions and elements necessary to discern interrelationships (e.g., analyzing requests for new electrical service involving consideration of the consumer's needs, availability of required voltages, availability of alternate sources of electrical service, and the attendant costs).

Level 4-4 225 points

Positions at this level require performance of varied duties requiring many different and unrelated processes and methods such as those relating to well-established aspects of an administrative field (e.g., supervisory functions such as assignment of work, training, and performance appraisal; budgetary functions such as formulation, modification, and monitoring of expenditures; public relations functions; and the coordination of work activities of subordinates). Decisions regarding what needs to be done include the assessment of unusual circumstances, variations in approach, and incomplete or conflicting data. The employee is often required to refine the methods and techniques to be used.

Factor 5: Scope and Effect

This factor measures the relationship between the nature of the work, i.e., the purpose, breadth, and depth of the assignment, and the effect of work products or services both within and outside the organization.

Effect measures such things as whether the work output facilitates the work of others, provides timely services of a limited nature, or impacts on major City programs. The concept of effect alone does not provide sufficient information to properly understand and evaluate the impact of the position. The scope of the work completes the picture, allowing consistent evaluations. Only the effect of properly performed work is to be considered.

Level 5-2   *75 points*

At this level, the purpose of the work is to perform specific procedures which typically comprise a complete segment of an assignment or project of broader scope (e.g., compiling a large body of data for use in a report of departmental activities; or serving as a customer service agent, identifying the needs of customers and serving as a liaison between the department and customer.

The work product or service affects the accuracy, reliability, or acceptability of further processes or services (e.g., accuracy of a report or acceptability of departmental services based on information supplied by customer service agent), and may affect the efficiency of other employees.

Level 5-3   *150 points*

At this level, the purpose of the work is to treat a variety of conventional problems, questions, or situations in conformance with established criteria. Examples include
- coordinating, directing, and supervising an organizational unit or work group involved in the performance of well-established programs or projects;
- directing all phases of the City's purchasing activity in compliance with well-established guidelines and procedures; or
- providing technical assistance in a specialized field of work such as grant research.

The work product or service typically affects the design or operation of systems or programs such as the City community development program or communications system; the adequacy of such activities as field investigations or testing operations; or the social, physical, and economic well-being of persons.

Level 5-4   *225 points*

At this level, the purpose of the work is to
- establish guidelines or criteria (e.g., for use by subordinates in coordinating programs; or for use by the general public in dealing with the department, participating in a program, or obtaining services provided);
- formulate major projects or programs of City concern (e.g., water or electrical distribution facility construction projects, or public safety projects such as fire suppression and prevention or law enforcement);
- assess program effectiveness; and/or
- investigate or analyze a variety of unusual conditions, problems, or questions.

The work product or service affects a wide range of departmental activities, major activities of community concern, or the operation of other departments and City government as a whole.

Factor 6: Personal Contacts

This factor includes the face-to-face contacts and telephone and radio dialogue with persons not in the supervisory chain. (NOTE: Personal contacts with supervisors are covered under Factor 2, Supervisory Controls; personal contacts with subordinates are covered under Factor 10, Supervisory Accountability). Levels described under this factor are based on what is required to make the initial contact, the difficulty of communicating with those contacted, and the setting in which the contact takes place (e.g., the degree to which the employee and those contacted recognize their relative roles and authority).

Above the lowest level, points should be credited under this factor only for contacts which are essential for successful performance of the work and which have a demonstrable impact on the difficulty and responsibility of the work performed.

The relationship of Factors 6 and 7 presumes that the same contacts will be evaluated for both factors. Therefore, use the personal contacts which serve as the basis for the level selected for Factor 7 as the basis for selecting a level for Factor 6.

Level 6-1   *10 points*

Personal contacts are primarily with co-workers in the immediate organizational unit but may also be with employees in related work units. Positions at this level are primarily involved in staff functions of a limited nature.

Level 6-2   *25 points*

Personal contacts are with employees of the City but outside the immediate organizational unit, such as directors of other departments. People contacted generally are engaged in different functions or kinds of work (e.g., staff persons or administrators of unrelated departments). There may also be contact with the general public in a moderately structured setting (e.g., the contacts are generally established on a routine basis, usually at the employee's work place; the exact purpose of the contact may be unclear at first to one or more of the parties; and one or more of the parties may be uninformed concerning the role and authority of other participants). Typical of contacts at this level are those with job applicants at the personnel office or with salespersons or vendors seeking to do business with the City.

Level 6-3   *60 points*

Personal contacts are with individuals or groups from outside City government in a moderately unstructured setting (e.g., the contacts are not established on a routine basis; the purpose and extent of each contact is different, and the role and authority of each party is identified and developed during the course of the contact). Typical of contacts at this level are those with officials of other government organizations; attorneys (other than the City attorney); contractors; consultants; or representatives of professional organizations, the news media, or public action groups.

Factor 7: Purpose of Contacts

Purposes of personal contacts range from factual exchanges of information to situations involving significant or controversial issues and differing viewpoints, goals, or objectives. The personal contacts which serve as the basis for the level selected for this factor must be the same as the contacts which are the basis for the level selected for Factor 6.

Level 7-1   *20 points*

Contacts are primarily for the purpose of providing services of a limited nature or obtaining, clarifying, or giving facts or information directly related to the work. Positions at this level are typically limited-function staff positions involved in projects requiring the compilation of data or similar activities.

Level 7-2   *50 points*

Contacts are primarily for the purpose of planning, coordinating, or advising on work efforts; or to resolve operating problems. Contacts typically involve influencing or motivating individuals or groups working toward mutual goals and having basically cooperative attitudes. Duties normally evaluated at this level include

- coordinating interdepartmental projects;
- advising personnel in other departments on correct procedures to follow (e.g., interpreting City Personnel Rules and Regulations in unusual or complex situations; or
- determining customer needs for such services as electrical power or solid waste collection.

Level 7-3   *120 points*

Contacts are primarily for the purpose of influencing, motivating, interrogating, or controlling persons (e.g., dealing with those who are in opposition to established policies or regulations in order to gain their compliance; or negotiating with contractors to settle contract disputes). At this level, individuals or groups contacted may be skeptical, hostile, and uncooperative.

Factor 8: Physical Demands

This factor covers the requirements and physical demands placed on the employee by the work assignment. This includes physical characteristics and abilities (e.g., specific agility and dexterity requirements) and the physical exertion involved in the work (e.g., climbing, lifting, pushing, balancing, stooping, kneeling, crouching, crawling, or reaching). To some extent, the frequency or intensity of physical exertion must also be considered, e.g., a job requiring prolonged standing involves more physical exertion than a job requiring intermittent standing.

Level 8-1   *5 points*

The work is primarily sedentary, although there may be some walking, bending, or carrying of light objects

Level 8-2   *20 points*

The work requires some physical exertion such as prolonged walking or standing, bending, crouching, or stooping. The employee frequently lifts light objects and occasionally objects weighing 25 to 50 pounds. The employee may be required to use tools or equipment requiring above-average dexterity (e.g., when training others in their use).

Factor 9: Work Environment

This factor considers the risks and discomforts in the employee's physical surroundings or the nature of the work assigned and the safety regulations required. Although the use of safety precautions can practically eliminate a certain danger or discomfort, such situations typically place additional demands upon the employee in carrying out safety regulations and techniques.

Level 9-1   *5 points*

The work is normally performed in an office setting. There are some positions which involve the occasional inspection of construction work requiring use of special safety precautions (e.g., hard hats). Work performed outdoors is under pleasant conditions.

Level 9-2   *20 points*

The work is typically performed both in an office and in the field. The employee is exposed to regular and recurring risks and discomfort such as machinery and its moving parts, noise, construction sites, or the unpleasant odor of garbage. The employee may also be exposed to inclement weather on an infrequent basis.

TECHNICIAN SERIES

Series Coverage

This series covers positions involving the supervision and performance of systematic procedures by which tasks are accomplished (such systematic procedures also being termed "techniques"). Technician positions typically require specialized training; the degree of this training will usually differ with the level of knowledges and skills required and the complexity of the task to be accomplished. While acknowledging that general problem-solving skills are readily transferable between jobs dissimilar in nature, this series focuses on techniques having specific and, sometimes, limited applications(e.g., operation of emergency communications equipment). Positions primarily involved with the administration or management of technically oriented programs or services are excluded from this series and are classified under the Staff/Administrative Series.

Occupational Information

Positions included in this series cover a wide variety of activities. Examples of these activities included

- operating electronic computer and peripheral equipment for production of utility service and tax billing, accounts payable checks, payroll and a variety of reports and other items; performing a number of chemical and bacteriological tests to insure the safety and potability of water supplied by the Water Department; and
- providing drafting services (including preparation of maps and location records).

Often procedure manuals, written specifically for the activity being performed, are available to guide the employee in choosing the correct action to be taken. Many positions in this series involve the operation of equipment varying widely in complexity. In some positions, the operation of this equipment is the primary responsibility while in others, equipment is utilized only as a means to accomplish the tasks, forming the employee's primary function. An example of the former might be the operation and maintenance of a water pumping station; an example of the latter might be the operation of emergency communications equipment in order to receive and record emergency communications and to dispatch public safety emergency units.

Factor-Level Descriptions

Factor-level descriptions are used to describe the characteristics of each job content factor used in the Factor Evaluation System of job classification. The factor-level descriptions used in the Primary Standard serve as a reference guide and are not written in terms of a specific occupation. Therefore, classification standards include factor-level descriptions which are more specific to an occupation (NOTE: Classification standards may be written for a narrowly defined occupation or for a group of related occupations). Classification standards do not change the essential meaning of Primary Standard factor-level descriptions; they merely redefine them in terms more descriptive of the occupation, allowing easier evaluation of the various job content factors.

Only those factor-levels that are applicable to positions in the occupation are described in the classification standard. For example, the highest levels of "Knowledge Required," as defined in the Primary Standard, would not exist in clerical work and, therefore, would not be described in the factor-levels for that occupation. If a position is encountered which does not fit well in any of the occupations for which classification standards exist, or if a position in an occupation appears to fall outside the established range of levels for a particular job content factor, then use of the Primary Standard is indicated and will permit evaluation.

Factor 1: Knowledge Required by the Position

This factor measures the nature and extent of information or facts which the worker must understand to do acceptable work (e.g., steps, procedures, practices, rules, policies, theories, principles, and concepts) and the nature and extent of the skills needed to apply those knowledges. This factor includes the knowledges and skills required to perform supervisory functions (e.g., training and performance appraisal); this differs from the responsibility placed on the employee for the activities of subordinates (covered in Factor 10, Supervisory Accountability). To be used as a basis for selecting a level under this factor, a knowledge must be required and applied.

Level 1-2   *200 points*

Positions at this level typically require a knowledge of basic or commonly used rules, procedures, or operations, obtained through some previous training or experience, to perform tasks such as

- assisting engineers in both field work (e.g., including setting up transits and tripods; holding level rod to establish elevation; driving construction stakes or other points to serve as guidelines or markers; and measuring and recording distances) and office work (e.g., including converting measurements from work sheets to land lot sheets or maps); or
- maintaining the operation of an automated water pumping station (e.g., including checking a variety of meters and gauges to ensure pumping station equipment is operating within safety limits; greasing pumps and motors as required; clearing debris from water supply; and shutting valves manually in case of power failure or other emergency).

The employee may demonstrate skill in operating equipment requiring some previous training or experience.

Level 1-3   *350 points*

Positions at this level typically require knowledge of a body of standardized rules, procedures, or operations obtained through considerable training and experience to perform the full range of standard assignments and resolve recurring problems associated with tasks such as

- drafting study plats for street improvements, permanent location plats for water and sewer lines, stubs, valves and other facilities, and land lot maps for City records (often based on mathematical calculations);
- fingerprinting and photographing persons (e.g., including processing and typing fingerprints and processing and printing both color and black and white film),
- receiving and dispatching emergency or other public safety communications using telephone, radio, and computer terminal equipment and monitoring alarm system control board; or
- performing a number of chemical and bacteriological tests on City water samples (e.g., including manganese, pH, fluoride, and turbidity tests).

The employee may demonstrate skill, acquired through considerable training and experience, to operate and adjust varied equipment for purposes such as performing numerous standardized tests or operations.

Level 1-4   *550 points*

Positions at this level typically require knowledge of an extensive body of rules, procedures, or operations in a technical field, acquired through extended training and experience, to perform a wide variety of interrelated or nonstandard procedural assignments and resolve a wide range of problems associated with, for example,

- directing, coordinating, and supervising the operations of a complex emergency and public safety communications -enter during assigned shift (e.g., including monitoring the actions of operators for propriety and compliance with procedures to be followed; handling unusually difficult communications problems or providing operators with technical assistance; and training operators in the function and use of communication equipment, such as computer terminals and radio, telephone, and alarm systems); or
- directing and managing the operation and maintenance of a water filter plant and several pumping stations (e.g., including- maintaining or completing all records or reports required by State and Federal law; checking operations to ensure proper chemical applications, sedimentation, filtration, and equipment operation; and providing technical assistance to plant operators and laboratory workers).

The employee may also demonstrate skill in adapting equipment when this requires considering the functioning characteristics of equipment; interpreting results of tests based on previous experience and observations (rather than directly reading instruments or other measures);or extracting information from various sources when this requires considering the applicability of information and the characteristics and quality of sources.

Factor 2: Supervisory Controls

- This factor covers the nature and extent of direct or indirect controls exercised by the supervisor, the worker's responsibility, and the review of completed work.
- Controls are exercised by the supervisor in the way assignments are made, instructions are given to the worker, priorities and deadlines are set, and objectives and boundaries are defined.
- The worker's responsibility depends on the extent to which the worker is ex-

pected to develop the sequence and timing of various aspects of the work, to modify or recommend modification of instructions, and to participate in establishing priorities and defining objectives

• The review of completed work depends upon the nature and extent of the review, e.g., close and detailed review of each phase of the assignment; detailed review of the finished assignment; spot-check of finished work for accuracy; or review only for adherence to policy.

Level 2-1   25 points

The supervisor typically provides specific and detailed instructions for both routine and nonrecurring assignments. These instructions cover all important aspects of the assignment.

The employee works as instructed; tasks are structured so that little or no initiative is required on the part of the employee (e.g., performing repetitive tasks under close supervision). Any deviations or situations not specifically covered by instructions are referred to the supervisor.

The work is closely controlled, both through the structured nature of the work and through review provided by the supervisor (e.g., which typically include review of work both in progress and upon completion for accuracy and adherence to instructions and established procedures).

Level 2-2   125 points

The supervisor typically provides continuing assignments by indicating generally what is to be done (e.g., persons to be photographed and fingerprinted). New or nonrecurring activities may be covered by specific instructions (e.g., revising land lot maps to include utility locations).

The employee uses initiative in carrying out recurring assignments independently according to established procedures and previous experience (e.g., following standard operating procedures in the receipt and dispatch of communications). The supervisor is available to provide additional instructions when new or unusual situations or problems are encountered.

The work is normally reviewed upon completion to ensure technical accuracy and compliance with established procedures. The work may be reviewed more closely for new or difficult assignments (e.g., investigation of crime scene which poses unusual technical problems).

Level 2-3   275 points

The supervisor makes assignments by defining objectives, priorities, and deadlines (e.g., objectives of water treatment; or priorities to be observed in handling emergency communications). At this level, technical assistance by the supervisor is provided only in unusual situations which do not have clear precedents (e.g., communications equipment failure).

The employee typically plans and carries out the successive steps in the assignment and handles most of the problems and deviations encountered according to departmental or City policy, accepted practices in the field of work, or previous experience.

The work may be reviewed by spot-checking for technical soundness or compliance with policy or requirements (e.g., reports to be submitted to other agencies).

Factor 3: Guidelines

This factor covers the nature of guidelines and the judgment needed to apply them. Guides used include, for example, equipment operating manuals; commonly used practices in the field of work (e.g., drafting principles and techniques); or standard operating procedures.

Individual jobs in different occupations vary in the specificity, applicability, and availability of the guidelines for performance of assignments. Consequently the constraints and judgmental demands placed upon employees also vary. For example, the existence of specific instruction, procedures, and policies may limit the opportunity of the employee to make or recommend decisions or actions. However, in the absence of procedures or under broadly stated objectives, employees in some occupations may use considerable judgment in researching literature or developing new methods.

Guidelines should not be confused with the knowledges described under Factor 1, Knowledge Required by the Position. Guidelines either provide reference data or impose certain constraints on the use of knowledges.

Level 3-1   *25 points*

Specific, detailed guidelines covering all important aspects of the assignment are provided to the employee (e.g., easily memorized equipment operating procedures). The employee works in strict adherence to the guidelines; any deviations must be authorized by the supervisor.

Level 3-2   *125 points*

The employee is provided a number of written and oral guidelines, most of which are directly applicable to the work. Typically, there are well-established procedures for performing the work. Guidelines which may be used include
- equipment operating manuals (e.g., for basic electronic data processing equipment);
- commonly used practices in the field of work (e.g., fingerprinting and photographing techniques and methods);
- standardized tests (e.g., fluoride content of treated water);
- Federal and State laws and regulations (e.g., U.S. Safe Drinking Water Act; Georgia Water Quality Control Act; and Environmental Protection Agency regulations applicable to municipal water treatment plants); or
- Reference sources (e.g., telephone and cross-reference directories; computer-accessed files such as those maintained by the Georgia Crime Information Center); or street locator files.

Judgment is required in locating and selecting the most appropriate guidelines and references. The employee may determine which of several established courses of action to take and may make minor deviations to adapt guidelines to specific situations; however, significant proposed deviations from the guidelines are referred to the supervisor.

Factor 4: Complexity

This factor covers the nature, number, variety, and intricacy of tasks, steps, processes, methods, or activities in the work performed; and the degree to which the employee must vary the work, discern interrelationships and deviations, or develop new techniques, criteria, or information.

Level 4-1   *25 points*

The work consists of tasks that are clear-cut and directly related (e.g., repetitive operation of simple or highly automated equipment; or performance of a few repetitive procedures). There is little or no choice to be made in deciding what needs to be done as actions to be taken are readily discernible.

Level 4-2   *75 points*

Positions at this level require performance of several duties involving consideration of choices of appropriate procedures or actions to be taken in a variety of situations (e.g., operating a variety of complex electronic equipment to receive and dispatch communications; monitoring alarm system control boards, emergency radio frequencies of other public safety communications systems, and the in-service status of various public safety units; and recording complaints or incidents as received). Assignments usually have many similar elements (e.g., drafting revised land lot sheets to include utility locations; drafting study plans for street improvements; and drafting official City street and zoning maps), thus limiting the need to use judgment in deciding what needs to be done.

Level 4-3   *150 points*

Positions at this level require performance of several duties involving different and unrelated processes or operations (e.g., coordinating and checking the operations of various water plant facilities including a water treatment plant; providing supervisory functions such as training, performance appraisal, counseling and technical assistance; and completing and maintaining various reports and records required by Federal and State law). There is typically a substantial amount of problem analysis involved in deciding what needs to be done; the chosen course of action may have to be selected from many alternatives. The employee is required to identify existing conditions and elements in order to discern interrelationships (e.g., identifying chemical, particle, and bacteriological content of nonpotable water and present treatment practices to ascertain necessary corrective action).

Factor 5: Scope and Effect

This factor measures the relationship between the nature of the work, i.e., the purpose, breadth, and depth of the assignment, and the effect of work products or services both within and outside the organization.

Effect measures such things as whether the work output facilitates the work of others, provides timely services of a limited nature, or impacts on major City programs. The concept of effect alone does not provide sufficient information to properly understand and evaluate the impact of the position. The scope of the work completes the picture, allowing consistent evaluations. Only the effect of properly performed work is to be considered.

Level 5-1   *25 points*

At this level, the purpose of the work is to perform specific, routine operations that include a few separate tasks or procedures (e.g., operating simple or highly automated equipment).

The work product or service is required to facilitate the work of others (e.g., preparing work materials for more highly skilled technicians); however, it has little impact beyond the immediate organizational or work unit or beyond the timely provision of limited services to others.

Level 5-2   *75 points*

At this level, the purpose of the work is to execute specific procedures or rules typically comprising a complete segment of an assignment (e.g., providing drafting services for the City; or assisting a city engineer in survey and office work).

Work efforts have an effect on the accuracy and reliability of the work of others (e.g., providing police identification services such as fingerprinting which affect the work of police personnel using these services). At this level, the work product or service may have a limited effect on information or similar systems of narrow scope.

Level 5-3   *150 points*

At this level, the purpose of the work is to handle a variety of conventional problems or situations in a technical area (e.g., collecting water samples and performing a series of bacteriological and chemical tests to ensure potability). The employee is provided with established criteria which define and direct the scope of work.

Work efforts typically affect the design or operation of systems or equipment (e.g., the filtration and treatment of water); the adequacy of testing operations; or the physical or economic well-being of persons.

Factor 6: Personal Contacts

This factor includes the face-to-face contacts and telephone and radio dialogue with persons not in the supervisory chain. (NOTE: Personal contacts with supervisors are covered under Factor 2, Supervisory Controls; personal contacts with subordinates are covered under Factor 10, Supervisory Accountability.) Levels described under this factor are based on what is required to make the initial contact, the difficulty of communicating with those contacted, and the setting in which the contact takes place (e.g., the degree to which the employee and those contacted recognize their relative roles and authority).

Above the lowest level, points should be credited under this factor only for contacts which are essential for successful performance of the work and which have a demonstrable impact on the difficulty and responsibility of the work performed.

The relationship of Factors 6 and 7 presumes that the same contacts will be evaluated for both factors. Therefore, use the personal contacts which serve as the basis for the level selected for Factor 7 as the basis for selecting a level for Factor 6.

Level 6-1   *10 Points*

Personal contacts are primarily with employees in the immediate work unit and occasionally those in related work units. Contacts are with both technical and nontechnical personnel.

Level 6-2   *25 points*

Personal contacts are with employees of the City but outside the immediate organizational unit; these employees are typically involved in other kinds of work (e.g., construction foreman using the technical services of a draftsman).

AND/OR

Contacts are with members of the general public in a moderately structured setting (e.g., the contacts are generally established on a routine basis either at the employee's work place or in the course of routine field work; the exact purpose of the contact may be unclear at first to one or more of the parties; and one or more of the parties may be uninformed concerning the role and authority of other participants). Typical of contacts at this level are residents from whom water samples are being collected or persons in need of public safety or emergency services.

Factor 7: Purpose of Contacts

Purposes of personal contacts range from factual exchanges of information to situations involving significant or controversial issues and differing viewpoints, goals, or objectives. The personal contacts which serve as the basis for the level selected for this factor must be the same as the contacts which are the basis for the level selected for Factor 6.

Level 7-1   *20 points*

Contacts are made primarily to exchange or clarify information about the work. Contacts may also be made in providing technical services.

Level 7-2   *50 points*

At this level, contacts are for the purpose of planning, coordinating, or advising on work efforts or to resolve problems (e.g., advising mechanics of the need for and coordinating the repair of equipment to minimize the effect on operations). The employee is often required to influence or motivate individuals (e.g., influencing individuals to provide information such as suspect descriptions or to identify themselves when reporting crimes, fires, or other emergencies). Persons contacted usually have cooperative attitudes.

Factor 8: Physical Demands

This factor covers the requirements and physical demands placed on the employee by the work assignment. This includes physical characteristics and abilities (e.g., specific agility and dexterity requirements) and the physical exertion involved in the work (e.g., climbing, lifting, pushing, balancing, stooping, kneeling, crouching, crawling, or reaching). To some extent, the frequency or intensity of physical exertion must also be considered, e.g., a job requiring prolonged standing involves more physical exertion than a job requiring intermittent standing.

Level 8-1   *5 points*

The work is primarily sedentary. The employee typically sits comfortably to do the work which may include operating equipment requiring average dexterity. There may be some walking, bending, or standing required in positions involving activities such as occasional inspections of operations.

Level 8-2   *20 points*

The work requires some physical exertion such as performing survey work or other field operations involving prolonged standing or walking over rough or uneven surfaces or frequent lifting of moderately heavy objects (e.g., weighing 25-50 pounds).

Factor 9: Work Environment

This factor considers the risks and discomforts in the employee's physical surroundings or the nature of the work assigned and the safety regulations required. Although the use of safety precautions can practically eliminate a certain danger or discomfort, such situations typically place additional demands upon the employee in carrying out safety regulations and techniques

Level 9-1   *5 points*

The work is usually performed in an office setting, although there are some positions which require a small amount of field work under pleasant conditions.

Level 9-2   *25 points*

The work involves regular and recurring exposure to moderate risks and discomforts such as high levels of noise or heat or adverse weather. There are some positions at this level which involve recurring psychological discomfort (e.g., monitoring several radio frequencies and other operators' transmissions while receiving and dispatching communications at peak intervals).

Index